Ultimate Certified Kubernetes Security Specialist (CKS) Certification Guide

Secure Kubernetes Clusters, Harden Applications, and Achieve CKS Certification with Hands-On Labs and Real-World Scenarios

Vijay Kumar

www.orangeava.com

First Published: September 2025

Published By: Orange Education Pvt Ltd, AVA®

Address: 9, Daryaganj, Delhi, 110002, India

275 New North Road Islington Suite 1314 London,

N1 7AA, United Kingdom

ISBN (PBK): 978-93-49888-60-9

ISBN (E-BOOK): 978-93-49888-01-2

Scan the QR code to explore our entire catalogue

www.orangeava.com

Dedicated To

My Beloved Wife,

Preeti Saini

My Lovely Mother,

Sushila Saini

And

My Kids, Atharv and Ved

About the Author

Vijay Kumar is a seasoned IT professional, with over 12 years of diverse experience in the IT industry. Throughout his career, he has worn multiple hats–serving as an IT Analyst, Consultant, and Project Lead–contributing to large-scale digital transformation initiatives. His expertise includes IT modernization, automation, and migration across high-demand sectors such as financial institutions, government agencies, telecom providers, and large enterprise clients across India, Europe, and the United States.

Vijay currently works as a Cloud Solution Architect specializing in application modernization, migration, cloud security and AI Solutions. He helps enterprises transition from legacy environments to cloud-native platforms, combining deep technical knowledge with practical problem-solving to guide their cloud transformation.

Vijay holds a Bachelor of Technology and is currently expanding his expertise in Machine Learning and Artificial Intelligence, with a focus on Generative AI. His commitment to continuous learning is evident in his extensive list of professional certifications, including architect-level accreditations from AWS, Google Cloud Platform (GCP), Oracle, and VMware. Additionally, he is a Certified Kubernetes Administrator (CKA), Certified Kubernetes Application Developer (CKAD), and a Certified Kubernetes Security Specialist (CKS), showcasing his end-to-end mastery of Kubernetes and cloud-native ecosystems.

Outside of work, Vijay actively contributes to several online forums and communities dedicated to cloud computing, DevOps, and Kubernetes. He also maintains a personal technology blog where he shares insights, tutorials, and the best practices on cloud architecture and container orchestration.

When he is not exploring cloud security or Kubernetes internals, Vijay enjoys reading about emerging technologies, writing technical content, and spending time outdoors. Passionate about knowledge-sharing, he actively mentors aspiring cloud engineers and architects.

This book is a continuation of his mission to empower the IT community–especially those pursuing the Certified Kubernetes Security Specialist (CKS) certification.

About the Technical Reviewer

Pramodh Kumar M is a seasoned DevSecOps Consultant with over five years of hands-on experience. He specializes in implementing and optimizing solutions across a wide range of cloud services and platforms. His expertise includes GitHub Enterprise, ServiceNow, Azure DevOps, LaunchDarkly, Octopus Deploy, SonarQube, JFrog Platform, and the Atlassian Stack.

Pramodh's focus is on delivering customized solutions that maximize value for clients. He draws on a comprehensive knowledge of DevSecOps and automation best practices to help organizations achieve their goals.

Acknowledgements

Writing this book has been an incredible journey, and I would like to take a moment to express my heartfelt gratitude to the many people, who supported me throughout this endeavor.

First and foremost, I am deeply thankful to my parents for their unwavering encouragement, values, and belief in the power of education. Their constant support has been a foundation for everything I have pursued.

I thank my wonderful wife for her endless patience, understanding, and support during the late nights and weekends spent writing and researching. Her belief in me kept me going, when the work seemed overwhelming. To my children, who bring joy and perspective into my life every day. Their little reminders to take breaks were more helpful than you know.

I would also like to thank my colleagues and mentors, whose insightful conversations, shared knowledge, and encouragement played a crucial role in shaping the content and technical accuracy of this book. Their contributions are truly appreciated.

Lastly, a special thanks to my publishing team at Orange Education Pvt Ltd, for their professional guidance, attention to detail, and continuous support. Their partnership made this book possible.

To everyone who walked with me on this journey—thank you. This book is as much yours, as it is mine!

Preface

As Kubernetes continues to be the dominating container orchestration and management platform, securing the Kubernetes environments, container images, network and platform is more critical than ever before. The book introduces the learning and certification path for Certified Kubernetes Security Specialist (CKS) exam. We will start with the introduction of all the topics covered in the exam to lay the groundwork for more complex topics.

The book then dives deep into every Kubernetes security domain which is part of the CKS exam. We will cover cluster setup, cluster hardening, Operating System security, Container and Container image security in detail. The book also introduces third party softwares, such as appArmor, SecComp, and gVisor which aids in securing the Kubernetes environment. We will also get a step-by-step guide to identify and mitigate security vulnerabilities, configuring network policies, RBAC and runtime security policies.

All the chapters in the book strictly align with the CKS curriculum and by the end of this book, you will not only fortify your knowledge to clear the CKS exam, but gain hands-on experience on security best practices. We will also introduce sample questions, tips and tricks, as well as troubleshooting techniques, throughout the chapters.

Chapter 1: This introduces the Certified Kubernetes Security Specialist (CKS) exam by providing a detailed overview of the exam. The chapter also covers the significance of the exam in the Kubernetes ecosystem, the learning path to the exam, and exam pre-requisites before they appear.

The chapter also covers the exam outlines, structure and format. It includes all the exam topics in brief, such as cluster setup, cluster hardening, RBAC, network policies, and so on. Thus, by the end of this chapter, you will have a clear understanding of the exam topics, format and its significance.

Chapter 2: This chapter will cover the first part of the exam curriculum, and focuses on the Kubernetes Cluster specific security practices. We will focus on mitigating network access risks, and securing inter pod communication with network policies. The chapter will dive deep into ingress security, endpoint and node security. It will also introduce CIS benchmarking, and how to run CIS Benchmark tools against Kubernetes clusters.

Chapter 3: will start with an introduction to Role Based Access Control (RBAC), implementation of RBAC in Kubernetes and how to leverage RBAC to limit access to the cluster and cluster resources. The chapter will also cover service accounts, and how to limit service account reach to reduce security threats. Lastly, we will see how to secure the Kubernetes API endpoint, and use cluster upgrades to mitigate known security threats.

Chapter 4: This chapter will focus on securing the host OS by disabling the unwanted services, and removing un-necessary software packages to reduce the OS footprint. An OS with small footprint provides a smaller attack surface for security threats. Next, we will look at ways to use Linux users, groups, permissions and RBAC to secure access to the services and resources. It will also showcase the use of firewall to control network traffic. Lastly, the chapter will cover the use of third party tools, such as AppArmor and SecComp to secure the operating system kernel.

Chapter 5: This chapter will focus on the best practices and security settings available for Kubernetes pods. We will start with a deep-dive into Post Security Policies (PSPs), and practical examples of how to use PSPs to secure Kubernetes pods. Next, we will focus on Kubernetes secrets, and how to use secrets to store confidential and sensitive information. In the last section of this chapter, we will understand how to effectively isolate workloads, within the cluster with practical examples of multitenancy, sandboxed containers, and gVisore.

Chapter 6: This chapter will delve into ways to secure the base container image. We will look at how to reduce the container image footprint, reduce the image layers, and scan images for security vulnerabilities, with practical examples. Next, we will explore techniques to secure the software supply chain, with the help of Software Bill of Material (SBOM), CI/CD pipelines and private repositories. Lastly we will also cover tools, such as Kubesec and KuberLinter for static analysis, as these tools will help identify misconfigured workloads and images, before these are deployed in production.

Chapter 7: This chapter will start with an introduction to behavioral analytics, and how Falco can be used for real time security and anomaly detection. Next, we will look at ways on how to detect security threats across different avenues, such as Physical Infrastructure, Network, Data, Users, and so on. We will also cover ways and examples of how to identify different phases of a security attack, and how to identify bad actors threatening the Kubernetes environment. Lastly, we will deep dive into securing the image by making it immutable, and to use audit logs to monitor who has access to the environment.

Chapter 8: This chapter aims to provide sample questions that you can practice, along with solution explanations to cement the knowledge which you gained throughout the chapters.

Get a Free eBook

We hope you are enjoying your recently purchased book! Your feedback is incredibly valuable to us, and to all other readers looking for great books.

If you found this book helpful or enjoyable, we would truly appreciate it, if you could take a moment to leave a short review with a 5 star rating on Amazon. It helps us grow, and lets other readers discover our books.

As a thank you, we would love to send you a free digital copy of this book, and a **30%** discount code on your next cart value on our official websites:

www.orangeava.com

www.orangeava.in (For Indian Subcontinent)

☑ **Here's how:**

Leave a review for the book on Amazon.

Take a screenshot of your review, and send an email to **info@orangeava.com** (it can be just the confirmation screen).

Once, we receive your screenshot, we will send you the digital file, within 24 hours.

Thank you so much for your support – it means a lot to us!

Downloading the code bundles and colored images

Please follow the links or scan the QR codes to download the ***Code Bundles and Images*** of the book:

https://github.com/ava-orange-education/Ultimate-Certified-Kubernetes-Security-Specialist-CKS-Certification-Guide

The code bundles and images of the book are also hosted on ***https://rebrand.ly/exk87ca***

In case there's an update to the code, it will be updated on the existing GitHub repository.

Errata

We take immense pride in our work at **Orange Education Pvt Ltd,** and follow best practices to ensure the accuracy of our content to provide an indulging reading experience to our subscribers. Our readers are our mirrors, and we use their inputs to reflect and improve upon human errors, if any, that may have occurred during the publishing processes involved. To let us maintain the quality and help us reach out to any readers who might be having difficulties due to any unforeseen errors, please write to us at :

errata@orangeava.com

Your support, suggestions, and feedback are highly appreciated.

DID YOU KNOW

Did you know that Orange Education Pvt Ltd offers eBook versions of every book published, with PDF and ePub files available? You can upgrade to the eBook version at **www.orangeava.com** and as a print book customer, you are entitled to a discount on the eBook copy. Get in touch with us at: **info@orangeava.com** for more details.

At **www.orangeava.com**, you can also read a collection of free technical articles, sign up for a range of free newsletters, and receive exclusive discounts and offers on Print Books and eBooks.

PIRACY

If you come across any illegal copies of our works in any form on the internet, we would be grateful if you would provide us with the location address or website name. Please contact us at **info@orangeava.com** with a link to the material.

ARE YOU INTERESTED IN AUTHORING WITH US?

If there is a topic that you have expertise in, and you are interested in either writing or contributing to a book, please write to us at **business@orangeava.com**. We are on a journey to help developers and tech professionals to gain insights on the present technological advancements and innovations happening across the globe and build a community that believes Knowledge is best acquired by sharing and learning with others. Please reach out to us to learn what our audience demands and how you can be part of this educational reform. We also welcome ideas from tech experts and help them build learning and development content for their domains.

REVIEWS

Please leave a review. Once you have read and used this book, why not leave a review on the site that you purchased it from? Potential readers can then see and use your unbiased opinion to make purchase decisions. We at Orange Education would love to know what you think about our products, and our authors can learn from your feedback. Thank you!

For more information about Orange Education, please visit **www.orangeava.com**.

Table of Contents

CHAPTER 1

Introduction to CKS Exam Curriculum

Introduction

As Kubernetes continues to be the dominating solution for container orchestration, securing Kubernetes components has become more critical than ever before. The ability to secure Kubernetes environments at every stage has become a vital skill for organizations as well as professionals.

The Certified Kubernetes Security Specialist (CKS) certification is a performance-based certification exam offered by Cloud Native Computing Foundation (CNCF), in collaboration with The Linux Foundation. The exam is aimed at validating a candidate's proficiency in Kubernetes and cloud security in a simulated environment.

This chapter will start with an introduction to the Kubernetes Certification path and briefly touch upon the prerequisites needed before you can appear for the exam, such as getting the Certified Kubernetes Administrator (CKA) certification. We will also look at the target audience that can benefit from the CKS certification. Then we will move on to the exam's key focus areas, such as Cluster Setup, Cluster Hardening, System Hardening, Supply Chain Security and Monitoring, Logging, and Runtime Security.

The exam has an open book format with access to Kubernetes documentation, Kubernetes GitHub repository, blogs, and a well-defined list of external tool documentation. We will cover these resources in detail and also get a brief overview of the exam environment. We will wrap this chapter by listing a couple of online resources that you can use to practice the exam questions, as well as ways to build a practice environment right on your workstation or laptop.

Structure

In this chapter, we will discuss the following topics:

- CKS Certification Path
- Target Audience
- Exam Objectives
- Curriculum
- Exam Resources
- Practice Resources

CKS Certification Path

Cloud Native Computing Foundation (CNCF) focuses on certifications for professionals who want to demonstrate their Kubernetes and cloud native skills. These include working knowledge of tools such as Istio, Cilium, Argo, as well as Kubernetes. CNCF offers five certificates focused on testing Kubernetes' working knowledge of individuals. These certification exams are broken into 3 levels based on the target audience.

- Associate
    - Kubernetes and Cloud Native Associate (KCNA)
    - Kubernetes and Cloud Security Associate (KCSA)
- Administrators
    - Certified Kubernetes Administrator (CKA)
    - Certified Kubernetes Security Specialist (CKS)
- Developer
    - Certified Kubernetes Application Developer

Figure 1.1 is a pictorial representation of these exams as per the audience for which they are intended.

Figure 1.1: *Available Kubernetes Certifications by target audience*

Let us take a brief look at these exams; though every exam is targeted at a different audience, some of these exams provide the groundwork for the others and can serve as a starting point for anyone interested in learning and validating their Cloud Native and Kubernetes knowledge.

Associate Exams

Associate exams are entry-level credentials for anyone looking to specialize in Cloud Native technologies and serve as stepping-stones to administrative-level exams. These exams test your knowledge on broader fundamentals of Cloud Native technologies.

Kubernetes and Cloud Native Associate (KCNA)

Kubernetes and Cloud Native Associate (KCNA) is an entry-level certification exam that focuses on basic Kubernetes fundamentals, such as Kubernetes architecture, basic principles behind cloud-native technologies, and an understanding of kubectl commands. This exam is online and multiple choice and does not focus on practical applications of cloud native fundamentals; rather, it aims to validate your basic knowledge of these principles and lays the groundwork by setting you up for the Certified Kubernetes Administrator (CKA) exam.

Kubernetes and Cloud Security Associate (KCSA)

Kubernetes and Cloud Security Associate (KCSA) is another entry-level certification with an emphasis on cloud native security. Instead of focusing on Kubernetes fundamentals, this exam focuses on measuring your knowledge of foundational cloud security skills such as hardening controls, monitoring security aspects, identifying and assessing risks and vulnerability. This exam is ideal for candidates who are looking to hone their cloud native security skills. This is again an online exam with multiple-choice questions.

Administrative Exams

Administrative exams are more advanced than associate-level exams and are aimed at validating your ability to solve real-world problems by implementing Kubernetes and third-party cloud solutions.

Certified Kubernetes Administrator (CKA)

Certified Kubernetes Administrator (CKA) has been designed to test your hands-on Kubernetes skills. The exam is performance-based, meaning you must showcase your Kubernetes knowledge by solving real-world challenges by applying your Kubernetes skills that range from Kubernetes cluster architecture, installation, and management to troubleshooting workloads and cluster deployments.

The exams ensure that CKAs have the knowledge, skills and competency to act as Kubernetes administrators. The exam is proctored, delivered online in a lab environment.

Certified Kubernetes Security Specialist (CKS)

Certified Kubernetes Security Specialist (CKS) is another performance-based exam which not only focuses on the Kubernetes fundamentals but also places greater importance on Kubernetes and Cloud Native security constructs. CKS covers a wide range of topics all the way from cluster security, workload security down to security monitoring and compliance. We will learn more about the exam throughout the upcoming chapters.

CKS is also the only Kubernetes-related exam offered by CNCF that requires a current CKA certification before you can appear for it. This makes sure that any CKS has the required knowledge to not only apply and maintain Kubernetes security, but they also have hands-on experience with Kubernetes administration and demonstrated skill with Kubernetes fundamentals.

Developer Exam

Cloud Native Computing Foundation (CNCF) offers a single exam focused on Kubernetes application developers.

Certified Kubernetes Application Developer (CKAD)

Certified Kubernetes Application Developer (CKAD) is specially focused on application developers and makes sure that CKAD not only have the necessary skills to develop performant, scalable, and secure applications but they can also manage cloud native applications on Kubernetes. CKAD is more focused on testing your skills on application resource definitions, use of core primitives, monitoring, and troubleshooting of application workloads running in a Kubernetes environment.

Like CKA and CKS, CKAD is also a skills-based exam and is delivered online in a lab environment.

Target Audience

Certified Kubernetes Security Specialist (CKS) is the only Kubernetes exam that has a pre-req for CKA, so by design, the exam is focused on Kubernetes Administrators who have strong foundational knowledge and want to expand or specialize in Kubernetes and cloud-native security. The primary focus of the exam is Kubernetes administrators, security engineers, DevOps engineers, and system architects. These roles are generally responsible for building, deploying, maintaining, and securing Kubernetes applications in the production environment.

Getting certified with CKS demonstrates that you have the skills to build and secure Kubernetes clusters, secure containerized workloads, and identify and mitigate vulnerabilities. It also validates your ability to respond to security threats effectively by leveraging a wide range of third-party security tools designed especially for containerized workloads.

Exam Objectives

Kubernetes is one of the fastest-growing open-source projects. As per CNCF, "The Cloud Native Computing Foundation is committed to growing the community of Kubernetes-knowledgeable security specialists, thereby enabling continued growth across the broad set of organizations using the technology."

Source: https://www.cncf.io/training/certification/cks/

CKS is primarily designed to validate your ability to secure a Kubernetes environment effectively. The exam also aims to ensure that you can implement security best practices right from cluster setup stage all the way to building and maintaining monitoring and logging solutions for the containerized application.

The exam's focus goes well beyond theoretical knowledge of the security concepts into practical problem-solving skills, which you must demonstrate in a simulated real-world environment. The exam also aims to arm you with knowledge about emerging security challenges with containerized applications by testing you on container image security, supply chain security, Role-Based Access Control (RBAC), and supporting tools such as AppArmor, Seccomp, Falco, and so on.

The ultimate goal for the CKS certification is to produce security specialists who are well-versed in Kubernetes administrations as well as capable of designing and maintaining secure Kubernetes environments and protecting workloads against an ever-increasing list of threats.

Curriculum

Cloud Native Computing Foundation (CNCF) has open-sourced the curriculum for all the exams that it conducts. At the time of writing this chapter, the curriculum is based on Kubernetes v1.31. The topics covered in the upcoming chapter will align with the current version (1.31) of the exam. All the examples, primitives, and third-party tools will also be in alignment with Kubernetes v1.31.

Kubernetes tends to have a fast release cycle, with Minor versions staying in support for around 14 months. It is possible that in the future, the exam will move to a different Kubernetes version. I would recommend always practicing on the latest supported Kubernetes version. You can always refer to the current CKS curriculum available at https://github.com/cncf/curriculum.

As per the current exam curriculum, the exam focuses on the following areas, also called domains; every domain in the exam curriculum has a specific score weight, which is listed along with the domain name.

- Cluster Setup - **15%**
- Cluster Hardening - **15%**
- System Hardening - **10%**
- Minimize Microservice Vulnerability - **20%**
- Supply Chain Security - **20%**
- Monitoring, Logging, and Runtime Security - **20%**

Cluster Setup

The cluster setup domain of the exam focuses on your ability to secure a cluster against unauthorized access by using Network Security policies as well as apply industry standards such as CIS benchmark to validate the security configuration of base Kubernetes components such as etcd, kubelet, kubedns, and kubeapi. The following is a detailed look at all the topics covered in this domain.

- **Use Network security policies to restrict cluster-level access:** This topic covers the use of network security policies to restrict communication between pods within the namespaces as well as across namespaces. The topic also deals with how to reduce exposure at the cluster level. You also need to be familiar with implementing ingress and egress traffic rules to isolate workloads and minimize cluster and workload exposure.

- **Use CIS benchmark for security review:** This topic covers how to use CIS Benchmarking tools such as kube-bench to evaluate the security configuration of Kubernetes components such as etcd, kubelet, kube-apiserver, and kube-dns. When you run kube-bench against a Kubernetes cluster, it generates a list of vulnerabilities along with recommendations on how to fix this. During the exam, you might be asked to run the tool and apply a specific recommendation from the results.
- **Properly set up ingress objects with TLS:** This topic primarily deals with deploying and securing Ingress objects by using TLS encryption and managing TLS certificates for secure application traffic.
- **Protect node metadata and endpoints:** The topic will test your ability to protect node metadata and sensitive endpoints such as metadata API. The topic will cover ways to limit permissions and securing access through firewall rules or node configurations.
- **Verify platform binaries before applying:** The last topic in the domain will test your knowledge on how to retrieve and validate checksums for the platform binaries and focus on the importance of using trusted sources for platform deployment by reducing the risk associated with compromised components.

Cluster Hardening

Once you have a Kubernetes cluster built on the security principles covered under the cluster setup domain, the next step is to reduce the cluster attack surface. You do this by ensuring that the right authentication and authorization policies are in place and only people who absolutely need to access the cluster resources are granted permission. You also need to ensure that the permissions are governed at a granular level. The cluster hardening domain deals with protecting a running cluster by reducing the attack surface as much as possible. The following topics are covered under this domain:

- **Using RBAC to minimize exposure:** Role Based Access Control allows you to define permissions for users, groups, and applications. This section of the domain focuses on your ability to implement permissions with the least privileges.
- **Working with Service Accounts:** Service accounts are either built in or can be created for use in the deployed application or deployment pipeline. This section of the exam helps you demonstrate your ability to apply best practices pertaining to service accounts such as avoiding granting unnecessary permissions to service accounts and avoiding cluster-level permissions for service accounts if not needed.
- **Restrict Access to Kubernetes API:** This part of the exam will test your knowledge about securing the Kubernetes API endpoint. The API endpoint is

the most vulnerable access point in the cluster, as it is generally available over a management network with a wide user base. In this section, you will be tested on how to implement authentication, authorization, RBAC, audit logging, and firewall/network policies to secure communication to the endpoint.

- **Upgrade Kubernetes to avoid vulnerabilities:** Kubernetes has a really fast release cycle; most minor versions of Kubernetes are only supported for about 14 months. Every new Kubernetes release is packed full of vulnerability fixes and security patches. It is important to keep the Kubernetes environment up to date with the latest supported version as well as apply any security or vulnerability fixes.

This section will focus on how efficiently you can execute and upgrade.

System Hardening

Kubernetes cluster does not live and run in isolation; the cluster functioning depends on multiple components which run in a host OS. Most often than not this OS tends to be some distribution of Linux. System hardening domain deals with securing the underlying operating system.

- **Minimize Host OS footprint:** Every operating system, even minimal Linux distros, comes pre-bundled with thousands of software packages. Some of these packages are used by Kubernetes clusters to operate properly; however, there are several packages which are not needed.
- In this section, you will demonstrate your knowledge of working with unnecessary software packages and unwanted services to reduce the operating system footprint, thus minimizing the available attack vectors.
- **Using least-privilege identity and access management:** In this section, you will learn and practice working with OS users, groups, services, and processes to implement a least privileged IAM model for the operating system.
- **Minimize external access to the network:** While we have secured the Kubernetes API endpoint in the last domain - Cluster Hardening, we still need to make sure that the cluster master and worker nodes are protected against network threats from the outside world. You will learn how to limit network access to cluster nodes with firewall and network policies, configure secure ingress, and limit the number of exposed ports.
- **Appropriately use kernel hardening tools such as AppArmor, Seccomp:** AppArmor and Seccomp are system hardening tools that are covered in the exam and can help secure a Kubernetes environment by constraining the application behavior. AppArmor is used to apply file access control policies, while Seccomp can restrict system calls available to a container. This reduces the surface for runtime attacks.

Minimize Microservice Vulnerabilities

So far, we have been focused on securing the Kubernetes cluster and reducing the cluster attack surface by implementing various security best practices. Now we will shift our focus and look at securing the application workload that runs on the Kubernetes cluster. In most cases, the application will have a microservices architecture with one or more pods working together in the form of deployment. In this section, we will concentrate on how to secure these workload components.

- **Use appropriate pod security standard:** Pod Security Standards are the evolution of Pod Security Policies, Pod Security Policies were deprecated in version 1.21, and Pod Security Admission, which governs the new Pod Security Standards framework, became a stable feature in Kubernetes version 1.25. Pod security standard provides three basic policies that you can choose from and apply to the namespace. These policies govern the isolation level for the pods. The isolation level can range from highly permissive to highly restricted, depending on the standard that you choose.

  This section will cover how to apply these standards and control pod behavior.

- **Manage Kubernetes secrets:** Kubernetes secrets allow you to store sensitive information such as API Keys, user credentials, tokens, and so on. Though secret information is base64 encoded, it is not encrypted and can be easily retrieved and manipulated.

  This section of the exam focuses on defining different types of secrets, securely managing these secrets using RBAC, and injecting these in the pods.

- **Understand and implement isolation techniques:** Sometimes you might want to isolate a workload pod for application or security reasons; for example, you might want to test a container image that is from an unknown source. In this case, you can make use of multi-tenancy or sandboxing. You can also use tools such as gVisor and Kata containers to further isolate the pods.

  This section of the exam will test your skills to use namespaces for isolation, quotas, sandboxed environments, and so on.

- **Implement Pod-to-Pod encryption using Cilium:** Cilium is an independent tool that can be used to enhance the Kubernetes security. Cilium provides advanced networking and security policies that allow you to secure pod-to-pod communication by encrypting the traffic.

  With Cilium, you can enforce security policies directly on the kernel; this puts less overhead on the application and on the Kubernetes cluster. This section will see to it that you can implement pod-to-pod transparent encryption for network traffic.

Supply Chain Security

The supply chain security domain emphasizes securing the software security chain. This domain is focused on maintaining the security and integrity of all the software components involved in the software build process, such as container images, code base, artifact repositories, and so on. The domain will equip you with the skills to identify supply chain security issues and guard against such challenges while ensuring compliance with security standards.

- **Minimize base image footprint:** Just like Kubernetes Host OS, Kubernetes pods are built using container images. These images start with a base layer and keep on adding more layers as you include more libraries or software to the image. It is necessary to keep the image footprint in check and remove unwanted tools, libraries, and software packages from the image. This not only reduces the size of the image but also reduces the number of attack vectors. This greatly enhances the image and container security.
- **Understand your supply chain:** A software supply chain can include several components such as Software Bill of Material (SBOM), CI/CD pipeline, artifact repositories, and so on. You need to demonstrate a thorough understanding of your supply chain and be able to map dependencies. A comprehensive knowledge of the build process gives you better visibility into potential security challenges and risks that you might have to protect against.
- **Secure your supply chain:** Once you understand the whole supply chain, you will be in a better position to implement policies restricting access to public repositories and registries and enforce the use of only permitted registries and repositories. You will also be able to use artifact signing and signature validation to make sure that the images and artifacts that you are using in the build process have not been tampered with.
- **Perform static analysis of user workloads and container images:** In this section, you will use tools such as Kubesec and KubeLinter to analyze workloads and images to ensure that they are not misconfigured and do not have any known vulnerabilities. These tools help with automating the security detection and compliance process. You will demonstrate how to use these tools to ensure that the workloads meet the security best practices laid out by your organization.

Monitoring, Logging, and Runtime Security

The last domain of the CKS curriculum focuses on post-deployment activities and tests your ability to analyze, identify, and mitigate security threats in the Kubernetes deployments. This domain makes sure that you have the know-how to use various monitoring and logging tools to gain visibility into the clusters as well as perform security audits as and when needed.

- **Perform behavioral analytics to detect malicious activities:** Behavioral analysis can help identify malicious activities within the cluster. You need to demonstrate the use of behavioral analysis tools such as Falco to identify anomalous patterns such as Pod privilege escalation, unauthorized API calls, and so on.
- **Detect threats within physical infrastructure, apps, networks, data, users, and workloads:** Apart from monitoring the application behavior, you need to ensure that all the other cluster components such as Host OS, network, user activities, and applications are monitored. You also need to ensure that security policies are in place for all the involved components.
- **Investigate and identify phases of attack and bad actors within the environment:** While keeping the environment secure and free from threats is the goal, it is also important that you know how to investigate a security threat and identify different phases of the attack such as reconnaissance, exploitation and lateral movement. Quickly being able to identify the attack stage and finding the bad actors can help to quickly devise a targeted response plan and implement preventive measures to protect against future threats.
- **Ensure immutability of containers at runtime:** In this section, you need to showcase your ability to make sure that the containers are immutable and do not change during or post-deployment. One way to do so is to use signed images and permitted libraries. Immutability ensures that the containers do not change at runtime and prevents tampering.
- **Use Kubernetes audit logs to monitor access:** In the last section, you need to showcase the use of Kubernetes audit logs to track user activities, API access, and other system events. Audit logs help you follow the activity trail and identify access patterns, detect policy violations, and detect security incidents. Audit logging greatly enhances the cluster monitoring and security posture.

Exam Resources

Similar to the Certified Kubernetes Administrator (CKA) exam, CKS is also a practice-based exam, and you are supposed to complete tasks in a live Kubernetes environment. The exam is based on an open-book format and has a predefined list of resources that can be leveraged during the exam. The following resources can be used when you appear for the exam.

- **Kubernetes Documentation:**
    - https://kubernetes.io/docs/
    - https://kubernetes.io/blog/

- **Tools Documentation:**
    - **Falco**

      https://falco.org/docs/
    - **BOM**

      https://kubernetes-sigs.github.io/bom/cli-reference/
    - **etcd**

      https://etcd.io/docs/
    - **NGINX Ingress Controller**

      https://kubernetes.github.io/ingress-nginx/user-guide/nginx-configuration/
    - **Cilium**

      https://docs.cilium.io/en/stable

Note: *You can use the search function on the documentation page; however, you can only open the search result if it has the domain matching the sites listed above.*

Exam Tip:

- You can bookmark the relevant document URLs to quickly jump to the required page instead of searching through the documentation site.
- Having the documents bookmarked also ensures that you will not visit a restricted site by mistake.

External Resources

Although CKS is designed to test your knowledge of Kubernetes security best practices, the exam also relies on certain third-party tools such as AppArmor, Seccomp, Cilium, and so on. You need to be proficient with these tools before you appear for the exam. Following is a list of third-party tools that are explicitly mentioned in the exam curriculum, along with the path to relevant Kubernetes documentation.

- **Kube-bench:** Kube-bench lets you run checks on your Kubernetes cluster and confirms whether the cluster is secure as per the CIS Kubernetes Benchmark. You can gather more details about kube-bench at the following GitHub page:

  Documentation: https://github.com/aquasecurity/kube-bench
- **AppArmor:** AppArmor or Application Armor, is a Linux kernel security module. AppArmor lets you create and apply profiles on the application level to control the application capabilities and permissions. The profile for the application decides which files and permissions the application needs. The following

tutorials page has detailed instructions on how to use AppArmor and configure permissions for Kubernetes workloads.

Documentation: https://kubernetes.io/docs/tutorials/security/apparmor/

- **Seccomp:** Seccomp stands for secure computing mode; it has been a Linux kernel feature since v2.6.12. Seccomp can be used to limit the privileges of a process by restricting which calls the process is allowed to make. This effectively lets you sandbox the application process. You can go through the following tutorial to get better equipped in using Seccomp profiles with Kubernetes.

  Documentation: https://kubernetes.io/docs/tutorials/security/seccomp/

- **Cilium:** Cilium is a networking, observability, and security solution. While Cilium offers a wide range of functionalities, in the CKS curriculum, it is only used to apply pod-to-pod transparent encryption. You can find the Cilium documentation at the following GitHub page:

  Documentation: https://github.com/cilium/cilium

- **Kubesec:** Kubesec is a security analysis tool that can be used to scan Kubernetes resources. Kubesec is used to scan the Kubernetes manifest files and outputs the results with a severity score and details for every identified security vulnerability. Kubesec is open source, you can find details on how to get started with Kubesec on the following documentation page:

  Documentation: https://kubesec.io/

- **KubeLinter:** KubeLinter is a static analysis tool for Kubernetes manifest files and Helm charts. KubeLinter checks the files against predefined best practices and focuses on production readiness and security. KubeLinter has a configurable architecture, so you can enable or disable certain checks to meet your application requirements. Follow the mentioned link to get started with KubeLinter:

  Documentation: https://docs.kubelinter.io/#/

- **Falco:** Falco is a cloud native security tool which can provide runtime security across hosts, containers, Kubernetes and cloud environments. It can be used to detect abnormal behavior and potential security risks in real time and alert against such threats. The following is the documentation link to start learning about Falco:

  Documentation: https://falco.org/docs/

Practice Resources

CKS is a lab-based exam where you need to work in a live environment; there is no substitute for practicing all the concepts repeatedly. It is also necessary that you know how to validate your work. To that effect, we can either build a Kubernetes lab on the workstation using tools such as Kind, Minikube, and so on. We can also use cloud Kubernetes offerings such as Elastic Kubernetes Service (EKS) by AWS or Oracle Kubernetes Engine (OKE) by Oracle Cloud.

CKS assumes that you have already passed your CKA exam, so we will not go into the details of building a new Kubernetes cluster from scratch, as we are already proficient at this. In the following, you will find a few resources that can help you build a local Kubernetes cluster on the workstation as well as in the cloud. You can use these to build either small test clusters or full-fledged multi-node clusters; all the options mentioned have detailed instructions on how to get started.

Cluster Deployment Resources:

- Minikube: https://minikube.sigs.k8s.io/docs/start
- VirtualBox: https://www.virtualbox.org/
- Vagrant: https://www.vagrantup.com/
- OKE Cluster (Using Free Oracle cloud credit): https://www.oracle.com/in/cloud/cloud-native/kubernetes-engine/
- GKE Cluster (Using Free Cloud Credit): https://cloud.google.com/kubernetes-engine
- EKS Cluster (Using Free Cloud Credit): https://aws.amazon.com/eks/
- AKS Cluster (Using Free Cloud Credit): https://learn.microsoft.com/en-us/azure/aks/

Exam Tips

- First and foremost, familiarize yourself with the exam content, format, and topics.
- Get comfortable with Kubernetes documentation and with how to search for specific topics and navigate the document website.
- The exam simulator can have multiple clusters and contexts. Make sure you are in the right context before attempting any question.
- Use Kubernetes imperative commands as much as possible; only attempt to create or copy YAML files from documentation if there is no imperative command available for the task.
- The Kubernetes CLI (kubectl) cheat sheet is one of the best resources at your disposal; make sure to use it.
- Use aliases such as **alias k=kubectl** to save time when running commands.
- More often than not, simple solutions are what you want. Avoid unnecessary, lengthy, complicated solutions as much as possible.

- Attempt the questions that you are confident about and can solve quickly.
- If you are stuck on any question, skip it for the time being and come back to it later with a fresh perspective.
- Your goal is to cross the 67% percent passing mark to crack the exam.
- Always take a backup of files that you are modifying to avoid losing the original content if you make a mistake.
- Do not rush to solve the question, as there will be some tricky questions.
- Make sure you validate your answers, script outputs, file locations, and so on.

Noteworthy Bookmarks

Although the exam covers a wide range of security subjects and best practices, it is hard to provide a comprehensive list of all the documents. Following is a list of documents that will serve as a good starting and reference point when you start preparing for the exam. However, do not rely on the bookmarks only; make sure you use these for support and validation.

- **Cluster Setup**
    - **Network Policies**: https://kubernetes.io/docs/concepts/services-networking/network-policies/
    - **Ingress with TLS**: https://kubernetes.io/docs/concepts/services-networking/ingress/#tls
    - **CIS Benchmarks for Kubernetes**: https://kubernetes.io/docs/setup/best-practices/certified-kubernetes/
    - **Verify Platform Binaries**: https://kubernetes.io/docs/setup/release/notes/#checksums
- **Cluster Hardening**
    - **Role-Based Access Control (RBAC)**: https://kubernetes.io/docs/reference/access-authn-authz/rbac/
    - **Service Accounts**: https://kubernetes.io/docs/tasks/configure-pod-container/configure-service-account/
    - **Securing the API Server**: https://kubernetes.io/docs/tasks/administer-cluster/securing-a-cluster/
    - **Upgrading Kubernetes Clusters**: https://kubernetes.io/docs/tasks/administer-cluster/cluster-upgrade/
- **System Hardening**
    - **Minimizing the Host OS Footprint**: https://kubernetes.io/docs/setup/best-practices/node-conformance/

  - **Node Security Best Practices**: https://kubernetes.io/docs/tasks/administer-cluster/securing-a-cluster/#node-security
  - **AppArmor**: https://kubernetes.io/docs/tutorials/clusters/apparmor/
  - **Seccomp**: https://kubernetes.io/docs/tutorials/clusters/seccomp/
- **Minimize Microservice Vulnerabilities**
  - **Pod Security Standards (PSS)**: https://kubernetes.io/docs/concepts/security/pod-security-standards/
  - **Managing Secrets**: https://kubernetes.io/docs/concepts/configuration/secret/
  - **Namespace Isolation**: https://kubernetes.io/docs/concepts/overview/working-with-objects/namespaces/
  - **Pod-to-Pod Encryption Using Cilium**: https://docs.cilium.io/en/stable/gettingstarted/encryption/
- **Supply Chain Security**
  - **Minimizing Base Images**: https://kubernetes.io/docs/concepts/containers/images/#best-practices
  - **SBOM Overview**: https://kubernetes.io/docs/concepts/overview/
  - **Image Signing and Validation**: https://kubernetes.io/docs/tasks/configure-pod-container/pull-image-private-registry/
- **Monitoring, Logging, and Runtime Security**
  - **Kubernetes Audit Logs**: https://kubernetes.io/docs/tasks/debug/debug-cluster/audit/
  - **Falco**: https://falco.org/
  - **Detecting Malicious Activities**: https://kubernetes.io/docs/tasks/debug/debug-cluster/
  - **Immutable Container Patterns**: https://kubernetes.io/docs/concepts/containers/#container-images
- **General References for All Domains**
  - **Kubernetes CLI (kubectl) Cheat Sheet**: https://kubernetes.io/docs/reference/kubectl/cheatsheet/
  - **Official Kubernetes API Reference**: https://kubernetes.io/docs/reference/kubernetes-api/
  - **Best Practices for Securing Clusters**: https://kubernetes.io/docs/tasks/administer-cluster/securing-a-cluster/

This collection will help you navigate the exam more efficiently while adhering to the allowed resources.

Conclusion

In this chapter, we have covered the CKS exam introduction and basic overview. You are now familiar with the exam curriculum, objectives, topics covered, pre-requisites, and target audience for CKS. CKS intends to validate your hands-on experience with Kubernetes and Cloud Native security constructs, starting from Cluster setup, hardening, and workload security to maintain security best practices for monitoring, logging, and auditing.

In the following chapters, we will cover all the CKS domains one by one. In every chapter, you will find practical examples of how the security primitives help with real-world security challenges. We will also include sample questions, answers, and practice questions at the end of every chapter that you can practice in your Kubernetes labs.

CHAPTER 2
Cluster Setup

Introduction

The first domain of the CKS exam focuses on critical security practices necessary to maintain a robust and secure Kubernetes cluster. With the ever-increasing adoption of Kubernetes over the last couple of years, production Kubernetes clusters have grown not only in scale but also in complexity. Making it paramount to understand, implement, and evolve essential security practices for containerized workloads.

Kubernetes has a wide array of tools and mechanisms to enhance cluster security.

First, we will look at Network Policies. By default, all pods within a cluster can talk to all other pods. Which is a huge security concern. Network policies arm you with the mechanism to control network traffic between pods. With these, you can ensure that only permitted traffic flows between the pods. You can define rules and policies to prevent unauthorized access and lateral traffic movement.

The second section of the Cluster setup domain takes advantage of CIS Benchmarking. Center of Internet Security (CIS) Benchmark is a set of comprehensive guidelines to secure a Kubernetes cluster. You can use CIS Benchmark to identify potential security gaps in the cluster; the benchmark also provides recommendations to fix the identified gaps.

Next, we will cover ingress security, which is another critical area that deals with external access to services within the cluster. Ingress is one of the most exploited targets for attackers, as most often, ingress is connected to an external network with internal services at the backend. We will look at how to secure ingress with TLS. Transport Layer Security (TLS) is one of the most popular methods to encrypt communication and protect data in transit.

Cluster nodes are the basic building blocks of any scalable Kubernetes Cluster, so protecting these building blocks is equally important. In this section, we will review the techniques to protect node metadata and endpoint. We will also cover how to verify platform binaries before building the cluster to ensure that the binaries have not been compromised.

Throughout the chapter, you will also find practical, hands-on, scenario-based questions to reinforce the concepts covered in the different sections. By the end of this chapter, you will have a comprehensive understanding of Kubernetes cluster security best practices. The chapter is designed to start you off with a solid foundation of Kubernetes security best practices and their practical implementation in production Kubernetes environments.

Structure

At an elevated level, this chapter covers the following concepts:

- Network Policies
    - Understanding Network Policies
    - The Need for Network Policies
    - Using Network Policies
- CIS Benchmark
    - Getting Started with CIS Benchmarking
    - CIS Benchmark Best Practices
- Ingress and TLS Security
- Securing Node metadata and endpoint
- Verify platform binaries
- Practice questions

Network Policies

Imagine that you are in a utopian city, the city is bustling with activity, and has many grand buildings. By default, there are no rules in the city for resident movement. Residents of any building are free to enter all other buildings without any restriction. Although this sounds like a utopian state with absolute freedom of movement for all its residents, this is a nightmare from a security point of view. If everyone is free to go everywhere, how do you ensure that a resident visiting the building has no malicious intentions?

So, for the security and functioning of the entire city, you need to have some rules and regulations in place that govern which resident is allowed to enter which building and in which buildings access will be restricted. These rules ensure that only authorised residents enter the buildings, protect against lateral access challenges, as well as enhance the security of the overall city.

When a new pod is created, it is assigned an ephemeral IP address from the pod IP range. This IP address is dynamic and changes with every pod restart, which is one of the main reasons why it is advised to implement a pod-to-services communication and not pod-to-pod communication.

Just like our imaginary city, Kubernetes clusters also allow unrestricted pod-to-pod communication within the cluster. This unchecked communication is a security risk which needs to be mitigated to not only secure the pod-pod communication but to secure cluster level access as well.

Understanding Network Policies

By default, pods are non-isolated and can accept traffic from any other source, and just like our imaginary utopian city, this is a security risk that must be mitigated by implementing rules of communication between pods.

Network Policies in Kubernetes let you do just that. With Network Policies, you can define communication rules similar to firewall rules. These rules control the traffic direction as well as target ports. The policies can govern traffic flow either within a namespace or across namespaces as well.

At their core, network policies are quite similar to firewall rules, but unlike firewall, which relies on IP Address and port numbers to filter, allow, or restrict the traffic, network policies control communication at the pod level. Network policies have the following components:

- Which pods are allowed to communicate
- Direction of Traffic
- Protocol – TCP/UDP, and so on
- Port number

There are some other parameters in the network policies that you can use for granular control over traffic. We will look at these in detail in the following sections.

The Need for Network Policies

By default, all pods in the cluster can communicate with each other. Network policies allow you to restrict this communication. This creates a more secure environment by limiting the communication to only necessary pods, which reduces the available attack surface.

You can also use network policies to segment the cluster into different network zones and then control the traffic between these zones. This is especially useful when you have sensitive and non-sensitive applications running on the same cluster and you want to isolate the sensitive applications from non-sensitive applications. Network policies also help you implement the least privilege security principle, where communication is only allowed when necessary, and all unnecessary communications are blocked by default.

Many industries such as Finance and Healthcare also have strict compliance guidelines that the application must adhere to meet the regulation. These regulations can also mandate network segmentation and controlled access which can be achieved with carefully planned network policies.

Using Network Policies

Before we look at how to use the network policies in real-world applications, let us look at the basic network policies definition. The following is the format for the network policies manifest file:

```
apiVersion: networking.k8s.io/v1
kind: NetworkPolicy
metadata:
  name: <policy_name>
  namespace: <namespace_name>
spec:
  podSelector:
    matchLabels:
      <key>:<value>
  policyTypes:
  - Ingress
  - Egress
  ingress:
  - from:
    - ipBlock:
        cidr: <CIDR>
    - namespaceSelector:
        matchLabels:
          <key>: <value>
    ports:
    - protocol: <TCP/UDP>
      port: <port_number>
  egress:
  - to:
    - ipBlock:
        cidr: <CIDR>
    ports:
    - protocol: <TCP/UDP>
      port: <port_number>
```

You can visit https://kubernetes.io/docs/concepts/services-networking/network-policies/ for details on network policies.

Let us start with a sample 3-Tier application, the application has 3 pods running across 3 namespaces. The application consists of a frontend pod, running in the frontend namespace, backend pod running in backend namespace and database pod running in database namespace.

We are going to keep the deployment simple and not add any bloat. The app is made up of just 3 simple httpd containers without any actual application hosted. All 3 pods have the same image and port exposed for ease of deployment. The following is the manifest file:

```
---
apiVersion: v1
kind: Namespace
metadata:
  name: frontend
  labels:
    tier: frontend
---
apiVersion: v1
kind: Namespace
metadata:
  name: backend
  labels:
    tier: backend
---
apiVersion: v1
kind: Namespace
metadata:
  name: database
  labels:
    tier: database
---
apiVersion: v1
kind: Pod
metadata:
  name: frontend-pod
  namespace: frontend
  labels:
    app: frontend
    tier: frontend
spec:
  containers:
  - name: frontend
    image: httpd:latest
    ports:
    - containerPort: 80
---
```

```
apiVersion: v1
kind: Pod
metadata:
  labels:
    app: frontend
    tier: frontend
  name: frontend-test
  namespace: frontend
spec:
  containers:
  - image: alpine:latest
    name: frontend-test
    args:
    - /bin/sh
    - -c
    - while true; do sleep 5; done;
---
apiVersion: v1
kind: Pod
metadata:
  name: backend-pod
  namespace: backend
  labels:
    app: backend
    tier: backend
spec:
  containers:
  - name: backend
    image: httpd:latest
    ports:
    - containerPort: 80
---
apiVersion: v1
kind: Pod
metadata:
  name: database-pod
  namespace: database
  labels:
    app: database
    tier: database
spec:
  containers:
  - name: database
    image: httpd:latest
    ports:
    - containerPort: 80
```

Apply the manifest file.

```
$ kubectl apply -f sample
namespace/frontend created
namespace/backend created
namespace/database created
pod/frontend-pod created
pod/frontend-test created
pod/backend-pod created
pod/database-pod created
```

After you deploy the manifest, you should have 3 namespaces with 2 pods in the frontend namespace and 1 pod each in the backend and database namespace. By default, all the pods can communicate with each other. Let us validate this:

```
$ kubectl get ns
NAME                  STATUS   AGE
backend               Active   106s
database              Active   106s
frontend              Active   106s

% kubectl get po -n frontend -o wide
NAME              READY    STATUS     RESTARTS    AGE      IP             NODE
frontend-pod      1/1      Running    0           25m      10.0.10.114     10.0.10.14
frontend-test     1/1      Running    0           2m12s    10.0.10.117    10.0.10.238

% kubectl get po -n backend -o wide
NAME            READY    STATUS     RESTARTS    AGE    IP            NODE
backend-pod     1/1      Running    0           25m    10.0.10.148    10.0.10.194

% kubectl get po -n database -o wide
NAME             READY    STATUS     RESTARTS    AGE    IP            NODE
database-pod     1/1      Running    0           26m    10.0.10.118    10.0.10.238

Let's try to access the database pod from the frontend namespace.
% kubectl exec --stdin --tty frontend-test -n frontend -- /bin/sh
# wget http://10.0.10.118
Connecting to 10.0.10.118 (10.0.10.118:80)
saving to 'index.html'
index.html           100%
|*********************************************************************************
**************|    45  0:00:00 ETA
'index.html' saved
#
```

As we can see that the frontend-test pod is able to access the database pod. Which is not the way it should be. We do not want anyone with access to the frontend namespace to be able to access the database directly. Let us fix this with the following scenarios:

Scenario 1

Let us assume that you want to apply a bottom-up approach for the application deployment and want to restrict all ingress communication in the namespaces frontend, backend, and database.

This can be done by creating a deny-all ingress policy for these namespaces. There are a couple of examples available at https://kubernetes.io/docs/concepts/services-networking/network-policies/. The following is the manifest file to create a deny-all-ingress policy for all namespaces:

```
---
apiVersion: networking.k8s.io/v1
kind: NetworkPolicy
metadata:
  name: deny-all-ingress
  namespace: frontend
spec:
  podSelector: {}
  policyTypes:
    - Ingress
---
apiVersion: networking.k8s.io/v1
kind: NetworkPolicy
metadata:
  name: deny-all-ingress
  namespace: backend
spec:
  podSelector: {}
  policyTypes:
    - Ingress
---
apiVersion: networking.k8s.io/v1
kind: NetworkPolicy
metadata:
  name: deny-all-ingress
  namespace: database
spec:
  podSelector: {}
  policyTypes:
    - Ingress
```

If you notice the policy type is Ingress however, we have not defined anything in the ingress section, this means all ingress traffic will be blocked. We also have not defined anything in the podSelector section, meaning the policy will apply to all pods in the namespace.

```
% kubectl apply -f default-deny-np.yaml
networkpolicy.networking.k8s.io/deny-all-ingress created
networkpolicy.networking.k8s.io/deny-all-ingress created
networkpolicy.networking.k8s.io/deny-all-ingress created
% kubectl describe networkpolicy deny-all-ingress -n database
Name:         deny-all-ingress
Namespace:    database
Created on:   2024-12-30 15:01:56 +0000 UTC
Labels:       <none>
Annotations:  <none>
Spec:
  PodSelector:     <none> (Allowing the specific traffic to all pods
in this namespace)
  Allowing ingress traffic:
    <none> (Selected pods are isolated for ingress connectivity)
  Not affecting egress traffic
  Policy Types: Ingress
```

Once you apply the policy, all ingress traffic to all pods in 3 namespaces will be restricted.

Let us validate this with the help of the frontend-test pod again.

```
% kubectl exec --stdin --tty frontend-test -n frontend -- /bin/sh
/ # wget --timeout=5 http://10.0.10.118
Connecting to 10.0.10.118 (10.0.10.118:80)
wget: download timed out
```

As you can see, the connection from the frontend to the database pod is now timing out.

Practice Question: Deploy a pod named backend-test in the backend namespace using alpine:latest image. Open an interactive shell to this pod. Check whether you can connect to the database pod from the backend-test pod.

Scenario 2

Now that we have the default deny policy applied on all namespaces. The application is useless as nothing can communicate with anything else. So, let us consider following network flow which the application needs to function properly:

- Outside traffic should be allowed to communicate with the frontend.
- Only Frontend traffic should be allowed to reach the backend.
- Only backend traffic should be allowed to reach the database.

Let us build the required network policies.

1. Allowing outside traffic to the frontend pod.

   ```
   apiVersion: networking.k8s.io/v1
   kind: NetworkPolicy
   metadata:
     name: allow-ingress-to-frontend
     namespace: frontend
   spec:
     podSelector:
       matchLabels:
          tier: frontend
     policyTypes:
       - Ingress
     ingress:
     - from:
       - ipBlock:
           cidr: 0.0.0.0/0
       ports:
       - protocol: TCP
         port: 80
   ```

   The foregoing policy will allow incoming traffic on port 80 for the pod frontend in the frontend namespace.

2. Allow frontend to backend communication

   ```
   apiVersion: networking.k8s.io/v1
   kind: NetworkPolicy
   metadata:
     name: allow-frontend-to-backend
     namespace: backend
   spec:
     podSelector:
       matchLabels:
          tier: backend
     policyTypes:
       - Ingress
     ingress:
     - from:
       - namespaceSelector:
           matchLabels:
             tier: frontend
       - podSelector:
           matchLabels:
             tier: frontend
       ports:
   ```

```
      - protocol: TCP
        port: 80
```

3. Allowing backend to database traffic

```
apiVersion: networking.k8s.io/v1
kind: NetworkPolicy
metadata:
  name: allow-frontend-to-backend
  namespace: database
spec:
  podSelector:
    matchLabels:
       tier: database
  policyTypes:
    - Ingress
  ingress:
  - from:
    - namespaceSelector:
        matchLabels:
          tier: backend
    - podSelector:
        matchLabels:
          tier: backend
    ports:
    - protocol: TCP
      port: 80
```

Let us apply the manifests and build the network policies as per the scenario.

```
$ kubectl apply -f frontend.yaml
networkpolicy.networking.k8s.io/allow-ingress-to-frontend created
$ kubectl apply -f frontend-to-backend-traffic.yaml
networkpolicy.networking.k8s.io/allow-frontend-to-backend created
$ kubectl apply -f backend-to-database-traffic.yaml
networkpolicy.networking.k8s.io/allow-frontend-to-backend created

Once you apply these policy manifests, only the needed traffic will flow between
the pods and namespaces. All unwanted traffic is blocked and not permitted by
the default deny policy. Let us test this:

$ kubectl get pods -n database -o wide
NAME           READY   STATUS    RESTARTS   AGE   IP            NODE
database-pod   1/1     Running   0          62m   10.0.10.118   10.0.10.238
$ kubectl get pods -n backend -o wide
NAME          READY   STATUS    RESTARTS   AGE   IP            NODE
backend-pod   1/1     Running   0          62m   10.0.10.148   10.0.10.194
$ kubectl exec --stdin --tty frontend-test -n frontend -- /bin/sh
```

```
/ # wget --timeout=5 http://10.0.10.118
Connecting to 10.0.10.118 (10.0.10.118:80)
wget: download timed out
/ # wget --timeout=5 http://10.0.10.148
Connecting to 10.0.10.148 (10.0.10.148:80)
saving to 'index.html'
index.html           100%
|**********************************************************************
***********************************************************************
|    45  0:00:00 ETA
'index.html' saved
/ #
```

As you can see, the connection from the frontend-test pod to the backend pod was successful. However, the connection from the frontend-test pod to the database pod timed out.

This gives you granular control over the traffic flow between namespaces and pods to ensure better security.

Practice Question

Use the backend-test pod that you had deployed in the last practice question and test the connectivity from backend-test to the database pod.

Practice Question

In some cases, instead of blocking the ingress traffic, you might want to control the outgoing traffic. This is especially useful when you want to prevent data exfiltration. You need to use the same deployment and build the following scenario:

- The database pod can only communicate with the backend pod; all other egress should be blocked.
- The backend pod should only be able to communicate with the frontend pod; all other egress should be blocked.

Practice Question: Namespaces, with the right policies in place, can be used to isolate the workloads and share the cluster resources with multiple users. You need to implement the following scenario using the same deployment.

- All the pods in the frontend namespace should be able to communicate with and only with all pods in the backend namespace.
- All the pods in the backend namespace should be able to communicate with and only with all the pods in the database namespace.
- All other ingress and egress to/from the backend and database namespaces should be blocked.

Best Practices for Network Policies

Network policies give you granular control over all traffic that flows between pods and namespaces. However, you need to ensure that the Network Policies are used with caution. Wrongly configured network policies can disrupt the whole application flow and bring the cluster to a halt. The following are a couple of best practices that you need to keep in mind when working with network policies:

- Start with a default deny policy for all workloads. This ensures that only the required communication is enabled down the line and this also avoids the challenges with default allow policies which are trickier to maintain as you need to identify all traffic that needs to be blocked.
- Ensure that the pods, namespaces, hosts, deployments, and services are labelled properly and that there is no overlap in labels to ensure that the policy will only impact the traffic that it is intended for.
- Do not apply all the network policies at once; use a gradual approach. With a gradual approach, it is easier to measure the impact of the changes, and it is also easier to fix things if you know what has changed recently.
- Test the network policies beforehand in the test, dev environment. Do not apply the policies directly in production until you ensure that the policies work as intended.

CIS Benchmark

Center for Internet Security (CIS) benchmark has developed a comprehensive security benchmark for multiple IT Systems, this includes benchmark for Kubernetes as well. These benchmarks are developed in a collaborative process which includes Cybersecurity experts, subject matter experts and different organizations around the world.

CIS leverages a consensus-based approach while establishing the standard security controls for the IT systems. These controls help organizations to protect against known security vulnerabilities and threats.

CIS benchmark for kubernetes offers comprehensive guidelines on how to secure Kubernetes Clusters, these guidelines span from Control plane security, policies, RBAC to Logging and monitoring. By adhering to these standards, you can reduce the risk of attacks as well as protect your system based on industry best practices.

CIS benchmark for Kubernetes organizes the Kubernetes security components and aspects in multiple sections, with every section dealing with a particular area. Here is a brief on the principal areas covered by the CIS Benchmark:

- **Kubernetes Cluster Configuration:** This area deals with the configuration of the control plane components. The components covered by this section are API Server, etcd server, controller manager, and so on.

- **Worker Node Configuration:** This area deals with worker nodes as well as components running on these worker nodes, such as kubelet and CRE.
- **Network Policies:** The area focuses on the network policies used to control network traffic between pods, services, and namespaces.
- **Pod Security:** Pod security aspects focus on the capabilities that a running pod has, such as running the processes as root, running privileged containers, or allowing access to node parameters that are not needed.
- **Role Based Access Control:** This deals with securing access to the cluster and cluster components by way of limiting access to authorized users and services.
- **Secrets:** Secrets store sensitive data used by the pods or the cluster itself. It is important that these secrets are properly protected to avoid leaking sensitive information.
- **Logging and Monitoring:** This area provides recommendations on how to set up logging and monitoring for the cluster and cluster components to ensure that security issues are detected promptly.
- **Container Security:** This includes the use of trusted images, trusted image sources, and applying least privilege for the containers.

Getting Started with CIS Benchmarking

There are a lot of tools that can be used to evaluate your cluster against CIS Benchmarks. However, we will use kube-bench, which is specifically designed to check the clusters against the CIS Benchmark.

Kube-bench can be used in a variety of ways, as per kube-bench documentation at https://aquasecurity.github.io/kube-bench/dev/installation kube-bench can be installed directly on the host, it can run as a container, which installs kube-bench on the host, or you can install it from the binaries or compile it directly from the source.

However, the easiest way to use kube-bench is to run it as a pod on the Kubernetes cluster as part of a job. The kube-bench GitHub page https://github.com/aquasecurity/kube-bench?tab=readme-ov-file has all the supported job files to quickly get started with kube-bench, along with the instructions on how to run the job.

You can also create your own job file, which includes certain benchmarks and forgoes others. However, for the exercise, we will stick to the supplied main job file. The following are the steps to run kube-bench on a Kubernetes cluster using the job file available at the kube-bench GitHub page:

You can either download the job file and save it on the workstation or use the raw URL to directly apply it to the Kubernetes cluster.

```
% kubectl apply -f https://raw.githubusercontent.com/aquasecurity/
kube-bench/refs/heads/main/job.yaml
job.batch/kube-bench created

Look at the pods created by the job.
% kubectl get pods
NAME               READY   STATUS      RESTARTS   AGE
kube-bench-bfhtt   0/1     Completed   0          77s

Once the pod status shows Completed, you can download the logs from
the pod.

% kubectl logs kube-bench-bfhtt
```

The pod logs contain the summary of the test performed, following are some of the key components that you will see in the results:

- **Node Info:** Type of node (control plane or worker node) on which the test was performed.
- **Component Info**: Information about the components on the node that were inspected.
- **Passed Checks:** List of checks that were passed on the node.
- **Failed Checks:** List of checks that failed on the node.
- **Warnings:** List of checks that had a warning status.
- **Summary:** This is a high-level summary of the results.
- **Remediation Recommendation:** The tool provides a list of recommendations based on the test result on how to fix the failed and warning tests.

The following is an excerpt from the logs returned by the last command:

```
[INFO] 1 Control Plane Security Configuration
[INFO] 1.1 Control Plane Node Configuration Files
[PASS] 1.1.1 Ensure that the API server pod specification file
permissions are set to 600 or more restrictive (Automated)
[PASS] 1.1.2 Ensure that the API server pod specification file
ownership is set to root:root (Automated)
[FAIL] 1.1.19 Ensure that the Kubernetes PKI directory and file
ownership is set to root:root (Automated)
[WARN] 1.1.20 Ensure that the Kubernetes PKI certificate file
permissions are set to 600 or more restrictive (Manual)
[WARN] 1.1.21 Ensure that the Kubernetes PKI key file permissions are
set to 600 (Manual)
.
```

```
.
== Remediations master ==
1.1.19 Run the below command (based on the file location on your system)
on the control plane node.
For example,
chown -R root:root /etc/kubernetes/pki/
1.2.5 Follow the Kubernetes documentation and setup the TLS connection
between
the apiserver and kubelets. Then, edit the API server pod specification
file
/etc/kubernetes/manifests/kube-apiserver.yaml on the control plane
node and set the
--kubelet-certificate-authority parameter to the path to the cert file
for the certificate authority.
--kubelet-certificate-authority=<ca-string>
== Summary policies ==
0 checks PASS
6 checks FAIL
29 checks WARN
0 checks INFO

== Summary total ==
57 checks PASS
19 checks FAIL
54 checks WARN
0 checks INFO
```

Every Kubernetes cluster is different, and no two clusters might have the same results when running kube-bench. The results might be lengthy with lots of information and action items. However, as part of the exam, you will be expected to only apply a certain recommendation, but you need to ensure that you can quickly run kube-bench as per the provided scenario, look at the results, and apply the given recommendation to fix this.

Tip: *Always make sure that you run the kube-bench again after fixing the issue and make sure that the test for the issues is passed, ensuring that the fix has been applied as per the remediation recommendation.*

Tip: *kube-bench is a great tool to ensure compliance with the CIS benchmark for self-managed clusters; however, cloud solutions such as EKS, AKS, and OKE are managed solutions, so you need to ensure that you use the right job file for the managed cloud clusters.*

Let us look at two examples of kube-bench recommendations and how to fix and validate the results.

CIS Benchmark Best Practices

The following are the key areas of CIS Benchmark best practices:

- CIS benchmark is frequently updated with newer versions to address newer vulnerabilities and to address new best practices. You need to ensure that you update the benchmark version to keep up with the changes introduced in the newer releases.
- Make sure that all the changes that you are making in the cluster configuration are well documented. The document should contain the details of what has changed, why it has changed, and when the change was implemented to ensure that the impact can be easily traced, justified, and reversed if needed.
- As mentioned in the first point, newer versions bring newer guidelines and address the latest known vulnerabilities. You need to ensure that you regularly audit the cluster against the latest CIS Benchmarks to ensure compliance.

Practice Question:

- Run kube-bench in your Kubernetes cluster and look for the following test in the output.

  ```
  1.1.11 Ensure that the etcd data directory permissions are set to
  700 or more restrictive (Automated)
  ```

- Apply the accompanying recommendation for the test if the test had failed and re-run the test. Validate that the test passes.

Practice Question:

- The following is the test result from kube-bench along with the recommendation to fix the warning:

  ```
  [WARN] 1.3.1 Ensure that the --terminated-pod-gc-threshold argu-
  ment is set as appropriate (Manual)
  ```

Recommendation

- 1.3.1 Edit the Controller Manager pod specification file **`/etc/kubernetes/manifests/kube-controller-manager.yaml`** on the control plane node and set the **`--terminated-pod-gc-threshold`** to an appropriate threshold, for example, **`--terminated-pod-gc-threshold=10`**
- Apply the recommendation in your cluster, run kube-bench, and validate that the warning goes away.

Ingress and TLS Security

Ingress in Kubernetes allows you to manage external access to services within a cluster. It is used for HTTP or HTTPs services. Unlike Load Balancer service, which uses one IP address per service, ingress can expose multiple services using a single IP address. Ingress relies on rules to control the traffic flow to backend services.

Kubernetes, by default, does not have a controller for ingress, and you need to deploy one externally. Ingress is part of both CKAD and CKA exams, and CKS only deals with the ingress security aspect, so we are not going to cover the ingress setup in detail.

CKS is primarily focused on configuring the ingress object with TLS termination, which ensures that the traffic coming in from the outside is secured and the data exchanged between the client and service is encrypted to prevent eavesdropping and tampering. The internal ingress to service traffic can still use http. This alleviates the need to configure end-to-end encryption for service traffic.

Getting Started with Ingress and TLS

The following practice exercise assumes that you have already configured an ingress controller. Ingress in Kubernetes cannot work without the controller. Depending on the environment that you are using, you can use either a self-managed ingress controller, such as NGINX, or use managed services such as cloud application gateways for ingress controllers.

To set up Ingress with TLS, we need to perform the following steps:

1. Set up backend service and deployment
2. Create Self-Signed certificate with key
3. Create Kubernetes Secret
4. Create Ingress with TLS Secret

Set up backend service and deployment

In Kubernetes, services are the go-to method to expose anything, either within the cluster or outside the cluster. This holds true for ingress as well; to configure an ingress, we will need a backend service that exposes the application or service running on the pod on a port.

Another best practice is to deploy the pods using deployments for easy management. Let us build a deployment for nginx pods and expose a container port using a service.

```
apiVersion: v1
kind: Namespace
metadata:
  name: ingress-ns
---
apiVersion: apps/v1
kind: Deployment
```

```
metadata:
  name: ingress-nginx
  namespace: ingress-ns
  labels:
    tier: ingress-nginx
spec:
  replicas: 1
  selector:
    matchLabels:
      tier: ingress-nginx
  template:
    metadata:
      labels:
        tier: ingress-nginx
    spec:
      containers:
      - name: demo-nginx
        image: nginx:latest
        ports:
        - containerPort: 80
---
apiVersion: v1
kind: Service
metadata:
  name: demo-ingress-backend
  namespace: ingress-ns
spec:
  selector:
    tier: ingress-nginx
  ports:
    - protocol: TCP
      port: 80
      targetPort: 80
```

Apply the manifest file and view the deployed resource.

```
% kubectl apply -f ingress_deployment.yaml
namespace/ingress-ns created
deployment.apps/ingress-nginx created
service/demo-ingress-backend created
```

Let us quickly make sure that the nginx service is exposed on the Cluster-IP.

```
% kubectl get pods -n ingress-ns
NAME                             READY   STATUS    RESTARTS   AGE
ingress-nginx-54cc566894-ctbk6   1/1     Running   0          42s
```

```
% kubectl get service -n ingress-ns
NAME                   TYPE        CLUSTER-IP      EXTERNAL-IP   PORT(S)   AGE
demo-ingress-backend   ClusterIP   10.102.61.174   <none>        80/TCP    34s
% kubectl describe service demo-ingress-backend -n ingress-ns
Name:              demo-ingress-backend
Namespace:         ingress-ns
Labels:            <none>
Annotations:       <none>
Selector:          tier=ingress-nginx
Type:              ClusterIP
IP Family Policy:  SingleStack
IP Families:       IPv4
IP:                10.102.61.174
IPs:               10.102.61.174
Port:              <unset>  80/TCP
TargetPort:        80/TCP
Endpoints:         10.244.0.25:80
Session Affinity:  None
Events:            <none>
```

Create Self-Signed certificate with key

For a production environment, you will generate a CSR and then provide this CSR to a Certificate Authority, which in turn will generate a TLS certificate and key and provide it to you. You can use this TLS Certificate to secure the network communication.

However, in the practice lab, we will use a self-signed certificate. The certificate type does not really impact the process. You can use tools such as OpenSSL to generate this self-signed certificate along with the TLS key.

```
% openssl req -x509 -nodes -days 365 -newkey rsa:2048 -keyout ingress.
key -out ingress.crt -subj "/CN=nginx-ingress.com/O=nginx-ingress"
.....+....+++++++++++++++++++++++++++++++++++++++++*.+.........+......+.
+...+.....+......+.......+.....+............+..+.......+..+......+...
+..........+.........+......+++++++++++++++++++++++++++++++++++++++++*
...............+......+.+.....-----
```

Create Kubernetes Secret with TLS

Kubernetes has a secret of type TLS to store TLS certificates and keys. This secret can then be referenced in other Kubernetes objects to inject the certificate and key data in respective objects.

You can use the following imperative command to create this secret.

```
% kubectl create secret tls ingress-tls-secret --key=ingress.key
--cert=ingress.crt --namespace=ingress-ns
secret/ingress-tls-secret created
```

This command will create a TLS secret in ingress-ns namespace with the name ingress-tls-secret.

If you want to use a yaml file to create the secret. Then you can use the following yaml definition file.

```
apiVersion: v1
kind: Secret
metadata:
  name: ingress-tls-secret
  namespace: ingress-ns
type: kubernetes.io/tls
data:
  tls.crt: <base64 encoded tls.crt>
  tls.key: <base64 encoded tls.key>
```

To use the yaml file, you will first have to encode the ingress.crt and ingress.key file and update the output in the data segment under their respective sections.

Create Ingress with TLS Secret

Once we have the TLS certificate and key in the secret format, we can use this to create an ingress object and inject the secret into the ingress.

For this exercise, we have deployed a Kubernetes cluster using minikube and have enabled the ingress addon. The minikube ingress addon is based on nginx. You can enable this by running the following command:

```
minikube addons enable ingress
```

The following is the YAML file to create the ingress object with TLS Secret:

```
apiVersion: networking.k8s.io/v1
kind: Ingress
metadata:
  name: frontend-ingress
  namespace: ingress-ns
  annotations:
       nginx.ingress.kubernetes.io/rewrite-target: /
spec:
  tls:
  - hosts:
    - ingress-demo.localhost
    secretName: ingress-tls-secret
```

```
rules:
- host: ingress-demo.localhost
  http:
    paths:
    - path: /
      pathType: Prefix
      backend:
        service:
          name: demo-ingress-backend
          port:
            number: 80
```

Apply the manifest file after which we can look at the ingress details.

```
% kubectl apply -f ingress-with-tls.yaml
ingress.networking.k8s.io/frontend-ingress created
```

Testing Ingress with Certificate

Let's look at the ingress object.

```
% kubectl get ingress -n ingress-ns
NAME               CLASS   HOSTS                    ADDRESS        PORTS     AGE
frontend-ingress   nginx   ingress-demo.localhost   192.168.49.2   80, 443   64s
% kubectl describe ingress frontend-ingres -n ingress-ns
Name:              frontend-ingress
Labels:            <none>
Namespace:         ingress-ns
Address:           192.168.49.2
Ingress Class:     nginx
Default backend:   <default>
TLS:
  ingress-tls-secret terminates ingress-demo.localhost
Rules:
  Host                       Path  Backends
  ----                       ----  --------
  ingress-demo.localhost
                             /   demo-ingress-backend:80 (10.244.0.25:80)
Annotations:                 nginx.ingress.kubernetes.io/rewrite-target: /
Events:
  Type    Reason  Age                 From                      Message
  ----    ------  ----                ----                      -------
  Normal  Sync    49s (x2 over 83s)  nginx-ingress-controller  Scheduled for sync
```

To check the connection to ingress, we will need to create an entry in the hosts file that points the ingress host URL to the minikube internal IP. You can check the minikube node internal IP by running the following command:

```
% kubectl get nodes -o wide
NAME       STATUS   ROLES           AGE   VERSION   INTERNAL-IP    EXTERNAL-IP
OS-IMAGE            KERNEL-VERSION   CONTAINER-RUNTIME
minikube   Ready    control-plane   29h   v1.31.0   192.168.49.2   <none>
Ubuntu 22.04.4 LTS   6.6.30-0-virt    docker://27.2.0
```

Note down the internal ip and create the hosts file entry as follows:

```
% vi /etc/hosts
# localhost is used to configure the loopback interface
# when the system is booting. Do not change this entry.
192.168.49.2    ingress-demo.localhost
```

After this, you can use curl to check access to the URL with HTTPS by running the following command:

```
% curl -vvv -k https://ingress-demo.localhost/
* Host ingress-demo.localhost:443 was resolved.
* Connected to ingress-demo.localhost (127.0.0.1) port 443
* ALPN: curl offers h2,http/1.1
* (304) (OUT), TLS handshake, Client hello (1):
* (304) (IN), TLS handshake, Server hello (2):
* (304) (IN), TLS handshake, Unknown (8):
* (304) (IN), TLS handshake, Certificate (11):
* (304) (IN), TLS handshake, CERT verify (15):
* (304) (IN), TLS handshake, Finished (20):
* (304) (OUT), TLS handshake, Finished (20):
* SSL connection using TLSv1.3 / AEAD-CHACHA20-POLY1305-SHA256 /
[blank] / UNDEF
* ALPN: server accepted h2
* Server certificate:
*  subject: CN=TRAEFIK DEFAULT CERT
*  start date: Dec 29 11:00:24 2024 GMT
*  expire date: Dec 29 11:00:24 2025 GMT
*  issuer: CN=TRAEFIK DEFAULT CERT
*  SSL certificate verify result: unable to get local issuer certificate
(20), continuing anyway.
* using HTTP/2
* [HTTP/2] [1] OPENED stream for https://ingress-demo.localhost/
* [HTTP/2] [1] [:method: GET]
* [HTTP/2] [1] [:scheme: https]
* [HTTP/2] [1] [:authority: ingress-demo.localhost]
* [HTTP/2] [1] [:path: /]
* [HTTP/2] [1] [user-agent: curl/8.7.1]
* [HTTP/2] [1] [accept: */*]
```

```
> GET / HTTP/2
> Host: ingress-demo.localhost
> User-Agent: curl/8.7.1
> Accept: */*
>
* Request completely sent off
< HTTP/2 404
< content-type: text/plain; charset=utf-8
< x-content-type-options: nosniff
< content-length: 19
< date: Mon, 30 Dec 2024 16:45:40 GMT
<
* Connection #0 to host ingress-demo.localhost left intact
```

As you can see, we are able to connect to the backend service using ingress with TLS certificate.

Ingress Controller Security Best Practices

By default, when you deploy an ingress controller, it does not have any restrictions on how it runs. Most ingress controllers run as deployments on the Kubernetes cluster and should be governed by the same security policies as any other application deployment. The following are some of the best practices that you should adhere to when deploying the controller on the cluster:

- Make sure that the controller is running as a non-root user. This ensures that the controller does not have unnecessary privileges and cannot elevate privileges.
- Not all namespaces in the cluster will require an ingress, you should limit the controller to specific namespaces to reduce the attack surface for example generally only the web tier in a 3-tier application needs an ingress and the app and db tier do not need an ingress. So, you can limit the ingress controller access to only the web or frontend namespace.
- Enable audit logging in the controller to ensure that access logs are tracked and stored. These can then be used to track user activity.
- You should also implement periodic review of audit logs to detect unusual and unauthorized access attempts; you can implement a monitoring and notification system to the same effect.
- You should also conduct regular penetration testings to identify and address security weaknesses in the ingress configurations.

Practice Question: Deploy a pod named webpage, use httpd:latest image. Expose this pod via a load balancer service named webpage-service. Create a new TLS Certificate and Key with CNAME webpage.localhost, and use the generated certificate and key to create a new tls secret using the YAML file. Create a new ingress object and use this TLS secret in the ingress. Validate the connection over https to the ingress and backend service.

Securing Node Metadata and Endpoint

When you deploy a Kubernetes cluster, it does not just run in a vacuum, it is deployed on either physical or virtual machines. Each of these virtual machines runs the necessary services to manage the pods assigned to them. Each node also exposes multiple endpoints, either within the cluster or outside the cluster. Securing these endpoints is of utmost importance when building a security framework for Kubernetes.

Node and Endpoint security covers several practices such as protecting the nodes metadata, securing kubelet configuration and validating the integrity of platform binaries. In this section we are going to cover these one by one.

Securing the Nodes Metadata

Nodes metadata contains sensitive information about the nodes and how the nodes are configured; for example, the metadata endpoint might expose the deployment location, date, IP address, and in some cases even node authentication details, which allows access to other services without any restrictions. Depending on the node provider, the information made available via the metadata endpoint might be different; however, it is always a good practice to secure the metadata endpoints. This is especially true in scenarios where the nodes are deployed in a cloud environment, either on managed or controlled machines.

As part of the CKS exam, you should be aware of such endpoints and have a high-level idea of how to disable access to these.

Let us take an example of a Kubernetes cluster running on an AWS EC2 instance. By default, EC2 instances expose the metadata endpoint on an internal IP address **169.254.169.254**. You can easily read all instance properties by querying the endpoint.

Other cloud providers also use the same IP address, 169.254.169.254, to expose the metadata API endpoint. You can read more about querying metadata for other cloud providers using the links provided in the chapter appendix.

These documents also provide the details of the information that is published via these endpoints. There are many ways to protect the endpoint, and some of these are specific to the cloud provider; for example, in AWS, you can create an IAM role and assign the role to the EC2 instances running the EKS nodes to enforce restricted access to the metadata. However, that is not in scope of the CKS exam, and we will only focus on the method available to us within the scope of the Kubernetes cluster.

One way in which you can restrict access is by using egress network policies. You can create a default deny egress policy to metadata endpoints. This will ensure that all the traffic to the metadata endpoint from the pods is dropped.

Practice Question: Create an egress network policy that blocks all traffic to IP address 169.254.169.254 from frontend and backend namespaces.

Securing Node Endpoints

Kubernetes API endpoint is one of the most known service ports. By default, the Kubernetes API server uses port 6443. Any client can use this port to communicate with the API Server and either read information or make changes to existing deployments or create new deployments.

There are other ports and protocols that are open by default. You can find the complete list of such ports at https://kubernetes.io/docs/reference/networking/ports-and-protocols/.

Table 2.1 lists the ports for control plane nodes.

Protocol	Direction	Port Range	Purpose	Used By
TCP	Inbound	6443	Kubernetes API server	All
TCP	Inbound	2379-2380	etcd server client API	kube-apiserver, etcd
TCP	Inbound	10250	Kubelet API	Self, Control plane
TCP	Inbound	10259	kube-scheduler	Self
TCP	Inbound	10257	kube-controller-manager	Self

Table 2.1: *Ports for Kubernetes Control Plane Nodes*

Table 2.2 lists the ports for the worker nodes

Protocol	Direction	Port Range	Purpose	Used By
TCP	Inbound	10250	Kubelet API	Self, Control plane
TCP	Inbound	10256	kube-proxy	Self, Load balancers
TCP	Inbound	30000-32767	NodePort Services†	All

Table 2.2: *Ports for Kubernetes Worker Nodes*

Some of these ports, such as the API Server port, can be changed to custom ports, while others cannot be changed or have too large a range to be changed.

For the ports that support changes like the API Server port, you should always use a custom port instead of the default port. For ports that cannot be changed, consider using a firewall for all traffic to and from the cluster. You can either employ a central firewall to monitor and control traffic for the whole subnet or you can use the node firewall to also control which ports are allowed on the node.

Securing Kubelet Configurations

Kubelet is the primary agent running on each node. It is responsible for managing all the containers that run on that node. Securing kubelet is also vital to prevent unauthorized access to the containers and to ensure the integrity of the node.

Restricting Kubelet permissions involves disabling anonymous access and enabling authentication and authorization mechanisms. By default, requests to the kubelet's HTTPS endpoint are not rejected by other configured authentication methods and treated as anonymous. This is a security issue, as even unauthorized users can make requests to the kubelet and get responses. You can change this behaviour by updating the kubelet configuration to disable anonymous authentication. There are many ways in which you can achieve this.

1. Start the kubelet service with --anonymous-auth=false flag by running the following command:

   ```
   systemctl restart kubelet --anonymous-auth=false
   ```

2. If you want to make the restart behaviour sticky and not worry about service restarts, you can update the kubelet configuration file and add the following configuration to the file:

   ```
   --anonymous-auth=false
   ```

Securing Graphical User Interface (GUI)

So far, in all examples we have used kubectl to view, manage and deploy new kubernetes objects, kubectl is quite versatile and powerful in that it provides granular control over all things Kubernetes. However, it is not the most user-friendly way of interacting with the Kubernetes objects. Some users prefer a graphical user interface (GUI) over CLI. It is also much easier to monitor objects in a GUI with click throughs.

While Kubernetes itself does not have a GUI, there are many options available that provide a graphical management and monitoring platform for Kubernetes. Kubernetes Dashboard is one such option. It is a free, web-based, highly functional option when you need a user interface to manage the Kubernetes cluster.

However, the dashboard opens another point of attack to the outside world and increases the attack surface. If the GUI is not well protected and configured with required access control it might end up compromising the security of the whole environment.

Installing Kubernetes Dashboard

Kubernetes dashboard is open-source, and the code is hosted on GitHub at https://github.com/kubernetes/dashboard. You can deploy the dashboard in many ways, such as using Helm or kubectl. The yaml manifest file for the dashboard is available at https://raw.githubusercontent.com/kubernetes/dashboard/v2.7.0/aio/deploy/recommended.yaml

To deploy Kubernetes Dashboard on the cluster, simply run the following command:

```
% kubectl apply -f https://raw.githubusercontent.com/kubernetes/
dashboard/v2.7.0/aio/deploy/recommended.yaml
namespace/kubernetes-dashboard created
serviceaccount/kubernetes-dashboard created
service/kubernetes-dashboard created
secret/kubernetes-dashboard-certs created
secret/kubernetes-dashboard-csrf created
secret/kubernetes-dashboard-key-holder created
configmap/kubernetes-dashboard-settings created
role.rbac.authorization.k8s.io/kubernetes-dashboard created
clusterrole.rbac.authorization.k8s.io/kubernetes-dashboard created
rolebinding.rbac.authorization.k8s.io/kubernetes-dashboard created
clusterrolebinding.rbac.authorization.k8s.io/kubernetes-dashboard
created
deployment.apps/kubernetes-dashboard created
service/dashboard-metrics-scraper created
deployment.apps/dashboard-metrics-scraper created
```

All these objects are deployed in a separate namespace called kubernetes-dashboard. Let us look at all the components in the kubernetes-dashboard namespace.

```
% kubectl get all -n kubernetes-dashboard
NAME                                            READY   STATUS    RESTARTS   AGE
pod/dashboard-metrics-scraper-6b96ff7878-9gt22  1/1     Running   0          111s
pod/kubernetes-dashboard-8696f5f494-vdzfc        1/1     Running   0          111s

NAME                                TYPE        CLUSTER-IP      EXTERNAL-IP
PORT(S)     AGE
service/dashboard-metrics-scraper   ClusterIP   10.97.26.33     <none>        8000/
TCP    111s
service/kubernetes-dashboard        ClusterIP   10.108.192.80   <none>        443/
TCP     111s

NAME                                        READY   UP-TO-DATE   AVAILABLE   AGE
deployment.apps/dashboard-metrics-scraper   1/1     1            1           111s
deployment.apps/kubernetes-dashboard        1/1     1            1           111s
```

```
NAME                                                    DESIRED   CURRENT   READY   AGE
replicaset.apps/dashboard-metrics-scraper-6b96ff7878   1         1         1       111s
replicaset.apps/kubernetes-dashboard-8696f5f494        1         1         1       111s
```

By default, ClusterIP service type is used for the dashboard service on port 80. For this reason, the dashboard can only be accessed from the nodes where it is running. However, you can use kubectl proxy to proxy the connection to the hosts from localhost. Run the following command to start the proxy:

```
% kubectl proxy
Starting to serve on 127.0.0.1:8001
```

The command will start the proxy on port 8001, and you can access the Dashboard UI on the following URL http://localhost:8001/api/v1/namespaces/kubernetes-dashboard/services/https:kubernetes-dashboard:/proxy

Figure 2.1 shows the Kubernetes dashboard login screen.

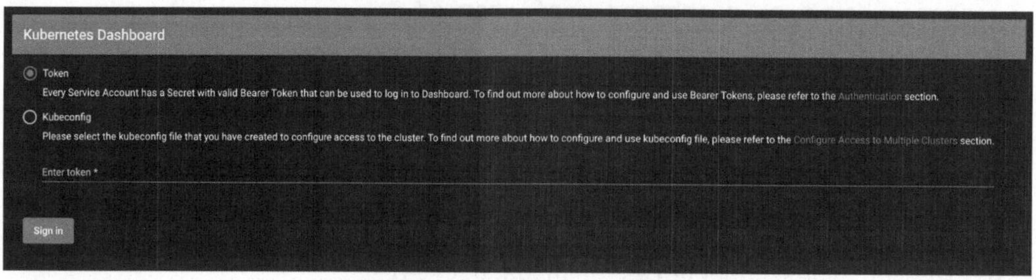

Figure 2.1: *Kubernetes Dashboard login screen*

However, once you access the URL, you will be asked to authenticate with either a token or with a kubeconfig file. The steps to create a sample user and access the dashboard are well-documented on the Kubernetes dashboard GitHub page https://github.com/kubernetes/dashboard/blob/master/docs/user/access-control/creating-sample-user.md

Using the steps from the foregoing link, create a Service Account and a ClusterRolebinding. The following is the combined yaml manifest for both:

```
---
apiVersion: v1
kind: ServiceAccount
metadata:
  name: admin-user
  namespace: kubernetes-dashboard

---

apiVersion: rbac.authorization.k8s.io/v1
kind: ClusterRoleBinding
```

```
metadata:
  name: admin-user
roleRef:
  apiGroup: rbac.authorization.k8s.io
  kind: ClusterRole
  name: cluster-admin
subjects:
- kind: ServiceAccount
  name: admin-user
  namespace: kubernetes-dashboard
```

Use the above YAML to create the Account and Rolebinding.

```
% kubectl apply -f dashboard-account-role-binding.yaml
serviceaccount/admin-user created
clusterrolebinding.rbac.authorization.k8s.io/admin-user created
```

After the ServiceAccount has been created you can use the following command to generate a Bearer Token for the **`ServiceAccount`**.

```
% kubectl -n kubernetes-dashboard create token admin-user
eyJhbGciOiJSUzI1NiIsImtpZCI6IlpyWE1CWnRtVGpZMTNsLUFleUpzT3RLbGQ-
3VXdRQ1l4WUtWSXRlamh2cEEifQ.eyJhdWQiOlsiaHR0cHM6Ly9rdWJlcm5ldGV-
zLmRlZmF1bHQuc3ZjLmNsdXN0ZXIubG9jYWwiXSwiZXhwIjoxNzM1NTgyMjY1LC-
JpYXQiOjE3MzU1Nzg2NjUsImlzcyI6Imh0dHBzOi8va3ViZXJuZXRlcy5kZWZhdWx-
0LnN2Yy5jbHVzdGVyLmxvY2FsIiwianRpIjoiOGM2YThhYjgtNWY0My00NzZlLT-
kxMzYtYWJkNjFjMGM5MDYwIiwia3ViZXJuZXRlcy5pbyI6eyJuYW1lc3BhY2UiOi-
JrdWJlcm5ldGVzLWRhc2hib2FyZCIsInNlcnZpY2VhY2NvdW50Ijp7Im5hb-
WUiOiJhZG1pbi11c2VyIiwidWlkIjoiZmFlNTljZWYtNGYzYS00MTEyLThjYWEt-
NWIxYWUxNWEzOGRmIn19LCJuYmYiOjE3MzU1Nzg2NjUsInN1YiI6InN5c3RlbT-
pzZXJ2aWNlYWNjb3VudDprdWJlcm5ldGVzLWRhc2hib2FyZDphZG1pbi11c2VyIn0.
XdbX55k47dGic7-
```

Access the generated token to login to the dashboard.

Figure 2.2 shows the Kubernetes Dashboard login screen with updated token.

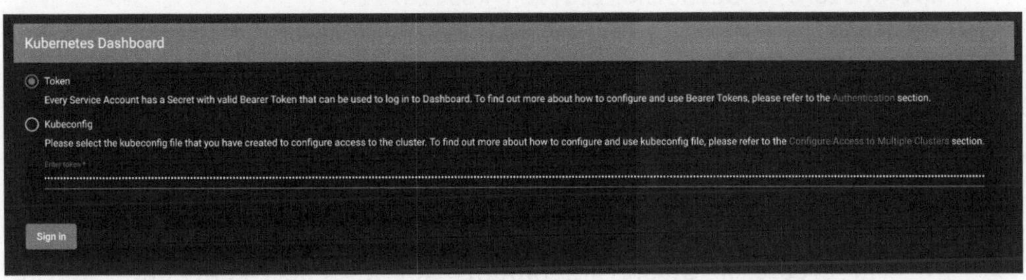

Figure 2.2: *Kubernetes Dashboard login screen with token*

From here, you can look at all your deployed objects, namespaces, services and even secrets. Having this level of access to the cluster is a security risk, if the service account gets compromised the whole cluster will be at risk.

Figure 2.3 shows the Kubernetes Dashboard home screen.

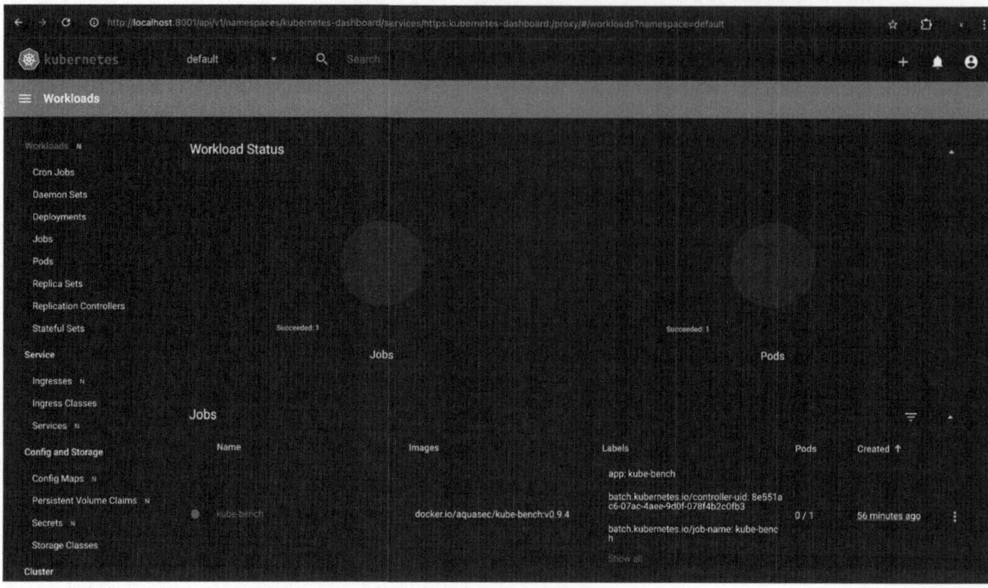

Figure 2.3: *Kubernetes Dashboard home screen*

Not all users in the cluster need access to all resources. Let us look at how we can reduce the access level for the user by applying access policies.

Let us create a separate service account for read-only access. Now we use imperative commands to save time.

```
% kubectl create sa read-only-sa -n kubernetes-dashboard
serviceaccount/read-only-sa created
```

Next create a ClusterRole with ReadOnly permissions on all objects.

```
kind: ClusterRole
apiVersion: rbac.authorization.k8s.io/v1
metadata:
  namespace: '*'
  name: read-only-clusterrole
rules:
- apiGroups: ["*"]
  resources: ["*"]
  verbs: ["get", "list", "watch"]
```

Next, we will create a ClusterRolebinding for the serviceAccount and the clusterrole.

```
% kubectl create clusterrolebinding read-only-sa-dashboard
--serviceaccount=kubernetes-dashboard:read-only-sa --clusterrole
=read-only-clusterrole
```

```
clusterrolebinding.rbac.authorization.k8s.io/read-only-sa-dash-
board created
```

Lastly, we can create the token for the service account using the command from the last section.

```
% kubectl -n kubernetes-dashboard create token read-only-sa
eyJhbGciOiJSUzI1NiIsImtpZCI6IlpyWE1CWnRtVGpZMTNsLUFleUpzT3RLbGQ-
3VXdRQ1l4WUtWSXRlamh2cEEifQ.eyJhdWQiOlsiaHR0cHM6Ly9rdWJlcm5ldGVzLm-
RlZmF1bHQuc3ZjLmNsdXN0ZXIubG9jYWwiXSwiZXhwIjoxNzM1NTgyODUzLCJpYXQiO-
jE3MzU1NzkyNTMsImlzcyI6Imh0dHBzOi8va3ViZXJuZXRlcy5kZWZhdWx0LnN2Yy-
5jbHVzdGVyLmxvY2FsIiwianRpIjoiM2IzMTdlNDAtNDVhZS00NDVhLTgzNWUtNW-
FjYzNhODQ5NWUyIiwia3ViZXJuZXRlcy5pbyI6eyJuYW1lc3
```

Use the token to log in to the dashboard. We can confirm the read-only behaviour by trying to deploy a hello-world pod from the dashboard.

Figure 2.4 shows the error when trying to deploy pod with a read-only user.

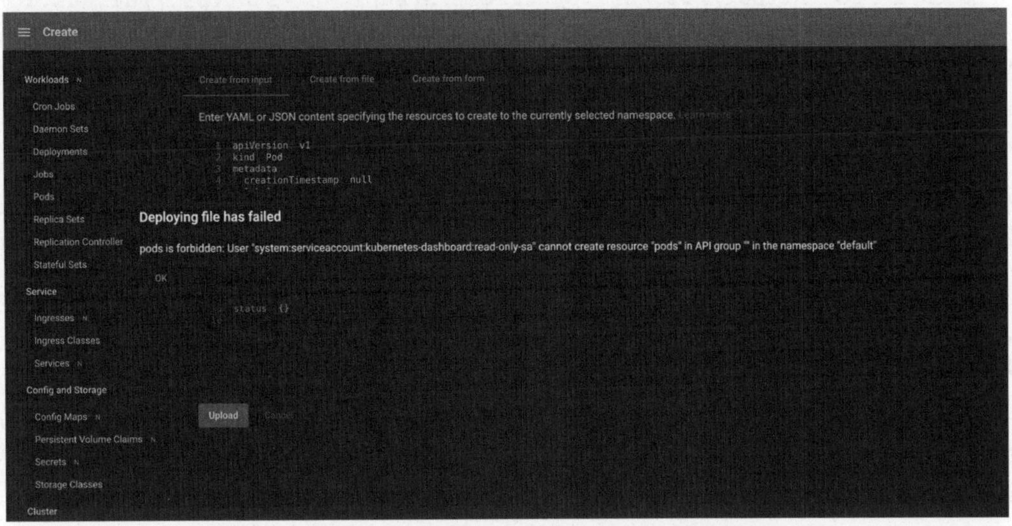

Figure 2.4: *Pod deployment error with read-only user*

Verifying Platform Binaries

There are many ways in which you can deploy a fresh Kubernetes cluster; you can either deploy the cluster with every component running as a service or use kubeadm to stand up the cluster with minimal configurations. Irrespective of how the cluster is deployed, ensuring that the binaries used in the deployment come from a trusted source is of utmost importance.

If the platform binaries are compromised, then the whole cluster and deployments will be at risk. An attacker can push malicious code in the binaries which when deployed in the cluster can expose the cluster to outside threats or even allow unfettered access to all the resources.

One of the ways to ensure that the binaries have not been tampered with is to validate the checksum for the binaries from the official Kubernetes page. If the checksums do not match, it would mean that either the binary was corrupted while downloading or has been tampered with. Avoid installing such binaries on the platform.

Example 1: Validating the checksum of kubectl

Let us download the latest **kubectl**

```
% curl -LO "https://dl.k8s.io/release/$(curl -L -s https://dl.k8s.io/release/stable.txt)/bin/linux/amd64/kubectl"
```

Download the **checksum**

```
% curl -LO "https://dl.k8s.io/release/$(curl -L -s https://dl.k8s.io/release/stable.txt)/bin/linux/amd64/kubectl.sha256"
```

Validate the **checksum**

```
% echo "$(cat kubectl.sha256) kubectl" | sha256sum --check
% kubectl: OK
```

Practice Question: Assume you are installing kubelet on a new node. Download the latest version of kubelet and validate its checksum to ensure that the file has not been tampered with.

Practice Questions

Throughout the chapter, we have added practice questions for you to try and get as much hands-on as possible. We are collating all the questions in this section for easy reference.

Question 1: Use the backend-test pod that you had deployed in the last practice question and test the connectivity from backend-test to the database pod.

Question 2: In some cases, instead of blocking the ingress traffic, you might want to control the outgoing traffic. This is especially useful when you want to prevent data exfiltration. You need to use the same deployment and build the following scenario:

1. The database pod can only communicate with the backend pod, all other egress should be blocked.
2. The backend pod should only be able to communicate with the frontend pod, all other egress should be blocked.

Question 3: Namespace Isolation: Namespaces, with the right policies in place, can be used to isolate the workloads and share the cluster resources with multiple users. You need to implement the following scenario using the same deployment.

1. All the pods in the frontend namespace should be able to communicate with and only with all pods in the backend namespace.
2. All the pods in the backend namespace should be able to communicate with and only with all the pods in the database namespace.
3. All other ingress and egress to/from the backend and database namespaces should be blocked.

Question 4: Create a new namespace called practice. Create a **`default-deny NetworkPolicy name default-deny`**. The policy should deny all egress traffic from the namespace practice.

Question 5: You need to ensure that anonymous access to the API server is not enabled. Update the API Server Configuration file to use the following flag.

```
--anonymous-auth=false
```

Question 6: Create a new namespace called development, create a new Deployment with **`busybox:latest`** image, set the replica count to 3. Create a new **`serviceAccount`**, **`Role`** and **`Rolebinding`** for Kubernetes Dashboard. Ensure that the serviceAccount only has read-only access to resources deployed in the development namespace.

Question 7: Download the binary for **`kubeadm`**, download the **`checksum`** for **`kubeadm`**, and validate the **`checksum`** for the file. Write the result in a text file called **`checksum_result.txt`**.

Question 8: Run **`kube-bench`** in your Kubernetes cluster and look for the following test in the output.

```
1.1.11 Ensure that the etcd data directory permissions are set to
700 or more restrictive (Automated)
```

Apply the accompanying recommendation for the test if the test had failed and re-run the test. Validate that the test passes.

Question 9: The following is the test result from kube-bench along with the recommendation to fix the warning:

```
[WARN] 1.3.1 Ensure that the --terminated-pod-gc-threshold
argument is set as appropriate (Manual)
```

Recommendation:

1.3.1 Edit the Controller Manager pod specification file **`/etc/kubernetes/manifests/kube-controller-manager.yaml`** on the control plane node and set the **--terminated-pod-gc-threshold** to an appropriate threshold, for example, **--terminated-pod-gc-threshold=10**

Apply the recommendation in your cluster, run **kube-bench**, and validate that the warning goes away.

Question 10: Create an egress network policy that blocks all traffic to IP address 169.254.169.254 from frontend and backend namespaces.

Question 11: Assume you are installing kubelet on a new node. Download the latest version of kubelet and validate its checksum to ensure that the file has not been tampered with.

Conclusion

The Cluster Setup domain of the CKS exam requires a deep understanding of the Kubernetes deployment process as well as thorough knowledge of security best practices. In this chapter, we have covered practical ways of securing the cluster endpoints, protecting endpoints, controlling network traffic, ensuring compliance with CIS benchmarking, and making sure that the platform is built with trusted binaries.

In the upcoming chapter, we will focus on hardening an existing cluster with the use of Role Based access control, service account management, and Kubernetes upgrade.

Resources

- Instance Metadata Endpoint in AWS: https://docs.aws.amazon.com/AWSEC2/latest/UserGuide/instancedata-data-retrieval.html.
- Instance Metadata Endpoint in Azure: https://learn.microsoft.com/en-us/azure/virtual-machines/instance-metadata-service?tabs=windows
- Instance Metadata Endpoint in GCP: https://cloud.google.com/compute/docs/metadata/querying-metadata
- Instance Metadata Endpoint in OCI: https://docs.oracle.com/en-us/iaas/Content/Compute/Tasks/gettingmetadata.htm

CHAPTER 3
Cluster Hardening

Introduction

In the previous chapter, we had covered the first building block for securing a Kubernetes environment, the cluster setup. Now that you have built a new Kubernetes cluster, keeping the security best practices in mind, it is time to delve deeper and ensure that the cluster is kept as secure as possible. The second domain of the CKS exam focuses on hardening a Kubernetes cluster against security threats by ensuring that access is provided based on user roles, providing access to only users who actually need it, and protecting the built-in as well as custom service accounts.

Cluster hardening relies on the principle of **least privilege**, which ensures users have only the necessary permissions to perform their tasks, reducing the impact of attacks. Kubernetes implements this through Role-Based Access Control (RBAC), allowing granular permissions from cluster-wide to pod-specific levels. RBAC will be detailed in upcoming sections.

The CKS exam covers Service account security, which is vital for applications in a Kubernetes cluster. These accounts often have higher permissions than user accounts, making their security crucial. You should already be familiar with creating and using service accounts from the CKA exam. This chapter will focus on securely using service accounts by limiting their scope and following best practices for managing credentials and tokens.

The next aspect of this domain is the Kubernetes API endpoint. The API server is the most important endpoint when it comes to Kubernetes clusters, as it serves as a gateway into the cluster and acts as the heart of the cluster. Safeguarding the API endpoint is crucial a compromised endpoint can allow access to all other resources of the cluster. As part of this chapter, we will see how to secure the API server communication by limiting access to the API endpoint and implement authentication and authorization mechanisms to protect communication with the API server.

In the last section of the chapter, the importance of keeping the cluster up to date for maintaining a secure Kubernetes environment will be discussed. Kubernetes has frequent upgrades and a small release window. Each new upgrade or patch addresses known security vulnerabilities and exploits. Kubernetes support is provided only for n-2 versions, and no new patches, updates, or upgrades are released for older versions, which increases the risk of exploitation. This section will cover how to plan and execute safe and efficient cluster upgrades, rollback mechanisms, testing, and upgrade validations.

By the end of this chapter, you will have a comprehensive understanding of how to harden a Kubernetes cluster to protect it against a wide range of known and emerging threats. By implementing the strategies discussed in the chapter, you can not only clear the CKS exam but also enhance the security of your application and protect the infrastructure as well from threats.

Structure

At an elevated level, this chapter covers the following concepts:

- Role-Based Access Control (RBAC)
    - RBAC Fundamentals
    - RBAC Implementation in Kubernetes
    - How to Use RBAC to Reduce Security Exposure
- Securing Service Accounts
- Securing the Kubernetes API Endpoint
- Cluster Upgrade
- Practice Questions

Role-Based Access Control (RBAC)

Let us take our example of the utopian city from *Chapter 2, Cluster Setup*, just like last time, the city has no rules in place for what a resident is allowed to do once they are inside the city. They are free to roam the city and interact with any and everything. Even a guest visiting the city is allowed into the city hall and can tamper with the city records. Which is again not what you want if you want to keep the city secure and ensure that residents or guests do not mess up the critical infra and bring the whole utopia down.

So you decide to implement an access control mechanism that controls which resident/guest is allowed to visit, interact with, or change things in the city. You do this by creating different groups of residents and visitors based on their role and function, for example the visitors are only allowed to visit the city museum and only allowed to look at the public exhibit while the security operators are allowed access to the private parts of the museum and can also make rules to allow or restrict certain visitors from entering in the museum.

After implementing such a mechanism, you can rest assured that residents and guests only interact with features and buildings that they are authorised to, greatly enhancing the security of our utopian city.

Just like our imaginary city, we also want to make sure that our Kubernetes cluster is secure and all the users who have access to the cluster only interact with what they need and nothing else. Before we look at how to implement the access control mechanism in a Kubernetes environment, let us look at the fundamentals of Role-Based Access Control (RBAC).

RBAC Fundamentals

The principle of least privilege is the guiding principle behind Role-Based Access Control. The least privilege principle says that access to resources should be provided only to the users who absolutely need it, and the operations should be limited. No user should be provided unnecessary permission. Let us take a look at the concepts involved with RBAC.

- **Subjects**

  Subjects are the entities that request access to a resource. The subject could be a user, group, a machine, a bot, or anything else that wants to interact with the resources. In the Kubernetes context, a subject can be one of the following.

  - **User:** A human user who has an account in the system.
  - **Service Account:** These are special accounts created to represent an application.
  - **Groups:** Collection of users or service accounts.
- **Roles**

  Roles are a set of permissions allowing a subject to perform listed operations on the objects. Roles are typically defined at the namespace level however you can also cerate clusterroles which allow permissions at the cluster level.
- **Objects**

  Objects are the resources on which a subject is requesting permissions. In Kubernetes, an object can be:

  - Pods
  - Deployment
  - Services
  - Namespaces
  - Secrets

    - And many more....
- **Permissions**

  Permissions are the actions that a subject is authorized to perform on an object. Kubernetes lists the permissions as verbs in the role definitions. Some of the common verbs that you must have used in Kubernetes when preparing for the CKA exam are:

    - Get
    - List
    - Watch
    - Create
- **Role Bindings**

  Role bindings associate a particular role with a subject. In the Kubernetes context, rolebinding are created at the namespace level; however, you can create cluster role bindings to allow a subject permissions at the cluster level.

RBAC implementation in Kubernetes

Now that we are familiar with the basics of RBAC, lets dive into how this can be implements in Kubernetes cluster. For this exercise, we would implement the following scenario, creating all the involved components and validating the configurations as well.

Scenario 1:

We have a new Kubernetes cluster with two namespaces, named finance-app and mobile-app. A simple nginx application is deployed in both of the namespaces with 3 pods each. A developer named fin-dev should have access to the finance-app namespaces and should be able to view, create, update, and delete the pods in the namespace. Another developer named mob-dev should have similar permissions on the mobile-app namespace. Our goal is to create the necessary roles and rolebindings for this scenario.

We will build the first part of scenario 1, starting with the user key, csr, and certificate generation, then we will build the role, and finally assign the role to the user using a rolebinding in their respective namespaces.

1. **Generating user private key**

By default, Kubernetes users are identified based on a private key and certificate. To generate the key and certificate pair, we start by generating the private key that we will use for user identification. You can use **openssl** to generate the private key.

```
$ openssl genrsa -out fin-dev.key 2048
```

2. **Generate user CSR**

Next, we need to create a CSR, which will then be used to generate the K8s CSR object and generate the user certificate.

```
$ openssl req -new -key fin-dev.key -out fin-dev.csr
You are about to be asked to enter information that will be
incorporated
into your certificate request.
What you are about to enter is what is called a Distinguished
Name or a DN.
There are quite a few fields but you can leave some blank
For some fields there will be a default value,
If you enter '.', the field will be left blank.
-----
Country Name (2 letter code) [AU]:
State or Province Name (full name) [Some-State]:
Locality Name (eg, city) []:
Organization Name (eg, company) [Internet Widgits Pty Ltd]:Lab
Organizational Unit Name (eg, section) []:TestPrep
Common Name (e.g. server FQDN or YOUR name) []:fin_dev
Email Address []:fin-dev@cksprep.local
Please enter the following 'extra' attributes
to be sent with your certificate request
A challenge password []:
An optional company name []:
```

3. **Generate K8s CSR Object**

Once we have the CSR file, we need to encode this file in **base64** and pass this to the CSR Object definition file. We will use the CSR definition file to create the CSR object, which an admin can view, validate, and approve.

You can get the **base64** encoded value for the fin-dev.csr file using the following command:

```
$ cat fin-dev.csr | base64 | tr -d "\n"
LS0tLS1CRUdJTiBDRVJUSUZJQ0FURSBSRVFVRVNULS0tLS0KTUlJQ3lUQ0NBY….
```

Once we have the **base64** value, we need to create a CSR object that will be used to request a signed certificate. You can read about the Certificates and CSR's in detail at https://kubernetes.io/docs/reference/access-authn-authz/certificate-signing-requests/. We will use the process listed in the document to create a CSR object.

```
$ cat <<EOF | kubectl apply -f -
apiVersion: certificates.k8s.io/v1
kind: CertificateSigningRequest
metadata:
  name: fin-dev
```

```
spec:
  request: LS0tLS1CRUdJTiBDRVJUSUZJQ0FURSBSRVFVRVNULS0tLS0KTUl-
JQ3lUQ0NBY….
  signerName: kubernetes.io/kube-apiserver-client
  expirationSeconds: 86400  # one day
  usages:
  - client auth
EOF
certificatesigningrequest.certificates.k8s.io/fin_dev created
```

NOTE: *Make sure to update the* **csr base54** *encoded value in the preceding command before execution.*

4. **Approve CSR and extract certificate**

Once the CSR object is created, you can view this object using the **kubectl** command and approve or reject it based on whether it meets the requirement and is genuine. After the CSR is approved, you need to extract the certificate from the certificate object. This certificate then needs to be passed on to the user who will use it along with the private key file to authenticate to the Cluster API.

```
$ kubectl get csr
NAME      AGE   SIGNERNAME                             REQUESTOR          RE-
QUESTEDDURATION   CONDITION
fin_dev   39s   kubernetes.io/kube-apiserver-client   kubernetes-admin   24h
Pending
$ kubectl certificate approve fin-dev
certificatesigningrequest.certificates.k8s.io/fin-dev approved
$ kubectl get csr
NAME      AGE   SIGNERNAME                             REQUESTOR
REQUESTEDDURATION   CONDITION
Fin-dev   89s   kubernetes.io/kube-apiserver-client   kubernetes-admin   24h
Approved,Issued
$ kubectl get csr fin-dev -o jsonpath={.status.certificate} | base64 -d > fin_dev.
crt
```

5. **Updating kubeconfig file**

You can add a new context to the **kubeconfig** file for the user and switch to that context when you need to use that user for validation.

```
$ kubectl config set-credentials fin-dev --client-certificate=fin_
dev.crt --client-key=fin-dev.k
ey --embed-certs=true
User "fin-dev" set.
$ kubectl config set-context fin-dev --user=fin-dev --cluster=-
kind-ckspractice
Context "fin-dev" created.
```

6. **Create Role and RoleBinding**

After we have the user in place, we will create the role as per the scenario and bind the user that we created earlier to this role using **RoleBinding**. Just like a lot of other Kubernetes objects, you can either use imperative commands to create the **Role** and **RoleBinding** or use the yaml file. To save time, we will use the imperative command for the scenario and also list the yaml file. Feel free to use any method that you are comfortable with. You can also read about the role and rolebinding in detail at https://kubernetes.io/docs/reference/access-authn-authz/rbac/.

Role YAML:

```
apiVersion: rbac.authorization.k8s.io/v1
kind: Role
metadata:
  namespace: fin-dev
  name: fin-dev-role
rules:
- apiGroups: [""] # "" indicates the core API group
  resources: ["pods"]
  verbs: ["list", "get", "create", "update", "delete"]
```

RoleBinding YAML:

```
apiVersion: rbac.authorization.k8s.io/v1
kind: RoleBinding
metadata:
  name: fin-dev-rolebinding
  namespace: fin-dev
subjects:
- kind: User
  name: fin-dev
  apiGroup: rbac.authorization.k8s.io
roleRef:
  kind: Role #this must be Role or ClusterRole
  name: fin-dev-role
  apiGroup: rbac.authorization.k8s.io

$ kubectl create role fin-dev-role --verb=get --verb=create --ver-
b=update --verb=delete --resource=pods --namespace=finance-app
role.rbac.authorization.k8s.io/fin-dev-role created
$ kubectl create rolebinding fin-dev-rolebinding --role=fin-dev-
role --user=fin-dev --namespace=finance-app
rolebinding.rbac.authorization.k8s.io/fin-dev-rolebinding created
```

7. **Validate the role and rolebinding**

Let us list all the available contexts and switch to the **fin-dev** context that we had created earlier. Once we are working in the right context, we can use kubectl to test the role and rolebinding.

```
$ kubectl config get-contexts
CURRENT   NAME               CLUSTER            AUTHINFO           NAMESPACE
          fin_dev            kind-ckspractice   fin-dev
*         kind-ckspractice   kind-ckspractice   kind-ckspractice
$ kubectl config use-context fin-dev
Switched to context "fin-dev".
$ kubectl get pods -n finance-app
NAME                                  READY   STATUS    RESTARTS   AGE
fin-app-deployment-b5fdd557b-27jmc    1/1     Running   0          10m
fin-app-deployment-b5fdd557b-c8bz6    1/1     Running   0          10m
fin-app-deployment-b5fdd557b-fkjpr    1/1     Running   0          10m
ckspractice@DESKTOP-LGCOG3B:~$ kubectl get pods -n mobile-app
Error from server (Forbidden): pods is forbidden: User "fin-dev" cannot list
resource "pods" in API group "" in the namespace "mobile-app"
```

From the preceding result, you can see that the fin-app user can list the pods in the finance-app namespace; however, the user is forbidden to perform the same action in the mobile-app namespace.

Practice Question: We have built the first part of scenario 1; as part of the practice exercise, you need to build the other half and validate the permissions granted to the mob-dev user in mobile-app namespace. You also need to ensure that the permissions are limited to the mobile-app namespace and do not bleed into other namespaces.

Scenario 2:

We will work with the same cluster; however, this time we have a Kubernetes admin named **k8s-oper**, the user is responsible for managing all deployments in the cluster across all namespaces. He should be able to view all the pods, services, deployments, configmaps and secrets across all namespaces.

1. **Generating user private key, CSR, and K8s CSR Object**

We will use the commands mentioned in the last scenario to generate the new private key for the k8s-oper user, use the key to generate the CSR and K8s CSR Object.

```
$ openssl genrsa -out k8s-oper.key 2048
$ openssl req -new -key k8s-oper.key -out k8s-oper.csr
You are about to be asked to enter information that will be
incorporated
into your certificate request.
What you are about to enter is what is called a Distinguished
Name or a DN.
```

```
There are quite a few fields but you can leave some blank
For some fields there will be a default value,
If you enter '.', the field will be left blank.
-----
Country Name (2 letter code) [AU]:
State or Province Name (full name) [Some-State]:
Locality Name (eg, city) []:
Organization Name (eg, company) [Internet Widgits Pty Ltd]:Lab
Organizational Unit Name (eg, section) []:TestPrep
Common Name (e.g. server FQDN or YOUR name) []:k8s-oper
Email Address []:k8s-oper@cksprep.local

Please enter the following 'extra' attributes
to be sent with your certificate request
A challenge password []:
An optional company name []:
```

2. **Generate K8s CSR Object**

Let us encode the CSR file in **base64** and generate the CSR Object.

```
$ cat k8s-oper.csr | base64 | tr -d "\n"
LS0tLS1CRUdJTiBDRVJUSUZJQ0FURSBSRVFVRVNULS0tLS0KTUl….
$ cat <<EOF | kubectl apply -f -
apiVersion: certificates.k8s.io/v1
kind: CertificateSigningRequest
metadata:
  name: k8s-oper
spec:
  request: LS0tLS1CRUdJTiBDRVJUSUZJQ0FURSBSRVFVRVNULS0tLS0KTUl….
  signerName: kubernetes.io/kube-apiserver-client
  expirationSeconds: 86400  # one day
  usages:
  - client auth
EOF
certificatesigningrequest.certificates.k8s.io/k8s-oper created
```

NOTE: *Make sure to update the* **csr base64** *encoded value in the preceding command before execution.*

3. **Approve CSR and extract certificate**

```
$ kubectl get csr
NAME       AGE   SIGNERNAME                                      REQUESTOR
REQUESTEDDURATION   CONDITION
fin_dev    54m   kubernetes.io/kube-apiserver-client   kubernetes-admin   24h
Approved,Issued
k8s-oper   53s   kubernetes.io/kube-apiserver-client   kubernetes-admin   24h
Pending
```

```
$ kubectl certificate approve k8s-oper
certificatesigningrequest.certificates.k8s.io/k8s-oper approved
$ kubectl get csr
NAME       AGE     SIGNERNAME                                  REQUESTOR
REQUESTEDDURATION   CONDITION
fin_dev    56m     kubernetes.io/kube-apiserver-client   kubernetes-admin
24h                 Approved,Issued
k8s-oper   2m20s   kubernetes.io/kube-apiserver-client   kubernetes-admin
24h                 Approved,Issued
$ kubectl get csr k8s-oper -o jsonpath={.status.certificate} | base64 -d >
k8s-oper.crt
```

4. **Updating kubeconfig file**

```
$ kubectl config set-credentials k8s-oper --client-certificate=k8s-
oper.crt --client-key=k8s-oper.key --embed-certs=true
User "k8s-oper" set.
$ kubectl config set-context k8s-oper --user=k8s-oper --cluster=-
kind-ckspractice
Context "k8s-oper" created.
```

5. **Create `ClusterRole` and `ClusterRoleBinding`**

Just like the last scenario, we will provide the yaml for **`ClusterRole`** and **`ClusterRoleBinding`** for reference. However, unlike the last scenario, let us use the yaml for deployments this time around.

```
$ vi k8s-oper-role.yaml
apiVersion: rbac.authorization.k8s.io/v1
kind: ClusterRole
metadata:
 name: k8s-oper-role
rules:
- apiGroups: [""]
  resources: ["pods","services","deployments","configmaps","secrets"]
  verbs: ["get", "watch", "list"]
$ kubectl apply -f k8s-oper-role.yaml
clusterrole.rbac.authorization.k8s.io/k8s-oper-role created
$ vi k8s-oper-rolebinding.yaml
apiVersion: rbac.authorization.k8s.io/v1
kind: ClusterRoleBinding
metadata:
  name: k8s-oper-rolebinding
subjects:
- kind: User
  name: k8s-oper
  apiGroup: rbac.authorization.k8s.io
roleRef:
  kind: ClusterRole
```

```
    name: k8s-oper-role
    apiGroup: rbac.authorization.k8s.io
$ kubectl apply -f k8s-oper-rolebinding.yaml
clusterrolebinding.rbac.authorization.k8s.io/k8s-oper-rolebinding
created
```

6. **Validate the role and rolebinding**

Finally, let us switch to the right context and try to validate the **clusterrole** binding.

```
$ kubectl config get-contexts
CURRENT   NAME               CLUSTER            AUTHINFO           NAMESPACE
          fin_dev            kind-ckspractice   fin_dev
          k8s-oper           kind-ckspractice   k8s-oper
*         kind-ckspractice   kind-ckspractice   kind-ckspractice
$ kubectl config use-context k8s-oper
Switched to context "k8s-oper".
$ kubectl get services -A
NAMESPACE     NAME         TYPE        CLUSTER-IP    EXTERNAL-IP   PORT(S)
AGE
default       kubernetes   ClusterIP   10.96.0.1     <none>        443/TCP
10h
kube-system   kube-dns     ClusterIP   10.96.0.10    <none>        53/UDP,53/TCP,9153/TCP
10h
$  kubectl get configmaps -A
NAMESPACE            NAME                                                   DATA   AGE
default              kube-root-ca.crt                                       1      10h
finance-app          kube-root-ca.crt                                       1      75m
kube-node-lease      kube-root-ca.crt                                       1      10h
kube-public          cluster-info                                           2      10h
kube-public          kube-root-ca.crt                                       1      10h
kube-system          coredns                                                1      10h
kube-system          extension-apiserver-authentication                     6      10h
kube-system          kube-apiserver-legacy-service-account-token-tracking   1      10h
kube-system          kube-proxy                                             2      10h
kube-system          kube-root-ca.crt                                       1      10h
kube-system          kubeadm-config                                         1      10h
kube-system          kubelet-config                                         1      10h
local-path-storage   kube-root-ca.crt                                       1      10h
local-path-storage   local-path-config                                      4      10h
mobile-app           kube-root-ca.crt                                       1      75m
$  kubectl get nodes
Error from server (Forbidden): nodes is forbidden: User "k8s-oper" cannot list resource
"nodes" in API group "" at the cluster scope
```

As seen from the foregoing output, we can view the services and configmaps using the new user and clusterrole; however, we can not view the nodes.

Practice Question: Validate all the permissions for cluster role k8s-oper-role and confirm that only the allowed primitives are visible for the user.

Practice Question: Delete the cluster role and clusterrolebindings created in the foregoing scenario and recreate both using imperative commands instead of yaml files.

Service Account Security

All the example that we have seen so far are built assuming a user i.e., a real human being who is authenticating and performing tasks on a Kubernetes cluster. However, not all users are human, in some cases you might be dealing with a tool or automation task which runs as a pod and needs to interact with the Kubernetes cluster API. In this case, Kubernetes offers service accounts as a way to interact with the Kubernetes API from within the pod.

Service accounts are essentially accounts that are assigned to certain tools, processes, or services in the Kubernetes cluster to grant them specific permissions on API resources. Service accounts provide an easier mechanism to interact with the cluster resources by employing the primitives similar to regular users. However, Service Accounts also pose security challenges similar to regular user accounts and need to be managed and secured properly.

One of the most common security risk with service accounts is misconfigured RBAC. In cases when a service account has excessive permissions, if the account gets compromised it puts the whole cluster at risk, attackers can use the service account to access cluster resources which should not have been in scope of the current account.

For example, consider a CI/CD pipeline that is used to automate the build, testing, and deployment of a new application within a Kubernetes cluster. The service account used in the integration, at a minimum, has permissions to create deployment, pods, services, secrets, config maps, and any other Kubernetes object/primitive that is part of the application.

If the service account is compromised, the attacker can access the underlying data, secrets, and other sensitive information. To avoid this, service accounts should follow the principle of least privilege and should only have the absolute minimum permissions needed to perform the task.

Just like the normal user accounts, you need to implement robust credential management to protect the service account. Service account credentials must be kept secret and should also be rotated on a regular basis to avoid stale credentials.

Working with Service Accounts

By default, every namespace in the Kubernetes cluster has a service account named

default. If you do not specify any service account while creating the pod, the default service account for that namespace is mounted in the pod and can be used to communicate with the API Server.

However, by default, this service account does not have any role assigned, so it can not perform any operations on the cluster but if you assign a role to this service account it is propagated to all the pods in the namespace, this is a big security concern and it is best to avoid using the default service account and work with custom service account which are purpose built for the application. You can get more details on working with service accounts at https://kubernetes.io/docs/tasks/configure-pod-container/configure-service-account/ and https://kubernetes.io/docs/reference/access-authn-authz/service-accounts-admin/.

Let us see the workings of a service account with an example scenario.

Scenario 3:

We have an nginx pod name sa-test running in the namespace sa-demo. We first need to make sure that the default service account can not be used to list pods and services in the cluster. After that, we need to create a new service account which has view permissions for pods and services and use this service account with nginx pod. Finally, we also need to validate that we can list pods and service from within the pod.

Let us take a look at the pod definition file.

```
apiVersion: v1
kind: Pod
metadata:
  name: sa-test
  namespace: sa-demo
spec:
  containers:
  - name: sa-test
    image: nginx:latest
```

This is a simple pod manifest; we have not defined any service account for the pod. Let us now look at the pod details.

```
$ kubectl get pods -n sa-demo
NAME      READY   STATUS    RESTARTS   AGE
sa-test   1/1     Running   0          10s
$ kubectl get pod -n sa-demo sa-test -o yaml
apiVersion: v1
kind: Pod
metadata:
  annotations:
    kubectl.kubernetes.io/last-applied-configuration: |
```

```
      {"apiVersion":"v1","kind":"Pod","metadata":{"annota-
tions":{},"name":"sa-test","namespace":"sa-demo"},"spec":{"con-
tainers":[{"image":"nginx:latest","name":"sa-test"}]}}
  name: sa-test
  namespace: sa-demo
spec:
  containers:
  - image: nginx:latest
    imagePullPolicy: Always
    name: sa-test
    volumeMounts:
    - mountPath: /var/run/secrets/kubernetes.io/serviceaccount
      name: kube-api-access-ln8sg
      readOnly: true
      recursiveReadOnly: Disabled
  serviceAccount: default
  serviceAccountName: default
  volumes:
  - name: kube-api-access-ln8sg
    projected:
      defaultMode: 420
      sources:
      - serviceAccountToken:
          expirationSeconds: 3607
          path: token
      - configMap:
          items:
          - key: ca.crt
            path: ca.crt
          name: kube-root-ca.crt
      - downwardAPI:
          items:
          - fieldRef:
              apiVersion: v1
              fieldPath: metadata.namespace
            path: namespace
```

NOTE: *The output is truncated to fit. The actual output will have a lot of other information not needed for the current discussion.*

As per the underlined text, the default serviceAccount was automatically applied to the pod. You can look at the details of this **serviceAccount**.

```
$ kubectl get serviceaccount default -n sa-demo
NAME      SECRETS   AGE
default   0         11m
```

As per the output, there is no secret associated with the **serviceAccount** by default.

This was a security enhancement done in Kubernetes v1.22, earlier kuberentes versions used to have a secret associated with every serviceaccount, which was then mounted in the pod. You can get more details on this behaviour at https://kubernetes.io/docs/tasks/configure-pod-container/configure-service-account/.

By default, the service account is mounted at the path /var/run/secrets/Kubernetes.io/serviceaccount inside every container. This can be validated in the preceding pod yaml output.

```
$ kubectl exec --stdin --tty sa-test -n sa-demo -- /bin/bash
root@sa-test:~# cd /var/run/secrets/kubernetes.io/serviceaccount/
root@sa-test:/var/run/secrets/kubernetes.io/serviceaccount# ls -ltrh
total 0
lrwxrwxrwx 1 root root 12 Jan 22 15:09 token -> ..data/token
lrwxrwxrwx 1 root root 16 Jan 22 15:09 namespace -> ..data/namespace
lrwxrwxrwx 1 root root 13 Jan 22 15:09 ca.crt -> ..data/ca.crt
root@sa-test:/var/run/secrets/kubernetes.io/serviceaccount# cat token
eyJhbGciOiJSUzI1NiIsImtpZCI6Ik11ZjlFUlVVSFd0dm1NbUw2bE9h-
RXA5emhyUlowa214aW1xNWQ0SUlXMjgifQ.eyJhdWQiOlsiaHR0cHM6Ly9rdWJlcm-
5ldGVzLmRlZmF1bHQuc3ZjLmNsdXN0
root@sa-test:/var/run/secrets/kubernetes.io/serviceaccount# curl -s
-k -m 5 -H "Authorization: Bearer $(cat /var/run/secrets/kubernetes.
io/serviceaccount/token)" https://kubernetes.default.svc.cluster.
local/api/v1/namespaces/sa-demo/pods
{
  "kind": "Status",
  "apiVersion": "v1",
  "metadata": {},
  "status": "Failure",
  "message": "pods is forbidden: User \"system:serviceaccount:-
sa-demo:default\" cannot list resource \"pods\" in API group \"\" in
the namespace \"sa-demo\"",
  "reason": "Forbidden",
  "details": {
    "kind": "pods"
  },
  "code": 403
}
```

As per the preceding output, we can access the Kubernetes API endpoint; however, the account does not have any permission. Let us create a new serviceaccount, role and rolebinding, and mount the service account in the pod. We will again perform the pods test once we have the service account in place. Here is the yaml manifest for all the components that we need to create.

```
apiVersion: v1
kind: ServiceAccount
metadata:
```

```
  name: sa-test
  namespace: sa-demo
---
apiVersion: v1
kind: Pod
metadata:
  name: sa-test
  namespace: sa-demo
spec:
  serviceAccountName: sa-test
  containers:
  - name: sa-test
    image: nginx:latest
---
apiVersion: rbac.authorization.k8s.io/v1
kind: Role
metadata:
  name: sa-test-role
  namespace: sa-demo
rules:
- apiGroups: [""]
  resources: ["pods"]
  verbs: ["list"]
---
apiVersion: rbac.authorization.k8s.io/v1
kind: RoleBinding
metadata:
  name: sa-test-rolebinding
  namespace: sa-demo
subjects:
- kind: ServiceAccount
  name: sa-test
roleRef:
  kind: Role
  name: sa-test-role
  apiGroup: rbac.authorization.k8s.io
```

Let us create the resources and test the pod access.

```
$ kubectl apply -f sa-test.yaml -n sa-demo
serviceaccount/sa-test created
pod/sa-test created
role.rbac.authorization.k8s.io/sa-test-role created
$ kubectl exec --stdin --tty sa-test -n sa-demo -- /bin/bash
root@sa-test:/# curl -s -k -m 5 -H "Authorization: Bearer $(cat /
var/run/secrets/kubernetes.io/serviceaccount/token)" https://ku-
bernetes.default.svc.cluster.local/api/v1/namespaces/sa-demo/pods
{
```

```
    "kind": "PodList",
    "apiVersion": "v1",
    "metadata": {
      "resourceVersion": "314941"
    },
    "items": [
      {
        "metadata": {
          "name": "sa-test",
          "namespace": "sa-demo",
          "uid": "9862675d-81f3-4d9c-b31d-70d4bca3d0de",
          "resourceVersion": "314817",
          "creationTimestamp": "2025-01-22T15:52:14Z",
          "annotations": {
            "kubectl.kubernetes.io/last-applied-configuration":
  "{\"apiVersion\":\"v1\",\"kind\":\"Pod\",\"metadata\":{\"an-
  notations\":{},\"name\":\"sa-test\",\"namespace\":\"-
  sa-demo\"},\"spec\":{\"containers\":[{\"image\":\"nginx-
  :latest\",\"name\":\"sa-test\"}],\"serviceAccountName\":\"-
  sa-test\"}}\n"
          },
```


Now we are getting the pods list, but what about the other objects.

```
root@sa-test:/# curl -s -k -m 5 -H "Authorization: Bearer $(cat /
var/run/secrets/kubernetes.io/serviceaccount/token)" https://kuber-
netes.default.svc.cluster.local/api/v1/namespaces/sa-demo/services
{
  "kind": "Status",
  "apiVersion": "v1",
  "metadata": {},
  "status": "Failure",
  "message": "services is forbidden: User \"system:serviceaccount:-
sa-demo:sa-test\" cannot list resource \"services\" in API group
\"\" in the namespace \"sa-demo\"",
  "reason": "Forbidden",
  "details": {
    "kind": "services"
  },
  "code": 403
}
```

We cannot list the services from the pod; that is not what we want. Per our scenario we should be able to list pods and services, so here is a practice question for you to complete the scenario question.

Practice Question: Create a new pod named **`sa-test-1`** in the sa-demo namespace, the pod should have permissions to view pods, services, configmaps, and secrets. Create a new **`serviceAccount`**, role and rolebinding when solving the question.

As we saw in the last scenario, Kubernetes automatically places the service account token, certificate, and namespace details in the filesystem tree of each container in the pod at /var/run/secrets/kubernetes.io/serviceaccount.

Although this behavior is useful, in the sense that it makes it easier for pods to interact with the API Server, this can result in a large attack surface. Not every pod needs to interact with the API server, so not every pod needs the service account token. We can disable this automatic behavior in one of two ways.

1. **By updating the service account**

You can opt out of automounting the API Credentials when defining the **`serviceAccount`**. Here is the updated yaml file for the service account with **`autoMountServiceAccountToken`** flag set to false.

```
apiVersion: v1
kind: ServiceAccount
automountServiceAccountToken: false
metadata:
  name: sa-test
  namespace: sa-demo
```

2. **By updating the pod definition**

You can also opt to disable the automount for select pods and control the configuration at much granular level. Here is the updated yaml manifest for the pods with **`autoMountServiceAccountToken`** flag set to false.

```
apiVersion: v1
kind: Pod
metadata:
  name: sa-test
  namespace: sa-demo
spec:
  serviceAccountName: sa-test
automountServiceAccountToken: false
  containers:
  - name: sa-test
    image: nginx:latest
```

NOTE: *If both the ServiceAccount and the Pod's specify a value for automountServiceAccountToken, the Pod spec takes precedence.*

Service Account for external applications

So far, the service accounts that we have seen were all used within a pod running in the same Kubernetes cluster. However, that is not the only use case for service accounts. In certain use cases, the application that needs access to the Kubernetes cluster might be running outside the cluster. An example of such an application is monitoring or automation applications, where the application needs to access the cluster resources to either monitor the objects or automate the deployment process.

In this case, you can use a service account to provide necessary permissions to the application. Instead of directly using the service account in the application, you will generate a service account token that can be used for authenticating against the API server. Let us look at this use case with the help of a scenario.

Scenario 4:

You have a service account sa-token-test in the namespace sa-demo. Role and Rolebinding to list the pods in the namespace are already created for the service account. You need to create a token for the service account. The token should be valid for 15 minutes. You need to validate that you can list pods in the namespace using the generated token.

1. Let us start by listing the **serviceaccount**.

```
$ kubectl get serviceaccount sa-token-test -n sa-demo
NAME            SECRETS   AGE
sa-token-test   0         2m41s
```

2. Next, we need to create a new token for the service account with a 15-minute validity.

```
$ kubectl create token sa-token-test -n sa-demo –duration 15m > sa-
token-test
ckspractice@DESKTOP-LGCOG3B:~$ cat sa-token-test
eyJhbGciOiJSUzI1NiIsImtpZCI6Ik11ZjlFUlVVSFd0dm1NbUw2bE9h-
RXA5emhyUlowa214aW1xNWQ0SUlXMjgifQ…
```

3. Now let us use the token to call the cluster api and validate if we can list the pods.

```
$ curl -s -k -m 5 -H "Authorization: Bearer $(cat sa-token-test)"
https://127.0.0.1:36541/api/v1
/namespaces/sa-demo/pods
{
  "kind": "PodList",
  "apiVersion": "v1",
  "metadata": {
    "resourceVersion": "321585"
  },
  "items": [
```

```
{
  "metadata": {
    "name": "sa-test",
    "namespace": "sa-demo",
    "uid": "9862675d-81f3-4d9c-b31d-70d4bca3d0de",
    "resourceVersion": "314817",
    "creationTimestamp": "2025-01-22T15:52:14Z",
```

So the generated token is working and we can list the pods; however, did you notice a security issue with the way the solution was implemented? The token was saved in a text file and then used in the API call; however, that is a huge security concern. Ideally the token should be kept safe with robust privacy policy such as a credential manager. Another option is to create a secret for the service account that can be used to store the token within the cluster. In the following is the command to create a secret for the service account:

```
kubectl apply -f - <<EOF
apiVersion: v1
kind: Secret
metadata:
  name: <secret_name>
  annotations:
    kubernetes.io/service-account.name: <service_account_name>
type: kubernetes.io/service-account-token
EOF
```

Practice Question: You need to create a new service account named **`secret-view-sa`**, which can list other service accounts and secrets in the cluster across all namespaces. You also need to create a secret name **`view-sa-secret`** for the service account, which will hold the service account token, and lastly, extract the token from the secret and validate that you can list the secrets in the cluster via curl. You can use the above yaml to generate the secret and the curl command given in the foregoing scenario for testing. Make sure to modify the API endpoint address to point to secrets and not pods.

Securing the Kubernetes API Endpoint

The Kubernetes API server is the central nervous system of the Kubernetes environment. The API server is responsible for all operational coordination, management, and security. You interact with the API server through the API endpoint, which serves as the gateway to the Kubertentes server. There are three main ways in which you can connect to the API gateway, you can use the kubectl, use client libraries, or make REST calls to the endpoint. Kubernetes provides ways to access the API endpoint for both human as well as machine users via service accounts.

When a request is made to the API endpoint, it goes through 3 main stages, namely Authentication, Authorization, and Admission control.

Figure 3.1 shows the Kubernetes authentication flow through different plugins.

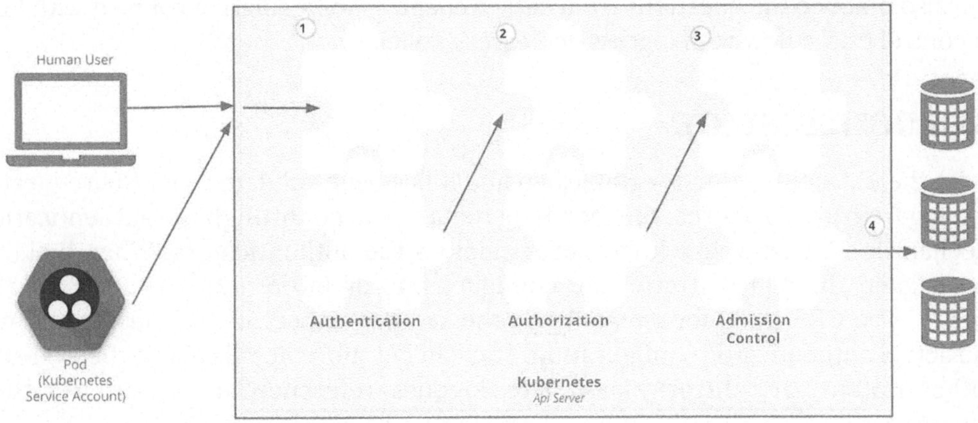

***Figure 3.1**: Kubernetes Authentication and Authorization Flow*

We need to make sure that the communication to the API endpoint is secured at every stage, right from the communication channel down to the user permissions. Let us take a look at how we can secure the API server across different stages of communication.

Securing Network Communication with TLS

The initial step in securing an API endpoint is to ensure that the communication channel between the user and the endpoint is protected. In a Kubernetes cluster, the API server endpoint, by default, listens on port 6443. This communication is safeguarded using encryption, and a certificate is employed to establish trust.

When setting up the cluster, you have the flexibility to customize various configurations, including the port, address, certificate, and private key. These can be configured during the initial cluster build or modified later to suit your security requirements. One of the key configurations is the use of a private Certificate Authority (CA) and a custom certificate for the endpoint.

If you opt to use a private CA, it is essential that every user includes the root CA certificate in their kubeconfig file to facilitate trusted communication. Failure to provide a valid CA certificate will result in the breakdown of Transport Layer Security (TLS) communication, causing the connection to be untrustworthy and effectively blocked.

You can also control the traffic flow to the Kubernetes endpoint by using network policies. With network policies, you can control the ingress and egress traffic. We have already covered network policies in detail; you can review the network policy details at https://kubernetes.io/docs/concepts/services-networking/network-policies/ and also practice the questions from earlier chapters to familiarize yourself with how to control traffic flow with ingress and egress policies.

Authentication

Once the TLS connection is established and it has been validated that the request is coming from a valid source, the incoming request will go through the authentication mechanism. This is where Kubernetes employs the authenticators. When building the cluster, the administrator can configure one or more authenticators for the cluster. The CKS exam focuses only on the security aspect of the cluster and not the actual authenticator configuration. You can get more details about the available authenticator at https://kubernetes.io/docs/reference/access-authn-authz/authentication/.

Kubernetes has many authentication methods; however, as part of this section, we will only focus on three authentication methods that do not rely on any external service or provider.

Client Certificate

Client certificates are generally used for human users who interact with the cluster via **`kubectl`** or any other method. The client certificate is used to validate the authenticity of the user. The client certificate is validated against the configured certificate authority. Administrators can either use the Kubernetes internal CA or a private CA.

We have already seen how to use the client certificate for user authentication in scenario 1, where we had generated a new key, csr, and certificate for the user. Here is a practice question for you to refresh the concept.

Practice Question: You are onboarding a new member, Sneha, to your team. Sneha is joining as a Kubernetes administrator and will be responsible for managing the production Kubernetes cluster. As part of the onboarding process, you need to create a new private key, certificate, and new kubeconfig file with a default context for her. Use the following details when creating the mentioned objects:

- Private key length should be 2048
- Private key file should be named **`sneha_admin.key`**
- You must also generate new Certificate Signing Request (CSR) and set the subject name to **`sneha_k8admin`**.

- Use the CSR to generate a new certificate and kubeconfig file, which can be shared with Sneha.
- Make sure that there is only 1 context in the new **kubeconfig** file.

Bearer Tokens

Second method to interact with the API server is to use Bearer Token. Bearer token is the go to method when you want to interact with the kbuerentes server from inside a pod with service account or when you connect to the API Server from an external application such as the CI/CD tool that we had talked about in the earlier section.

When using bearer token for authentication, the token needs to be passed to the API server in the requests Authorization header; the token must be in the format Bearer <token>. We had seen bearer tokens in action while working with the service accounts. Here is another practice question for you to try.

Practice Question: You are responsible for managing and monitoring the production Kubernetes cluster for your organization, and as part of operational streamlining efforts, you are implementing a new monitoring solution. The solution runs as an external service for fault tolerance and needs a service account to read all the cluster resources. You need to create a new service account named k8s-monitoring-sa. As the account will be used by an external application, you need to disable the token automounting at the service account level. You also need to generate a new secret for the service account to hold the service account token. The secret will be named **`monitoring-sa-token`**. Once you have the secret, extract the token from the secret and save it in a file named **`service-account-token.txt`**.

Static Token File

Static token file is the most basic authentication method available in Kubernetes. It is the simplest to implement but is also the least secure one. Static token file authentication is based on storing the user authentication information in a csv file, which is passed to the API servers with **`-token-auth-file=<token file.csv>`**

The file has to have at least 3 fields: token, user name, and user uid. You can optionally define groups that the user is part of. Following is a sample token file.

```
token,user,uid,"group1,group2,group3"
dkfjdije,app_user,231, "admin_grp,monitor_grp,audit_grp"
ertqowkb,audit_user,239, "admin_grp,monitor_grp,audit_grp"
```

Other Authentication Methods

Apart from the three mentioned authentication methods, Kubernetes supports a couple of other authentication methods to help integrate Kubernetes with external authentication providers such as OIDC, Authentication Proxy, and so on. For the exam, we do not need to cover the external authentication providers. You can get details on all supported authentication methods at https://kubernetes.io/docs/reference/access-authn-authz/authentication/.

Authorization

Once the request successfully passes through the authentication check, it means that the request is coming from an authentic source; however, we still need to make sure that the subject has permissions to perform the task mentioned in the request. That is where the authorization comes into the picture. This stage validates whether the subject is authorized to access the path and verb. Authorization can be implemented with RBAC with roles and rolebindings defining which operations are allowed for a subject. As per the last section of this chapter, Roles and Rolebindings can be either namespaced or clusterwide and can be assigned to a human user or service account. Here is a practice question for you to refresh your understanding of the RBAC Concept:

Practice Question: Let us build up on our last question, you should now have a service account `k8s-monitoring-sa`, you need to build a new role with get, list, and view permissions for all pods, deployments, replicasets, services, configmaps and volumes in the cluster. Assign this role to the service account and use the token from last question to validate whether all operations are working. Also make sure that the service account can not get the secrets.

Admission Control

The last stage of the process is admission control. Admission control ensures that the request is well-formed and can also modify or reject the request. Admission control only applies to requests that create, modify, delete, or connect to an object. Read operations are not acted on by the admission controller. You can have multiple admission controller acting on the request, in case of multiple controllers, they are applied in order. You can get detailed info on the available admission controller at https://kubernetes.io/docs/reference/access-authn-authz/admission-controllers/.

Cluster Upgrade

Running and maintaining a Kubernetes cluster for production application is not a one-time job. So far, you have deployed a new cluster, made sure that it follows security best practices laid out by industry experts, and ensured proper access control. However, every software product inherently has flaws and a constant enhancement cycle, even if you start with the latest version of any software, it will become outdated or obsolete after some time, similarly when you deploy Kubernetes cluster, ideally, you would start with the latest release; however, over time new features, functionalities, enhancements and security fixes will be launched which will make the cluster outdated.

You need to make sure that all the components involved in the Cluster, including but not limited to the Operating System, Binaries, third-party plugins, and external applications that interact with the cluster, are patched and updated regularly to protect against known security vulnerabilities as well as benefit from platform enhancements. If the cluster is running with an older version, it might become susceptible to known security threats, which can be exploited by an attacker. Known security vulnerabilities are publicly disclosed and tracked in the Common Vulnerabilities and Exposure (CVE) database. You can explore the known CVE and how these can be exploited at https://cve.mitre.org/. As the CVE database works as a central location to track all publicly published known vulnerabilities in different products, it is a goldmine for attackers to learn about system weaknesses and ways in which these can be exploited. So it is imperative to keep the cluster patched with the latest security fixes and always run on a supported version.

Kubernetes Versioning and Release Cycles

Kubernetes versions are typically represented by X.Y.Z, with 1.32.1 being the latest release at the time of writing this chapter.

- X represents the major version and denotes a significant change in Kubernetes, often a new major version will be incompatible with older major versions. Latest major version is 1.
- Y represents the minor version, with every new minor version, new features, bug fixes, and enhancements are released. You can upgrade from one minor version to the next one.
- Z represents a new patch; the patches include minor bug fixes and security updates.

Kubernetes has a rapid release cycle, as per the Kubernetes release documentation available at https://kubernetes.io/releases/, Kubernetes maintains release branches for the most recent three minor releases, and new releases currently happen approximately three times per year.

Kubernetes upgrade is already a big part of the CKA exam so you must already be familiar with the process, procedure and best practices. We are going to cover the upgrade process and best practices in brief in the following section:

Kubernetes Upgrade Process

Just like any other software update/upgrade, a Kubernetes upgrade starts with thorough research and understanding of which version you are currently running and where you want to go. We can divide the Kubernetes upgrade process into the following steps:

Choose the Target Version

The very first thing you need to do is to identify which Kubernetes version you want to upgrade to. You need to ensure that you are familiar with the new version and have read and understood the release notes. After that, you need to map the upgrade path. Kubernetes is really sensitive to changes, and though it is possible to jump a couple of patches, it is not advisable and should be avoided. Upgrade from one minor release to another should be done in sequence, for example, you can upgrade from 1.28 to 1.29 and then 1.30 and so on, but jumping from 1.28 to 1.31 is a strict no. Doing so can have drastic and unexpected effects on the cluster.

Testing in the Test environment

Make sure to thoroughly test the upgrade procedure, upgrade path, and application compatibility of the new version in a testing environment and avoid upgrading the production setup until all the kinks have been ironed out in the testing environment and you have a well-defined plan.

Rollback Strategy

You should also have a clear rollback strategy in case the upgrade fails. The strategy could involve simply reverting the the old version if possible or recovering from a backup if the current setup is severely compromised.

Kubernetes documentation available at https://kubernetes.io/docs/tasks/administer-cluster/kubeadm/kubeadm-upgrade/ provides detailed steps to upgrade the cluster and the sequence that needs to be followed. At a high level, the upgrade process will follow the mentioned sequence:

1. **Control Node upgrade**
    a. Upgrade Kubeadm on control plane node
    b. Drain and cordon the node
    c. Plan upgrade with kubeadm upgrade plan
    d. Apply upgrade with kubeadm upgrade apply
    e. Upgrade kubelet and kubectl
    f. Restart kubelet
    g. Uncordon the node

2. **Worker Node upgrade**
    a. Drain and cordon the node
    b. Upgrade the kubeadm version
    c. Upgrade the ndoe with kubeadm upgrade node
    d. Upgrade kubelet and kubectl
    e. Restart kubelet
    f. Uncordon the node

Practice Questions

In the following is a list of new practice questions for you to practice the topics that we have learned. Make sure to try these as per the instructions and keep the naming convention given.

Question 1: You are given admin access to a new Kuberentes cluster, you need to share the access with a new user who has joined your team. Your task is to first create a new SSH key, CSR and certificate. The use is named mark.

Question 2: New user mark from last question needs to be able to list all the pods, services, configmaps, secrets, volumes, and volumeclaims. He should also be able to get the details of individual objects if needed. Create a new cluster-wide role and rolebinding with the names admin-view-role and admin-view-rolebinding for mark. Validate the rolebinding by getting the details of any configmap in the default namespace.

Question 3: Create a new service account named audit-view, which has view-only permissions on all objects in the cluster. Validate the permissions of the service account by mapping it to a new nginx pod and running a curl command from inside the container to list all the services in the cluster.

Question 4: Create a new nginx pod and map the audit-view service account to the pod. Make sure that automounttoken is disabled for the pod. Once the pod is up, run the same curl command to list all services from inside the container and note the difference between the current output and the output from Question 10.

Question 5: Create a new Kubernetes cluster with v1.30. Practice upgrading this cluster to the latest available release. You might have to perform the upgrade more than once, depending on the latest current Kubernetes release.

Conclusion

The second domain of the CKS exam deals exclusively with cluster hardening, with a major focus on protecting the cluster with the right set of permissions, network policies, and the right usage of service accounts.

We have covered Role-Based Access Control in detail to see how to effectively leverage this powerful mechanism to control who has access to what resource and what they can do with the resources once they access these. We also covered how to implement similar control for service accounts and how to secure service accounts by avoiding automatically mounting the service account tokens in the pods. We also touched upon how to secure the API endpoint by combining the security policies, certificates, encryption, and access control. Lastly, we covered the importance of keeping the Kubernetes clusters updated and on a supported version to avoid attacks by exploiting known security vulnerabilities.

In the next chapter, we will shift our focus towards the operating system on which the Kubernetes platform is hosted. We will look at how to reduce the host OS footprint to reduce the attack surface, secure access to the OS, and even use tools such as AppArmor and Seccomp to secure the OS Kernel.

CHAPTER 4
System Hardening

Introduction

In the previous chapters, we have covered the initial setup and security for the Kubernetes cluster. We saw how to create a secure cluster and secure the cluster access using network security policies along with Role-Based Access Control (RBAC) to ensure that only the authorised users, machines, and applications have access to cluster resources. However, only securing the cluster itself is not sufficient when it comes to holistic security of the Kubernetes environment. Kubernetes cluster runs on an operating system and is vulnerable to operating system security threats.

Going back to our utopian city analogy, the building is only as secure as its foundation. A robust Kubernetes deployment needs a secure platform to run on. This chapter will focus on the critical practices of system hardening and focus of the steps required to secure the host upon which the Kubernetes cluster is built. We will start the chapter with an emphasis on the importance of minimizing the OS footprint. When it comes to security, less is always more. If we go back to our utopian city, every entrance to the city represents a potential point of compromise. By closing off unnecessary entrances, you can concentrate your efforts on closely guarding the city.

A lean operating system, without unnecessary services and software packages, makes a smaller attack surface. Every unwanted service or software package is a potential security risk and can introduce vulnerabilities in the system, allowing malicious actors to enter the system. By removing or disabling the unwanted services and removing unnecessary bloatware, you effectively reduce the potential for system exploitation.

We will further discuss how we can leverage the Kubernetes Role-Based Access Control (RBAC) principles, which are generally used with the Kubernetes objects, to secure access to host-level resources. We will also explore how to leverage the Linux Native security features to implement RBAC-like controls at the host level. This not only ensures secure access to the system resources but also keeps the security practice consistent across the platform and Operating System.

We will further explore how to use network firewalls such as **iptables** and **firewalld** to regulate network traffic to Kubernetes nodes. By blocking unwanted traffic to the platform and only allowing required traffic type, we can essentially isolate the cluster from external threats. We will also discuss best practices for network ports.

To further enhance the host OS security posture, we will look into external security tools such as **AppArmor** and **Seccomp**. We can use tools such as these to restrict the processes' capabilities and limit the system calls available for consumption. AppArmor is an access control system that allows defining rules in profiles around which resources are available for a process. Seccomp, on the other hand, is a kernel-level security mechanism that enables us to filter system calls, further reducing the exploitable attack surface.

By the end of this chapter, you will gain a better understanding of a proactive approach to system hardening and how it is essential in protecting the system against external as well as internal threats.

Structure

At an elevated level, this chapter covers the following concepts:

- Reducing Host OS Footprint
  - Disable Unwanted Services
  - Remove Unnecessary Packages
- Secure Access to the Host Platform
  - Linux Users and Groups
  - Linux File and Directory Permissions and Ownership
- Secure Network Access
  - Working with System Firewall
  - Securing Network Ports
- Secure OS Kernel with External Tools
  - AppArmor
  - Seccomp

Reducing Host OS Footprint

When it comes to understanding the concept behind reduced OS footprint, the fundamental is elegantly simple: a smaller footprint means a reduced attack surface or kill-box. Even the smallest Linux distro comes pre-bundled with hundreds, if not thousands, of binaries that you will never use. Every extra tool or binary in the system introduces the possibility of vulnerabilities, misconfigurations, and exploits.

In this section, we will work through the practical steps of reducing the OS footprint and focus on two major areas: disabling unwanted services and removing unwanted packages. We will delve into the tools necessary to identify and eliminate these extraneous components.

Disable Unwanted Services

When you start with a new Kubernetes cluster installation, the first step is to select the Operating System that you will use for the platform. Linux is the most famous OS for Kubernetes, and the majority of Kubernetes clusters in use are built on Linux. When you start with the Linux deployment, even the most basic installation will have a lot of tools and packages that are not needed by the Kubernetes platform; these packages and services should be either disabled or completely removed from the system to secure the environment.

Most Linux distributions have a default package manager, such as yum or apt, to help manage the installed software packages. The distros also have a service manager to maintain the running and installed services. Most Linux distros use **systemd** as the service manager. This tool provides the necessary commands to list, enable, disable, and control services. **`Systemctl`** is the command line interface for the system; proficiency with systemctl commands is essential for any Linux as well as Kubernetes operator. In the following section, we will see how to first list and identify unwanted services using systemctl and then use the command line interface to disable the identified services.

Identifying Unwanted Services

The first step in disabling the services is to identify them. This requires a thorough understanding of the necessary services needed by the operating system as well as the Kubernetes platform. We do not want to start disabling the services indiscriminately.

Run the following command on the terminal to list all enabled services.

```
$ systemctl list-unit-files --type=service | grep enabled
accounts-daemon.service                                     enabled
atd.service                                                 enabled
auditd.service                                              enabled
autovt@.service                                             enabled
avahi-daemon.service                                        enabled
bluetooth.service                                           enabled
chrony_update.service                                       enabled
chronyd.service                                             enabled
cloud-config.service                                      enabled
cloud-final.service                                       enabled
cloud-init-local.service                                    enabled
```

```
cloud-init.service                                         enabled
crond.service                                              enabled
cups.service                                               enabled
```

The command will list all the service unit files that are currently enabled. Carefully analyze the output and look for the service that is not required by the Kubernetes operation. Examples of unnecessary services for a Kubernetes cluster include:

- **Bluetooth Services:** Unless your Kubernetes nodes require Bluetooth functionality, bluetooth.service can be safely disabled.
- **Printing Services:** Services such as cups.service are typically not needed in a server environment.
- **Desktop Environment Services:** If your nodes are running a headless server OS, desktop environment services are redundant and should be disabled.
- **Avahi Daemon:** Avahi, a system for service discovery, is often unnecessary in a Kubernetes cluster with its own service discovery mechanisms.

Disabling Unwanted Services

Once you have identified the service that you want to disable, use the **`sytemctl`** command to disable the service.

```
$ sudo systemctl disable avahi-daemon.service
Removed /etc/systemd/system/sockets.target.wants/avahi-daemon.socket.
Removed /etc/systemd/system/multi-user.target.wants/avahi-daemon.service.
Removed /etc/systemd/system/dbus-org.freedesktop.Avahi.service.
```

The command will prevent the service from starting automatically at system restarts, but it does not stop the service that is currently running.

Stopping Unwanted Services

You can list all the services that are currently running with the following **`systemctl`** command.

```
$ systemctl | grep running
  proc-sys-fs-binfmt_misc.automount
loaded    active running   Arbitrary Executable File Formats File System
Automount Point
  cups.path
loaded    active running   CUPS Scheduler
  init.scope
loaded    active running   System and Service Manager
  session-8.scope
loaded    active running   Session 8 of user opc
  session-c1.scope
loaded    active running   Session c1 of user ocarun
```

```
  atd.service
loaded    active running   Job spooling tools
  auditd.service
loaded    active running   Security Auditing Service
  avahi-daemon.service
loaded    active running   Avahi mDNS/DNS-SD Stack
  chronyd.service
loaded    active running   NTP client/server
  crond.service
loaded    active running   Command Scheduler
```

If the service is running, you can check its detailed status by running following command:

```
$ systemctl status avahi-daemon.service
● avahi-daemon.service - Avahi mDNS/DNS-SD Stack
   Loaded: loaded (/usr/lib/systemd/system/avahi-daemon.service; dis-
abled; vendor preset: enabled)
   Active: active (running) since Sun 2025-03-09 10:41:24 GMT; 13min
ago
 Main PID: 1535 (avahi-daemon)
   Status: "avahi-daemon 0.7 starting up."
    Tasks: 2 (limit: 95060)
   Memory: 1.0M
   CGroup: /system.slice/avahi-daemon.service
           ├─1535 avahi-daemon: running [linux.local]
           └─1551 avahi-daemon: chroot helper

Mar 09 10:41:24 localhost.localdomain avahi-daemon[1535]: Registering
new address record for fe80::17ff:fe02:6be9 on enp0s6.*.
Mar 09 10:41:24 localhost.localdomain avahi-daemon[1535]: Registering
new address record for 10.0.10.97 on enp0s6.IPv4.
Mar 09 10:41:24 localhost.localdomain systemd[1]: Started Avahi mDNS/
DNS-SD Stack.
Mar 09 10:41:25 localhost.localdomain avahi-daemon[1535]: Server startup
complete. Host name is linux.local. Local service cookie is 1315897224.
Mar 09 10:41:28 terrapyauto avahi-daemon[1535]: Withdrawing address re-
cord for fe80::17ff:fe02:6be9 on enp0s6.
Mar 09 10:41:28 terrapyauto avahi-daemon[1535]: Leaving mDNS multicast
group on interface enp0s6.IPv6 with address fe80::17ff:fe02:6be9.
Mar 09 10:41:28 terrapyauto avahi-daemon[1535]: Interface enp0s6.IPv6
no longer relevant for mDNS.
Mar 09 10:41:30 terrapyauto avahi-daemon[1535]: Joining mDNS multicast
group on interface enp0s6.IPv6 with address fe80::17ff:fe02:6be9.
Mar 09 10:41:30 terrapyauto avahi-daemon[1535]: New relevant interface
enp0s6.IPv6 for mDNS.
Mar 09 10:41:30 terrapyauto avahi-daemon[1535]: Registering new address
record for fe80::17ff:fe02:6be9 on enp0s6.*.
```

You can stop the service by running following command:

```
$ sudo systemctl stop avahi-daemon.service
Warning: Stopping avahi-daemon.service, but it can still be activated by:
  avahi-daemon.socket
```

Verifying the Service

Once you stop and disable the service, you can check it's status by running the following command:

```
$ systemctl is-enabled avahi-daemon.service
Disabled
```

If the service is disabled, the command will return disabled.

Practical Considerations

When you start working on a new operating system to reduce the OS footprint, make sure you keep the following in mind:

- **Thorough Analysis:** During the exam, when asked to disable or stop the service, carefully analyse the service and ensure that you are disabling the service as asked in the question. Disabling other services might break the cluster and make the exam environment unusable.
- **Document Changes:** Make sure you use the given notepad section in the exam interface to keep track of any changes that you make to the service to ensure you can revert the changes if needed.
- **Test and Validate:** Once you disable the service, make sure you validate the service status. If the question wants you to stop the service as well, make sure you stop it manually, as disabling the service does not stop the current instance.

Remove Unnecessary Packages

Once you have disabled the unwanted service in the system, the next step to secure the environment is to remove bloatwares from the system which are not needed for Kubernetes or system operations. Every time you install a new package, it comes with a number of binaries and packages, with each package and binary representing another attack vector for the malicious actors to exploit. By diligently identifying and removing these extraneous components, we can significantly enhance the security posture of the Kubernetes nodes.

The process of removing unnecessary packages, just like disabling services, requires a thorough understanding of the operating system packages, Kubernetes requirements, and package management system used by the Linux distribution that you are working with. Different Linux distributions prefer different package managers; for example, Debian/Ubuntu has **apt**, CentOS/RHELs have **yum** and **dnf**. Depending on your platform OS, you should be proficient with the package manager command line interface.

Just like disabling the unwanted services, we will start with identifying the unnecessary packages and then move to a demonstration of how to remove these packages.

Identifying Unnecessary Packages

Identifying unnecessary packages that are not needed by the operating system operations, as well as the Kubernetes environment, can be a challenging task as there are intricate dependencies between the packages; however, you can adopt a systematic approach to the exercise and start with the common packages not currently in use.

As part of the section, we are using CentOS and the commands are specific the CentOS. The commands for your workstation might be different, please ensure to find and practice the corresponding commands based on you Linux distribution.

Listing Installed Packages

Run the following command to list all the packages currently installed in the system:

```
$ rpm -qa
perl-Getopt-Long-2.50-4.el8.noarch
golang-bin-1.19.4-2.0.1.module+el8.7.0+20922+47ac84ba.aarch64
rsyslog-gnutls-8.2102.0-15.el8.aarch64
mysql-community-client-plugins-8.0.36-1.el8.aarch64
smc-fonts-common-6.1-10.el8.noarch
sssd-2.9.1-4.0.1.el8_9.5.aarch64
iptables-libs-1.8.5-10.0.1.el8_9.aarch64
gnome-shell-extension-horizontal-workspaces-3.32.1-35.el8.noarch
perl-threads-2.21-2.el8.aarch64
dotnet-templates-8.0-8.0.102-2.0.1.el8_9.aarch64
iproute-tc-6.2.0-5.el8_9.aarch64
lucene-8.4.1-5.module+el8.3.0+20129+7f91a1ba.noarch
osinfo-db-20230518-1.0.3.el8.noarch
iwl5150-firmware-8.24.2.2-999.31.el8.noarch
libcomps-0.1.18-1.el8.aarch64
firefox-115.8.0-1.0.1.el8_9.aarch64
python3-terminaltables-3.1.0-1.0.1.el8.noarch
ledmon-0.97-1.el8.aarch64
lucene-analysis-8.4.1-5.module+el8.3.0+20129+7f91a1ba.noarch
libwacom-data-1.6-3.el8.noarch
```

```
libwayland-client-1.21.0-1.el8.aarch64
boost-atomic-1.66.0-13.el8.aarch64
gnome-system-monitor-3.28.2-1.el8.aarch64
```

The output list has been truncated to fit the page space; however, on the workstation, you will get a complete list of all the packages. Analyze the output, looking for packages that are clearly not needed for Kubernetes.

Common Unnecessary Packages

Some of the common packages and package types not needed for the Kubernetes cluster are listed as follows:

- **Development Tools:** The production Kubernetes environment will not need any development tools such as compilers and debuggers unless specifically required.
- **Graphical User Interface:** If your environment is hosted in a headless server, you would not need any GUI components to run the cluster, and any GUI package can be safely removed.
- **Office Suites and Multimedia packages:** This one is pretty self-explanatory, you do not want any bulky suite, such as Libre or Multimedia package, on a server system.
- **Disabled Service package:** Once you disable a service, you can remove its corresponding package.

Removing Package

Once you have identified the package, you can remove it by running the following command:

```
$ sudo yum remove avahi
Dependencies resolved.
================================================================================
 Package                                     Architecture
Version                                               Repository
Size
================================================================================
Removing:
 avahi                                       aarch64
0.7-21.el8_9.1                                        @ol8_baseos_latest
1.3 M

Transaction Summary
================================================================================
Remove  1 Package
```

```
Freed space: 1.3 M
Is this ok [y/N]: y
Running transaction check
Transaction check succeeded.
Running transaction test
Transaction test succeeded.
Running transaction
  Preparing        :
                                                 1/1
  Running scriptlet: avahi-0.7-21.el8_9.1.aarch64
                     1/1
  Erasing          : avahi-0.7-21.el8_9.1.aarch64
                     1/1
  Running scriptlet: avahi-0.7-21.el8_9.1.aarch64
                     1/1
  Verifying        : avahi-0.7-21.el8_9.1.aarch64
                     1/1

Removed:
  avahi-0.7-21.el8_9.1.aarch64


Complete!
```

Practical Considerations with Package Management

As stated earlier, removing unwanted packages is no small feat, as a lot of times the dependency between packages is not clear, and removing a dependent package might wreak havoc on the entire system and make the system unusable. Keep the following points in mind when working with packages in the exam environment:

- **Dependency Management:** Before removing packages, make sure you are aware of the package dependencies. Removing one package might also remove the binaries used by other packages. During the exam, make sure to only remove the package explicitly mentioned in the question and not other components.
- **Backup and Testing:** If possible, take a backup of the package before removing the binary and test the cluster after removing the package for any breakage.
- **CLI Proficiency:** Get familiar with the package management commands such as apt, yum, and dnf for different Linux distributions.
- **Dry Run:** Some package managers have the dry-run option, which can give an overview of the package that will be removed before actually removing it.

Use this to ensure that only the packages mentioned in the question will be removed. For example, with dnf, you can use the following command:

```
dnf remove <package name> --dry-run
```

Secure Access to the Host Platform

Even after you disable all the unwanted services and remove all the unnecessary softwares from the Operating System, the system is still vulnerable to unauthorized access. It is equally important to control who and what can access the host system itself. In this section, we will look at the critical security practice of controlling access to the host platform and focus on the fundamental principle of User and Group Management. We will double-click on the Role-Based Access Control (RBAC) from the host Operating System's point of view.

Just like the Kubernetes environment, operating systems also have the concept of Users, Groups, and Permissions, which provides the fundamental building block to control access to files, directories, and system processes. We will look at how to create dedicated user accounts for Kubernetes components and services, and we will also ensure that each component operates with the least amount of privileges that are needed for the smooth functioning of the environment. Next, we will also see how to use the groups to organize users and streamline the permissions management.

Next, we will look into user permissions and how to use Linux CLI commands such as chmod and chown to restrict user access to sensitive files and resources. Similar to Kubernetes, we will aspire to build a system based on the principles of least privilege.

One thing to note before we dive into this section is that Kubernetes also has a Role-Based Access Control (RBAC) mechanism, which only covers the Kubernetes components and it is imperative to extend the same concepts to the host OS. We will look at using mechanisms such as sudoers and how they can help us build RBAC-like controls at the host level. This step involves carefully crafting sudoers rules to limit the commands that specific users can execute with elevated privileges.

By the end of this section, you will be able to establish a robust access control framework for the Kubernetes nodes.

Linux Users and Groups

Linux user accounts represent a distinct identity in the Linux operating system and provide a basic mechanism for resource sharing and individual identity. Every user is assigned a unique User ID (UID) which is used to identify the user throughout the system. Users also get their own home directories and settings.

Linux User Operations

Creating New Users

When working on the Kubernetes cluster, you might want to create separate user accounts for Kubernetes processes such as Kubelet and for real-world users with limited access to the system resources. You can use the following commands to add a new user in most Linux distributions:

```
$ sudo adduser kubelet-user
```

Note: *Depending on your Linux Distribution you might be asked to enter a new password for the user and also provide additional information about the user such as the user home directory and user shell.*

The default settings for the **useradd** command are stored in a config file, and you can view this by running the following command:

```
$ cat /etc/default/useradd
# useradd defaults file
GROUP=100
HOME=/home
INACTIVE=-1
EXPIRE=
SHELL=/bin/bash
SKEL=/etc/skel
CREATE_MAIL_SPOOL=yes
```

As per the preceding output, you can see that when a user is created with the **useradd** command, the user will by default have the bash shell assigned, and also the user home directory will be located under the **/home** location. You can change the **useradd** config in this file or manually provide the details in the **useradd** command in the following format:

```
Useradd -d <HOME_DIRECTORY> -g <INITIAL USER GROUP> -m <Create
Home Directory if it does not exist> -s <USER SHELL>
```

List Users

After you create or if you want to list existing users. You can use the following command to view all users in the system:

```
$ cat /etc/passwd
root:x:0:0:root:/root:/bin/bash
bin:x:1:1:bin:/bin:/sbin/nologin
daemon:x:2:2:daemon:/sbin:/sbin/nologin
adm:x:3:4:adm:/var/adm:/sbin/nologin
lp:x:4:7:lp:/var/spool/lpd:/sbin/nologin
kubelet-user:x:54323:54323::/home/kubelet-user:/bin/bash
```

The entries in the file have the following format:

```
User-name:password:UID:GID:HOME_DIR:SHELL
```

User-name: This is the human-readable username assigned to the user.

Password: An X in the password field indicates that an encrypted and salted password for the user is stored in the **/etc/shadow** file.

UID: Unique ID for the User.

GID: Primary group ID for the user; the details for this group are stored in the **/etc/group** file. Note that the user can be part of multiple other groups. This field only indicates the initial user group that was defined at the time of user creation.

HOME_DIR: Home directory path for the user.

SHELL: Path to the shell assigned to the user.

If you are creating a machine account or service account, you should not assign the user account any shell access; instead, **use /sbin/nologin** or **/usr/sbin/nologin** in the SHELL field to secure the account.

Deleting User Accounts

As the Kubernetes environment grows and your system and team become more dynamic, you might have service accounts that are not needed anymore or a user account for a team member who has transitioned out of the team. You need to ensure that you remove such accounts from the system in a timely manner to ensure that there are no ghost accounts left in the system, which can be used to compromise the system integrity. Use the following command to delete the user from the system:

```
$ sudo userdel -r kubelet-user
```

Specifying the **-r** option in the command will ensure that the user home directory is deleted along with the user account. If you only want to delete the user and retain the home directory contents, remove the **-r** switch from the command.

Linux User Group Operations

Consider a scenario where you have to manage a large Kubernetes cluster that is shared among multiple teams with multiple members in every team. Members of a team generally require similar permissions to the resources. So, it is much more convenient to manage the permissions for a group than for every individual user. Group permission management also helps in streamlining the overall process with fewer chances of misconfiguring user access.

Just like members are grouped in different teams, you can group different user accounts in groups and maintain RBAC at a higher level while maintaining granular control over the permissions assigned to every user. Let us take a look at how to manage user groups in a Linux system.

Create Groups

Just like **useradd**, Linux offers **groupadd** command, which you can use to add a new group. Use the following as an example to create a new group:

```
$ sudo groupadd kubernetes-serviceaccounts
```

This will create a new group with no user assignment. The group will also be assigned a new GID which can be used to add users to the group. The group details are in a config file at **/etc/group**, we'll look at the file entry format in the next section.

Listing existing groups

You can view the details of all existing groups from the **/etc/group** file. Run the following command to view the details:

```
$ cat /etc/group
root:x:0:
bin:x:1:
daemon:x:2:
sys:x:3:
adm:x:4:cloud-agent,cloud-agent-updater,ocarun
kubernetes-serviceaccounts:x:54324:
```

The group file entries have the following format.

```
Group_name:password:GID:Group_List
```

Group Name: This is the name of the group that you provided in the groupadd command.

Password: Generally, groups do not have a password; however, a password can be used to implement privileged groups.

GID: Group ID for the group.

Group List: This is a list of users who are members of the given group. The list is comma-separated.

Assigning Users to Groups

Once you have the user and group in place, you can use the following command to assign group membership to the user.

```
$ sudo usermod -a -G kubernetes-serviceaccounts kubelet-user
```

The following is the description of the switches used:

- **-a (Append):** If you do not specify the append switch, then the user will be removed from any group that is not defined in the **-G** parameter.

- **`-G (Group List)`:** This is a list of groups that the user needs to be part of. You can define multiple groups in the list separated by a comma (,).

If you want to change the primary group for the user. Use the following command:

```
$ sudo usermod -g <Group_Name> <User_Name>
```

Notice that the switch here is lower-case g and not upper-case G.

Removing a Group

There might be instances where you want to delete the whole group. Before you remove the group from the system, you need to ensure that you remove the individual user accounts from the group. You can use the usermod command as shown in the last section to reassign the users.

Once the group is empty, use the following command to delete the group:

```
$ sudo groupdel kubernetes-serviceaccounts
```

Linux File and Directory Permissions and Ownership

So far, we have created new user, group and assigned the user to group. However, we still need a way to control access to the system files and directories. Linux uses file and directory permissions as gatekeepers of resource access.

Permissions define what actions an owner, group, or other account is allowed to perform on a file. Linux offers three types of permissions, which can be clubbed together in different combinations to control access. Before looking at how to assign the permissions to different files or directories, let us understand the basics of the Linux permission structure.

- **Linux Permission Types:**
  - **Read (r):**
    - For files, this allows the user to view the contents of the file.
    - For directories, this allows the user to list the directory contents.
  - **Write (w):**
    - For files, this permission allows a user to modify the contents of the file.
    - For directories, this permission allows a user to create, delete, or rename files within the directory.
  - **Execute(x):**
    - For files, allows the user to execute a file as a script or program file.

    - For directories, allows the user to enter the directory, that is, change directory (**cd**) to the directory.
- **Linux Permission Scope:** Linux permissions are assigned in three categories:
  - **Owner (u):** The user who owns the file or directory.
  - **Group (g):** The group that is associated with the file or directory.
  - **Others (o):** All other user accounts in the system that are neither the owner of the file/directory nor part of the group assigned to the file or directory.
- **Linux Permission Representation:** Permissions in a Linux system can be represented in one of the following two formats:
  - **Symbolic Notation**

In symbolic notation, the permissions are represented as a string of ten characters, with every character depicting a different aspect of the permission.

- The first character in the permission string can have one of two values;
  - **(dash symbol):** It represents a regular file.
  - **d (lower case letter d):** represents a directory.
- The next nine characters are grouped in three sets of three characters.
  - The first group represents the permissions for the **owner (u).**
  - The second group represents the permissions for the **group (g).**
  - The last group represents the permissions for **others (o).**
- Each group represents the permissions in the **Read, Write, Execute (rwx)** format in the same sequence.

Example: `-rwxr-xr`–represents the following permission:

Type: File

Owner: Read, Write, Execute

Group: Read and execute

Others: Read

- **Numeric or Octal Notation**

In Octal notation, every permission type is assigned a numerical value as follows:

- **Read (r):** 4
- **Write (w):** 2
- **Execute (x):**1

Permissions for every group are calculated by summing the values of the effective representation and can have one of the following values:

- **7** = rwx
- **6** = rw-
- **5** = r-x
- **4** = r--
- **3** = -wx
- **2** = -w-
- **1** = --x
- **0** = ---

So the above example can be rewritten as:

```
-rwxr-xr-- = 754
```

- **Assigning Permissions to files:** To assign permissions to files or directories, you can use the chmod command. The following are a couple of examples for permission assignment:
  - **Restricting Access to Sensitive Files:**
    - Use **`chmod 600 <file>`** to grant read and write permissions only to the owner.
    - This is very useful for configuration files that contain sensitive information.
  - **Granting Execute Permissions to Scripts:**
    - Use **`chmod +x <script>`** to grant execute permissions to a script.
    - This is a shortcut to **`chmod 755 <script>`** or **`chmod u+x <script>`**
  - **Directory Permissions:**
    - **`chmod 755 <directory>`** grants read, write, and execute permissions to the owner, and read and execute permissions to the group and others.
    - This is a common setting for directories that need to be accessible to multiple users.
    - **`chmod 700 <directory>`** grants full access only to the owner.
  - **Default File Permissions (umask):**
    - The umask command sets the default permissions for newly created files and directories.
    - It masks off certain permissions.

- For example, a umask of 022 will remove write permissions from group and other.

- **Recursive Permissions:**
  - Use the **-R** option with chmod to apply permissions recursively to all files and subdirectories within a directory.
  - chmod -R 755 <directory>

- **Viewing Permissions:** You can use the list command to view the permissions as well as the ownership of the file. Use the following command to view these details for all files and directories in a given path:

```
$ ls -l /tmp
$ ls -l /tmp
total 0
drwxr-xr-x. 2 root root  6 Mar 10 10:54 hsperfdata_root
drwx------. 3 root root 17 Mar  9 10:41 systemd-pri-
vate-3905969ab9df4dcbbd7f5b22b4d605c2-chronyd.service-GqXtHl
drwx------. 3 root root 17 Mar  9 10:41 systemd-pri-
vate-3905969ab9df4dcbbd7f5b22b4d605c2-ModemManager.service
-yedBsj
drwx------. 3 root root 17 Mar  9 10:41 systemd-private
-3905969ab9df4dcbbd7f5b22b4d605c2-rtkit-daemon.service-KXLHg3
drwx------. 3 root root 17 Mar  9 11:44 systemd-private
-3905969ab9df4dcbbd7f5b22b4d605c2-unified-monitoring-agent.
service-nnYJfx
```

The permissions are displayed in the symbolic notation as defined in the last section. You, the user, and the group assigned to the directory/file are also displayed. We will describe the file and directory ownership in the next section.

- **File and Directory Ownership:** With the file and directory permissions, you can define what actions can be performed on the object. Though we have talked about the owner and group when assigning the permissions, we have not introduced these so far.

In Linux, every file and directory is assigned an owner and group;

- **Owner (User):** The user who creates the directory or the file, by default, becomes the owner of that file/directory unless the ownership is manually assigned.
- **Group:** The group associated with the directory could be different from the group which owner is part of. The member of the file/directory group gets the group permissions on the resource.

- **Viewing Ownership:** Use the **`ls -l`** command to view the owner and group of files and directories.
  - Example: **`ls -l /path/to/file`**

  - The output will display the owner and group in the third and fourth columns, respectively.

- **Changing Ownership:** To change the ownership of a file or directory, you can use the chown and chgrp command. The following is an example of changing the ownership of a file from **`root`** to **`kubelet-user`** and **`Kubernetes-serviceaccounts`** group.

```
$ ls -l
total 0
-rw-rw-r--. 1 root root 0 Mar 10 18:13 test-file
$ sudo chown kubelet-user test-file
$ ls -l
total 0
-rw-rw-r--. 1 kubelet-user root 0 Mar 10 18:13 test-file
$ ls -l
total 0
-rw-rw-r--. 1 kubelet-user kubernetes-serviceaccounts 0 Mar 10
18:13 test-file
```

You can use the **`chown`** command to change both the user and group by providing the details as per the following example:

```
$ sudo chown root:root test-file
[opc@terrapyauto ~]$ ls -l
total 0
-rw-rw-r--. 1 root root 0 Mar 10 18:13 test-file
```

- **Recursive Ownership Changes:** : Use the **`-R`** option with chown to recursively change ownership of all files and subdirectories within a directory.

  Example: `sudo chown -R new_owner:new_group /path/to/directory`

Controlling Privilege Elevation with Sudoers

Not every system user is same; some users need more permissions than others, and some need to run commands or execute scripts using elevated permissions. Linux implements a privilege elevation mechanism with sudoers. The config file for sudoers is located at **`/etc/sudoers and controls`** which user or groups has the ability to execute commands with elevated privileges, typically as root.

In Kubernetes contxt, certain tasks may require elevated privileges, with sudoers you can control the privilege elevation at a granular level. Before we look at how to leverage this to secure the system, let us get a brief introduction to the file structure.

Run the following command to read the file.

```
$ sudo less /etc/sudoers
## Allow root to run any commands anywhere
root    ALL=(ALL)       ALL

## Allows members of the 'sys' group to run networking, software,
## service management apps and more.
# %sys ALL = NETWORKING, SOFTWARE, SERVICES, STORAGE, DELEGATING,
PROCESSES, LOCATE, DRIVERS

## Allows people in group wheel to run all commands
%wheel  ALL=(ALL)       ALL

## Same thing without a password
# %wheel        ALL=(ALL)       NOPASSWD: ALL

## Allows members of the users group to mount and unmount the
# %users  ALL=/sbin/mount /mnt/cdrom, /sbin/umount /mnt/cdrom
```

Above is a partial export of the file. Although the overall structure of the file is somewhat complex, for the purpose of the exam, you only need to understand the entry format. Every entry in the sudoers file has the following format:

`user MACHINE=(RUNAS) COMMANDS`

`user`: This is the user or group name that is getting the privileged access.

`MACHINE`: This column is generally left as ALL as it is supposed to be a list of hostnames on which the sudo entry is effective. In most cases, sudoers entries are limited to localhost, so you can use either localhost or ALL.

`RUNAS`: This is a list of users and/or groups. The user getting the privileged access can run the commands as any of the user/group defined in the list.

`COMMANDS`: This is a list of commands the user is allowed to run with privileged permissions.

Let us look at an example sudoers entry and interpret it.

`%users  ALL=/sbin/mount /mnt/cdrom, /sbin/umount /mnt/cdrom`

The above entry allows all users in group users to mount and unmount the cdrom on the system.

Best Practices and Practical Considerations

- **Dedicated Users and Groups:** You should create dedicated user accounts and groups for Kubernetes components and assign ownership of their files and directories to them.

- **System Files:** During the exam, when working with system files, take extreme caution while changing the permissions of system files. Incorrect permissions might make the system unstable.
- **CLI Proficiency:** Make sure you are familiar with different commands to work with users, groups, file permissions, and ownership, such as adduser, usermod, chown, chmod, and so on.

Secure Network Access

While the user, groups, permissions, and access control take care of activities that a user can perform once logged in to the system. It does not account for what kind of network traffic is flowing to and from the Kubernetes nodes.

In a distributed system such as Kubernetes, network security is paramount. Just like we had built strict rules around the pod and service communication using Kubernetes Network Security Policies, we need to also build similar structure around the Kuberenetes nodes to secure the traffic flowing between the nodes.

All Kubernetes nodes are interconnected, and the host OS might have other processes, applications, or services that either generate or listen to network traffic. We will explore the use of a system firewall, such as iptables, to control the network traffic at the host level. The system firewall acts as a gatekeeper, allowing only authorized traffic to pass through. We will look at some examples of how to build firewall rules to effectively isolate Kubernetes nodes from external threats.

Next, we will also look at another critical aspect of port security. Every open network port represents a potential entry into the system. We will explore ways to identify open ports, determine which services are using them, and their purpose, and look at ways to secure them. This primarily includes binding services to specific interfaces, disabling unwanted network ports, and ensuring that only authorized services are accessible from the network.

Working with System Firewall

The Operating System firewall is the first line of defence against unauthorized network access to your Kubernetes nodes. You can use the network firewall to filter traffic, allowing only authorized communication to pass through.

On Ubuntu, you have two options to work with the iptables firewall:

- **Iptables**: Linux includes the Netfilter subsystem, which can be used to identify and filter the network traffic going in and out of the system. Iptables is the user interface for the Netfilter subsystem, allowing administrators capabilities to manage it.

- **ufw (Uncomplicated Firewall):** ufw is the default firewall configuration tool for Ubuntu. It works as a friendly interface to configure IPv4 and IPv6 host-based firewall rules. Iptables is still the underlying firewall.

Enabling Firewall

When you first install the Operating System, the firewall is disabled by default. Run the following command to check the firewall status and enable it:

```
$ sudo ufw status
Status: inactive
$ sudo ufw enable
Command may disrupt existing ssh connections. Proceed with
operation (y|n)? y
Firewall is active and enabled on system startup
$ sudo ufw status
Status: active
```

Deny all traffic

Keeping in line with the principle of least privileges, the first step after you build the system is to disable all communication to and from the system.

However, before you disable all communication, make sure to enable ssh access to the system if you are connected via SSH, or you will lose the connection and will need direct access to the system console.

```
$ sudo ufw allow  ssh
Rule added
Rule added (v6)
$  sudo ufw default deny incoming
Default incoming policy changed to 'deny'
(be sure to update your rules accordingly)
$ sudo ufw default deny outgoing
Default outgoing policy changed to 'deny'
(be sure to update your rules accordingly)
```

Enable Kubelet and kube-apiserver traffic

Once you have the default deny policy in place, you can start allowing Kubernetes-specific traffic, such as kubelet and kube-apiserver, depending on the node type. Run the following command to enable both traffics on the node:

```
$ sudo ufw allow 6443/tcp
Rule added
Rule added (v6)
$ sudo ufw allow 10250/tcp
Rule added
Rule added (v6)
```

Listing Firewall rules

You can use the verbose switch with ufw status to list the current firewall rules.

```
$ sudo ufw status verbose
Status: active
Logging: on (low)
Default: deny (incoming), deny (outgoing), disabled (routed)
New profiles: skip

To                         Action      From
--                         ------      ----
22/tcp                     ALLOW IN    Anywhere
6443/tcp                   ALLOW IN    Anywhere
10250/tcp                  ALLOW IN    Anywhere
22/tcp (v6)                ALLOW IN    Anywhere (v6)
6443/tcp (v6)              ALLOW IN    Anywhere (v6)
10250/tcp (v6)             ALLOW IN    Anywhere (v6)
```

Deleting firewall rule

In some cases, you might have to delete an existing firewall rule. Use the following command to delete the existing firewall rule:

```
$ sudo ufw delete allow 6443/tcp
Rule deleted
Rule deleted (v6)
$ sudo ufw status verbose
Status: active
Logging: on (low)
Default: deny (incoming), deny (outgoing), disabled (routed)
New profiles: skip

To                         Action      From
--                         ------      ----
22/tcp                     ALLOW IN    Anywhere
10250/tcp                  ALLOW IN    Anywhere
22/tcp (v6)                ALLOW IN    Anywhere (v6)
10250/tcp (v6)             ALLOW IN    Anywhere (v6)
```

Securing Network Ports

Open network ports are potential entry points for attackers. To secure the network ports, we need to be able to list, identify common ports, and disable services that are not needed to stop listening on the network port. In this section, we will look at how to secure the open ports in the system.

Listing Open Ports

Services such as NTP, Web-Servers, DNS, and so on all have predefined standard ports that they use. When working with the ports, you need to be familiar with the common services and ports. Internet Assigned Numbers Authority (IANA) maintains a list of service names and transport port protocol numbers. You can refer to this list at https://www.iana.org/assignments/service-names-port-numbers/service-names-port-numbers.xhtml to search for common ports and services if you are unsure about which service is using a particular port.

On the Linux system, you can run the ss command to list all ports.

```
$ sudo ss -tnlp
State            Recv-Q            Send-Q                     Local Address:Port
Peer Address:Port            Process
LISTEN           0                 4096                          127.0.0.54:53
0.0.0.0:*                 users:(("systemd-resolve",pid=729,fd=17))
LISTEN           0                 4096                     127.0.0.53%lo:53
0.0.0.0:*                 users:(("systemd-resolve",pid=729,fd=15))
LISTEN           0                 4096                           0.0.0.0:111
0.0.0.0:*                 users:(("rpcbind",pid=712,fd=4),("systemd",pid=1,fd=103))
LISTEN           0                 4096                              [::]:111
[::]:*                  users:(("rpcbind",pid=712,fd=6),("systemd",pid=1,fd=105))
LISTEN           0                 4096                                *:22
*:*                   users:(("sshd",pid=1613,fd=3),("systemd",pid=1,fd=224))
```

From the list, you can identify the open ports and disable/stop any service that is not needed on the Kubernetes nodes.

Best Practices and Practical Considerations

- **Identify Unnecessary Port:** Make sure that you are familiar with the ports needed for the Kubernetes nodes and can quickly identify ports that are not required by the cluster and might be associated with other services.
- **Close Unnecessary Ports:** Any port that does not serve a specific purpose in the Cluster should be closed by either blocking the traffic via firewall or by disabling the associated service.
- **Proficiency with UFW:** Practice working with UFW and rule configuration, so that when asked during the exam, you can quickly build and test the rules.
- **Ensure Essential Communication:** Before applying a deny-all policy for incoming or outgoing traffic, ensure that you have allowed essential communication for the cluster; blocking all traffic might break the cluster if the nodes can not communicate with each other.
- **Ensure Testing:** Most distributed services, such as Kubernetes, have built-in timeouts and checks, so that even after the communication is blocked, the

service might not fail immediately. Ensure that you thoroughly test the cluster after making any changes in the firewall.

Securing OS Kernel with External Tools

Even after you secure the Operating System service, files, and network permissions, there is another aspect of the System Security that we need to manage. Pods that run on the node are allowed to use the underlying operating system resources and leverage the kernel to make system calls. This creates a huge security challenge as a pod can run any process irrespective of the container function.

In this section, we will explore how to restrict pods from accessing the underlying processes by limiting their capabilities, as well as restrict the system calls that the pod is allowed to make.

Kubernetes does not have a built-in mechanism to implement the necessary security measures and has to rely on external tools. For the CKS exam, you need to be familiar with two of these tools, AppArmor and Seccomp. We will discuss both of these tools in the upcoming sections.

AppArmor

AppArmor (Application Armor) is a Linux kernel security module that allows the system administrator to restrict program capabilities. Simply put, AppArmor restricts which resources, such as files and network capabilities, a program is allowed to access and use.

AppArmor can help extend the access control beyond the simple RBAC policies for users and groups. AppArmor is also not limited to just pods and containers, it is an OS construct and can be used beyond the Kubernetes use-cases. Before we move to practical implementation of AppArmor with pods, lets understand the main components of the configuration.

- **Mandatory Access Control (MAC):** MAC is a security architecture that is at the heart of AppArmor implementation. Unlike a traditional Discretionary Access Control (DAC) system, where users can control the permissions on their owned resources. MAC uses centrally controlled profiles to enforce security.
- **AppArmor Profiles:** AppArmor profiles are a set of rules that define what resources a process can access. The resources could be anything from simple files and directories to network sockets.
- **AppArmor Modes:** AppArmor provides two modes for profiles: **enforce** and **complain.** In complain mode, any unauthorized access is logged but not blocked. In enforce mode, unauthorized access is blocked by the system.

Now that we have the basics covered, let us look at how to use the profile with Kubernetes pods.

Listing AppArmor Profiles

In most Linux distributions, including Ubuntu, AppArmor is pre-installed, so you do not have to install it again. AppArmor will also be available in the CKS exam environments, depending on whether the question requires it. To list the current AppArmor profile, run the following command:

```
$ sudo aa-status
apparmor module is loaded.
127 profiles are loaded.
27 profiles are in enforce mode.
   /snap/snapd/22991/usr/lib/snapd/snap-confine
   /snap/snapd/22991/usr/lib/snapd/snap-confine//mount-namespace-cap-
ture-helper
   /usr/bin/man
   …
9 profiles are in complain mode.
   transmission-cli
   transmission-daemon
   …
3 processes have profiles defined.
1 processes are in enforce mode.
   /usr/sbin/rsyslogd (2489) rsyslogd
2 processes are in complain mode.
   /snap/cloud-agent/72/agent (1520) snap.cloud-agent.cloud-agent
   /snap/cloud-agent/72/updater/updater (1526) snap.cloud-agent.
oracle-cloud-agent-updater
```

The output will give you detailed information about all the profiles, their modes, which processes have the profile defined for them, and what mode those profiles are in.

Creating AppArmor Profile

AppArmor uses profiles to control which resources are available to the processes. The profile uses a format called AppArmor Profile Language; writing new CKS profiles is out of scope for the CKS exam. During the exam, you will be given a pre-configured profile that you will have to apply to a pod.

However, for the example, we are going to create a profile that will restrict the pods from writing any file to the host OS filesystem. The sample profile can be found at https://kubernetes.io/docs/tutorials/security/apparmor/. Use the sample profile and save it in a file named **`pod-deny-write`**.

```
#include <tunables/global>
profile pod-deny-write flags=(attach_disconnected) {
  #include <abstractions/base>

  file,

  # Deny all file writes.
  deny /** w,
}
```

Note: *When you create the profile, you have to create it on all Kubernetes nodes.*

After you create the profile, move it to **/etc/apparmor.d/** and parse it using **apparmor_parser**.

```
$ sudo mv pod-deny-write /etc/apparmor.d/
$ sudo apparmor_parser /etc/apparmor.d/pod-deny-write
$ sudo aa-status
apparmor module is loaded.
129 profiles are loaded.
29 profiles are in enforce mode.
   /snap/snapd/22991/usr/lib/snapd/snap-confine
   /snap/snapd/22991/usr/lib/snapd/snap-confine//mount-name-
space-capture-helper
   /usr/bin/man
   pod-deny-write
   ….
   ….
```

Attaching the policy to Kubernetes Pod

Before you can use the profile in the container, you have to ensure that:

- The AppArmor kernel module should be enabled on all the nodes. You can check the status by running the following command:

  ```
  $ cat /sys/module/apparmor/parameters/enabled
  Y
  ```

- Most container runtimes support AppArmor, including containerd and CRI-O. If you are sure about your container runtime, check the corresponding documentation.
- The profile should be loaded in all worker nodes, as the pod can be scheduled on any worker. The profile should be available there; otherwise, the pod will be rejected.

Once you have the pre-reqs validated, copy the following pod definition and run the container:

The AppArmor profile is defined under pod **spec** in **securityContext**, the **appArmorProfile** section defines the type of profile as well as the name of the profile to use. In our example, the type is **`localhost`**, and the name is

```
apiVersion: v1
kind: Pod
metadata:
  name: hello-apparmor
spec:
  securityContext:
    appArmorProfile:
      type: Localhost
      localhostProfile: pod-deny-write
  containers:
  - name: hello
    image: busybox:1.28
    command: [ "sh", "-c", "echo 'Hello AppArmor!' && sleep 1h" ]

$ kubectl create -f pod.yaml
pod/hello-apparmor created
$ kubectl get pod hello-apparmor
NAME             READY   STATUS    RESTARTS   AGE
hello-apparmor   1/1     Running   0          5s
```

Testing the AppArmor Profile

Once the container is in running state, you can check whether the profile is applied to the container or not by running the following command:

```
$ kubectl exec hello-apparmor – cat /proc/1/attr/current
k8s-apparmor-example-deny-write (enforce)
```

You can now try to create a new file and see how the profile behaves.

```
$ kubectl exec hello-apparmor – touch /tmp/test.txt
touch: /tmp/test: Permission denied
error: error executing remote command: command terminated with
non-zero exit code: Error executing in Docker Container: 1
```

Seccomp

Seccomp (Secure Computing Module) is another kernel-level security mechanism that can restrict the system calls that a process can make. With Seccomp, you can greatly reduce the attack surface and prevent potential system exploits by limiting the system calls available from the userspace.

Identifying the syscalls required by a workload is a difficult task and is not part of the CKS exam. During the exam, you will be provided the basic Seccomp profiles and asked to attach these to the pods.

However, as part of the exercise in the upcoming section, we will create a simple Profile, apply it to the pod, and test it.

Default Seccomp Profile

You can get started with Seccomp profiles with the default profile. While in general, the default profile is quite permissive and might not suit a lot of sensitive workloads, it blocks a lot of sensitive system calls. For Docker, you can refer to the blocked syscall at https://docs.docker.com/engine/security/seccomp/#significant-syscalls-blocked-by-the-default-profile.

To use the default Seccomp profile, you need to define **seccompProfile** in the **securityContext** of the pod manifest. The following is a pod manifest that uses the default profile:

```
apiVersion: v1
kind: Pod
metadata:
  name: default-pod
  labels:
    app: default-pod
spec:
  securityContext:
    seccompProfile:
      type: RuntimeDefault
  containers:
  - name: default-seccomp
    image: busybox:1.28
    command: [ "sh", "-c", "echo 'Using Default Seccomp Profile!'
&& sleep 1h" ]
    securityContext:
      allowPrivilegeEscalation: false

Let's create the pod and check it's status and logs.
$ kubectl apply -f default-seccomp
pod/default-pod created
$ kubectl get pods
NAME               READY   STATUS     RESTARTS   AGE
default-pod        1/1     Running    0          28s
$ kubectl logs default-pod
Using Default Seccomp Profile!
```

The pod is not making any restricted syscalls and is allowed to run without any issues.

Custom Seccomp Profile

If you have the details of syscalls that your pod needs, you can create a custom profile with only the required syscalls. Let us look at an example of a custom seccomp profile that will block all system calls from the pod. This is equivalent to a default deny policy.

Copy the following profile detail and save it to **/var/lib/kubelet/seccomp/default-deny.json**

```
{
    "defaultAction": "SCMP_ACT_ERRNO"
}
```

Next, let's create a new pod to use the default-deny profile.

```
apiVersion: v1
kind: Pod
metadata:
  name: default-deny
spec:
  securityContext:
    seccompProfile:
      type: Localhost
      localhostProfile: default-deny.json
  containers:
  - name: default-deny
     image: busybox:1.28
     command: [ "sh", "-c", "echo 'Using Default-Deny Seccomp
Profile!' && sleep 1h" ]
    securityContext:
      allowPrivilegeEscalation: false
```

Create the pod and check it's status

```
$ kubectl create -f default-deny
pod/default-deny created
$ kubectl get pod default-deny
NAME            READY   STATUS             RESTARTS   AGE
default-deny   0/1      CrashLoopBackOff   1          5s
```

As seen above, the pod will be created but will fail to start because the syscalls necessary for the echo command have not been allowed by the seccomp profile.

Audit Seccomp Profile

As mentioned in the last section, the pod failed because the necessary syscalls were not permitted by the profile. In this section, we will create a custom profile that will not block any syscalls but will log all the syscalls made by the pod, and the logs can be used to fine-tune the Profile.

Save the following file as **/var/lib/kubelet/seccomp/audit.json**.

```
{
    "defaultAction": "SCMP_ACT_LOG"
}
```

Now create another pod with following definition.

```
apiVersion: v1
kind: Pod
metadata:
  name: audit-syscall
spec:
  securityContext:
    seccompProfile:
      type: Localhost
      localhostProfile: audit.json
  containers:
  - name: audit-syscall
     image: busybox:1.28
     command: [ "sh", "-c", "echo 'Using audit Seccomp Profile!'
&& sleep 1h" ]
    securityContext:
      allowPrivilegeEscalation: false

$ kubectl apply -f audit
pod/audit-syscall created
$ kubectl get pods
NAME                  READY   STATUS      RESTARTS   AGE
audit-syscall           1/1     Running     0            54s
$ kubectl logs audit-syscall
Using audit Seccomp Profile!
```

Look at the syslogs on the node to check which calls were made by the pod.

```
$ cat /var/log/syslog | grep 'audit-syscall'
Mar 10 18:46:37 cks-demo-lab kernel: [369128.669452] audit: type=1326
audit(1594067860.484:14536): auid=4294967295 uid=0 gid=0 ses=4294967295
pid=29064 comm="echo" exe="/http-echo" sig=0 arch=c000003e syscall=51
compat=0 ip=0x46fe1f code=0x7ffc0000
Mar 10 18:46:37 cks-demo-lab kernel: [369128.669453] audit: type=1326
audit(1594067860.484:14537): auid=4294967295 uid=0 gid=0 ses=4294967295
pid=29064 comm="echo" exe="/http-echo" sig=0 arch=c000003e syscall=54
compat=0 ip=0x46fdba code=0x7ffc0000
Mar 10 18:46:37 cks-demo-lab kernel: [369128.669455] audit: type=1326
audit(1594067860.484:14538): auid=4294967295 uid=0 gid=0 ses=4294967295
pid=29064 comm="echo" exe="/http-echo" sig=0 arch=c000003e syscall=202
compat=0 ip=0x455e53 code=0x7ffc0000
Mar 10 18:46:37 cks-demo-lab kernel: [369128.669456] audit: type=1326
```

```
audit(1594067860.484:14539): auid=4294967295 uid=0 gid=0 ses=4294967295
pid=29064 comm="echo" exe="/http-echo" sig=0 arch=c000003e syscall=288
compat=0 ip=0x46fdba code=0x7ffc0000
...
```

Note: *The logs location on your workstation might be different.*

From the output, in the **syscall=<number>** field, we can identify the syscalls made by the process. You can search the syscall names with the number at https://filippo.io/linux-syscall-table/

Practice Question 1: Use the syscalls identified in the last exercise, look for their corresponding names at https://filippo.io/linux-syscall-table/, and create a new Seccomp profile with default deny action and only allow the required syscalls. Recreate the pod and validate that it runs as expected. Use the following custom-seccomp profile definition. Update the syscall-names with the actual syscalls identified by the audit profile.

```
{
    "defaultAction": "SCMP_ACT_ERRNO",
    "architectures": [
        "SCMP_ARCH_X86_64",
        "SCMP_ARCH_X86",
        "SCMP_ARCH_X32"
    ],
    "syscalls": [
        {
            "names": [
                "<syscall-name-1>",
   "<syscall-name-2>",
          "<syscall-name-3>",
   "<syscall-name-4>",
   "<syscall-name-5>"
            ],
            "action": "SCMP_ACT_ALLOW"
        }
    ]
}
```

Conclusion

In this chapter, we have covered the third domain of the CKS exam that deals with system hardening to secure the underlying Operating System platform against unwanted threats.

We began the chapter by focusing on reducing the host OS footprint, understanding that a lean Operating System minimizes the attack surface. We also looked at examples and steps on how to disable the unwanted services and remove un-necessary package not needed by the Kubernetes platform.

Next, we addressed another aspect of System Security covering the OS user, groups, and permissions. We also explored how to use the CLI tools such as chmod and chown to build a basic RBAC system, as well as the use of sudoers to manage the privilege elevation at the OS level.

We then shifted our attention to securing the network access with firewalls and network ports. We looked at the basics of port security and how to identify common ports.

In the last section, we delved into external tools, AppArmor, and Seccomp to further fortify the Operating System by allowing processors access to only the required system calls and capabilities.

In the next chapter, we will cover how to secure the workload running in the Kubernetes cluster by way of Pod Security Polices, Secrets, and Isolation techniques such as multitenancy and sandboxed containers.

CHAPTER 5
Minimizing Microservice Vulnerability

Introduction

In the preceding chapters, we have meticulously fortified the Kubernetes environment. We had started with the base deployment of the Kubernetes environment and worked our way to securing the underlying operating system. However, securing the environment is only part of the larger picture. In this chapter, we are going to cover another important piece of the security puzzle, the application microservices.

So far, we have diligently secured the underlying operating system, established robust access controls, and guarded the network perimeter. Yet, even within the most secure fortress, vulnerabilities can lurk within its inhabitants. In the context of Kubernetes, these inhabitants are our pods, the atomic units of deployment, and securing them is paramount to maintaining the overall integrity and resilience of our applications. We have learned that a lean and hardened environment reduces the attack surface. We have also understood the importance of controlled access and a secure network perimeter. Now, we must extend the same principles to the microservices to ensure that the pods are operating within a secure and confined environment.

By design, the pods are ephemeral, they are designed to be short lived and scalable. This poses a unique set of security challenges, unlike traditional applications pods need a security approach that is both flexible and robust. The microservices security standards must be adaptable to the changing landscape of the application while enforcing strict control to prevent unauthorized access and malicious activity.

The fourth pillar of the Certified Kubernetes Security (CKS) Specialist exam focuses on the security settings and best practices available for the Kubernetes pods. We will start the chapter by exploring the basics of Pod Security Standards (PSS) and Pod Security Admission (PSA). We will also implement these with the help of live examples in our

Kubernetes environment. PSS and PSA act as gatekeepers and define the security constraints that the pods must adhere to. We will examine how these standards can be used to enforce the least privilege principle and prevent the pods from running with excessive capabilities.

Next, we dive into Kubernetes Secrets and how to use these to manage sensitive data within Kubernetes. K8s Secrets provide a secure mechanism to store and distribute confidential information such as passwords, keys, certificates, and so on. Secrets make sure that this sensitive information is not stored in plain text either within the pod specification files or within the pod description output.

In the next section, we will delve into workload isolation and explore techniques such as multi-tenancy, sandboxed containers, and so on. We will learn how to effectively isolate workloads within the cluster and prevent them from interfering with each other, and limit the impact of a potential security breach.

In the last section, we will shift our focus to the communication between pods, examine the fundamentals of P2P communication, and understand how to encrypt this communication with Cilium.

Structure

At an elevated level, this chapter covers the following concepts:

- Pod Security Standards
    - Pod Security Standards Profiles
    - Pod Security Admission
    - Pod Security Standard Example
    - Practical Considerations
- Manage Kubernetes Secrets
    - Practical Considerations
- Isolation Techniques
    - Multitenancy
    - Sandboxed Containers
    - Isolating Containers with gVisor
    - Sandboxing with Kata Containers
    - Practical Considerations
- Securing Inter Pod Communication
    - Pod-to-pod Communication Basics
    - Securing p-2-p Communication with Cilium

- Enabling Transparent Encryption with IPSec
- Enabling Transparent Encryption with WireGuard

Pod Security Standards

In a Kubernetes environment, a Pod is the smallest unit of objects that you can manage. Pods are also the backbone of the microservices application and represent an individual component of an application microservice. Pods are the very heart of any microservices-based application; as such, their security posture directly impacts the overall resiliency and integrity of the application and the environment as well. Securing these workloads effectively requires a nuanced approach that balances the flexibility of Kubernetes with robust security controls.

The dynamic nature of Pods and Kubernetes means that operators or developers might unintentionally introduce security vulnerabilities by requesting excessive privileges or failing to adhere to best practices. This is where Pod Security Standards (PSS) plays an important role, PSS are a set of predefined security blueprints, each blueprint represents a distinct set/level of security assurance. These profiles are designed to establish clear and consistent security boundaries for the pods. They provide a standardized framework for defining the security requirements for the workloads.

By applying these standards to our namespaces, we can dictate the permissible configurations for our pods, preventing these pods from running with excessive privileges or accessing sensitive resources. This is crucial for mitigating the risk of privilege escalation, unauthorized access and other security vulnerabilities.

PSS defines three distinct security policies; each profile represents a progressively more restrictive security posture. The three PSS policies are: **Privileged**, **Baseline**, and **Restricted**. We will cover the policies individually and provide example usage in the upcoming sections.

Pod Security Standard Profiles

Pod Security Standard has three policies, these policies are cumulative in nature and covers the whole spectrum of security from highly permissive to highly-restrictive. Let us look at these policies individually.

Privileged Profile

This is the most permissive profile; it essentially allows the pods to run with unrestricted capabilities. It is intended for highly trusted workloads and should be used sparingly, if at all, in production environments. From a security perspective, this profile provides minimal protection and should be treated with extreme caution.

The policy is purposely open and completely unrestricted. It should generally be restricted for system and infrastructure level workloads and should be aimed at only privileged and trusted users.

Baseline Profile

Baseline policy is aimed at striking a balance between security and usability. The policy is designed to prevent known privilege escalation while also accommodating common container use cases. It is suitable for most application workloads.

The baseline profile provides a solid foundation for secure pod configuration, the profile enforces essential security controls without overly restricting functionality. The policy enforces certain restrictions on the pod capabilities. The following are two examples of allowed and restricted fields in the baseline profile:

- **Privileged Containers:** Privileged Pods disable most security mechanisms and must be disallowed.
    - Restricted Fields
        - `spec.containers[*].securityContext.privileged`
        - `spec.initContainers[*].securityContext.privileged`
        - `spec.ephemeralContainers[*].securityContext.privileged`
    - **Allowed Values**
        - `Undefined/nil`
        - `False`
- **HostPath Volumes:** HostPath volumes must be forbidden.
    - **Restricted Fields**
        - `spec.volumes[*].hostPath`
    - **Allowed Values**
        - `Undefined/nil`

You can find the detailed information about the baseline profile's allowed and restricted capabilities at https://kubernetes.io/docs/concepts/security/pod-security-standards/

Restricted

Restricted profile is the most restricted policy, this policy is designed to enforce current pod hardening best practices. It is intended for critical workload and environments with stringent security requirements. This profile provides the highest level of security assurance, minimizing the attack surface and mitigating the risk of sophisticated attacks.

This policy should be used for security-critical applications and for any user with lower trust. The following are two examples:

- **Volume Types:** The Restricted policy only permits the following volume types.
  - **Restricted Fields**
    - `spec.volumes[*]`
  - **Allowed Values**

    Every item in the spec.volumes[*] list must set one of the following fields to a non-null value:

    - `spec.volumes[*].configMap`
    - `spec.volumes[*].csi`
    - `spec.volumes[*].downwardAPI`
    - `spec.volumes[*].emptyDir`
    - `spec.volumes[*].ephemeral`
    - `spec.volumes[*].persistentVolumeClaim`
    - `spec.volumes[*].projected`
    - `spec.volumes[*].secret`
- **Running as Non-root** - Containers must be required to run as non-root users.
  - **Restricted Fields**
    - `spec.securityContext.runAsNonRoot`
    - `spec.containers[*].securityContext.runAsNonRoot`
    - `spec.initContainers[*].securityContext.runAsNonRoot`
    - `spec.ephemeralContainers[*].securityContext.runAsNonRoot`
  - **Allowed Values**
    - `true`

You can find the detailed information about the baseline profile's allowed and restricted capabilities at https://kubernetes.io/docs/concepts/security/pod-security-standards/#:~:text=since%20Kubernetes%201.29)-,Restricted,-The%20Restricted%20policy.

Pod Security Admission

In the last section, we looked at the Pod Security Standards (PSS) and different policies defined by PSS. Different PSS policies are aimed at different security levels and different security requirements. Depending on your application and user security requirements, you can choose one or more policies for the workload.

While PSS defines the security profile, Pod Security Admission is the mechanism that enforces these policies. It acts as an admission controller, intercepting requests to the

Kubernetes API server and ensuring that pods adhere to the specified security levels. This section will delve into the workings of Pod Security Admission, its configuration, and how it plays a crucial role in securing your Kubernetes workloads.

PSA evaluates pod requests against the PSS. It operates at the namespace level, allowing administrators to apply different security policies to different workloads within the same cluster. This granularity is essential for accommodating the diverse security requirements of modern applications. Before looking at the practical example, let us look at the basic concepts of PSA.

- **Enforcement Modes:** Just like PSS profiles, PSA also defines different enforcement modes, every mode has different implications when combined with the PSS profile. This also provides a much more granular control when it comes to security standard enablement. Following are the different modes supported by PSA:
    - **Enforce:** Pods that violate the specified PSS level are *rejected*. This is the most stringent mode, providing the strongest security guarantee.
    - **Audit:** Pods that violate the specified PSS level are *allowed*, but an *audit annotation* is added to the pod. This mode is useful for monitoring and identifying potential security violations without disrupting workloads.
    - **Warn:** Pods that violate the specified PSS level are *allowed*, but a *warning* is issued to the user. This mode provides a less disruptive way to introduce PSS, allowing developers to address security issues without immediate enforcement.

Namespace-Based Enforcement

PSA is configured per namespace; this means that different namespaces can have different security policies applied to them. This is crucial for multi-tenant environments or clusters with diverse workloads.

PSA is enabled by labeling namespaces with a specific format. The format is made up of 3 key parts and has the following format:

```
pod-security.kubernetes.io/<mode>: <level>
```

- **Prefix**: The prefix has the fixed value **`pod-security.kubernetes.io`**
- **Mode**: Mode can be one of any enforcement modes defined above and can be one of **enforce**, **audit**, or **warn**.
- **Level**: The level is the PSS profile and can be one of **privileged**, **baseline**, or **restricted**.

Pod Security Standard Example

In the last section, we looked at the theory of PSS and PSA. In this section, let us look at how to implement different policies and enforcement modes.

Let us start with creating 3 different namespaces. Use the following file to create the namespaces:

```
---
apiVersion: v1
kind: Namespace
metadata:
  name: psa-enforce-restrict
  labels:
    pod-security.kubernetes.io/enforce: restricted
---
apiVersion: v1
kind: Namespace
metadata:
  name: psa-audit-restrict
  labels:
    pod-security.kubernetes.io/audit: restricted
---
apiVersion: v1
kind: Namespace
metadata:
  name: psa-enforce-privileged
  labels:
    pod-security.kubernetes.io/enforce: privileged
```

```
$ kubectl apply -f namespaces.yaml
namespace/psa-enforce-restrict created
namespace/psa-audit-restrict created
namespace/psa-enforce-privileged created
$ kubectl get ns
NAME                     STATUS   AGE
default                  Active   10d
psa-audit-restrict       Active   11s
psa-enforce-privileged   Active   11s
psa-enforce-restrict     Active   11s
```

Next, let us create a pod in the respective namespaces and see how the deployment behaves.

```
---
apiVersion: v1
kind: Pod
metadata:
  name: busybox-enforce-restrict
  namespace: psa-enforce-restrict
spec:
  containers:
  - image: busybox:latest
```

```
    name: busybox-enforce-restrict
    command: ["sh", "-c", "sleep 3600"]
---
apiVersion: v1
kind: Pod
metadata:
  name: busybox-audit-restrict
  namespace: psa-audit-restrict
spec:
  containers:
  - image: busybox:latest
    name: busybox-audit-restrict
    command: ["sh", "-c", "sleep 3600"]
---
apiVersion: v1
kind: Pod
metadata:
  name: busybox-enforce-privileged
  namespace: psa-enforce-privileged
spec:
  containers:
  - image: busybox:latest
    name: busybox-enforce-privileged
    command: ["sh", "-c", "sleep 3600"]
```

Let us apply the pods file.

```
$ kubectl apply -f psa-pods.yaml
pod/busybox-audit-restrict created
pod/busybox-enforce-privileged created
Error from server (Forbidden): error when creating "psa-pods.yaml": pods "busybox-en-
force-restrict" is forbidden: violates PodSecurity "restricted:latest": allowPrivi-
legeEscalation != false (container "busybox-enforce-restrict" must set securityContext.
allowPrivilegeEscalation=false), unrestricted capabilities (container "busybox-enforce-re-
strict" must set securityContext.capabilities.drop=["ALL"]), runAsNonRoot != true (pod or
container "busybox-enforce-restrict" must set securityContext.runAsNonRoot=true), seccomp-
Profile (pod or container "busybox-enforce-restrict" must set securityContext.seccompPro-
file.type to "RuntimeDefault" or "Localhost")

$ kubectl get pods -A
NAMESPACE          NAME                          READY   STATUS    RESTARTS
AGE
default            hello-apparmor                1/1     Running   260 (52m
ago)   10d
kube-system        coredns-668d6bf9bc-w4bdt      1/1     Running   0
10d
kube-system        etcd-minikube                 1/1     Running   0
10d
```

```
kube-system             kube-apiserver-minikube            1/1     Running   0
10d
kube-system             kube-controller-manager-minikube   1/1     Running   0
10d
kube-system             kube-proxy-4hfvh                   1/1     Running   0
10d
kube-system             kube-scheduler-minikube            1/1     Running   0
10d
kube-system             storage-provisioner                1/1     Running   1 (10d ago)
10d
psa-audit-restrict      busybox-audit-restrict             1/1     Running   0
27m
psa-enforce-privileged  busybox-enforce-privileged         1/1     Running   0
27m
```

From the output, we can see that the privileged and audit restricted pod was created and is running successfully. However, the enforce-restrict pod was not allowed to run. Let us update the pod definition to include the security context as described in the error message.

```
apiVersion: v1
kind: Pod
metadata:
  name: busybox-enforce-restrict
  namespace: psa-enforce-restrict
spec:
  containers:
  - image: busybox:latest
    name: busybox-enforce-restrict
    command: ["sh", "-c", "sleep 3600"]
    securityContext:
      allowPrivilegeEscalation: false
      capabilities:
        drop: ["ALL"]
      runAsNonRoot: true
      runAsUser: 4000
      runAsGroup: 4000
      seccompProfile:
        type: RuntimeDefault
```

```
$ kubectl apply -f psa-pod.yaml
pod/busybox-enforce-restrict created
$ kubectl get pods -n psa-enforce-restrict
NAME                       READY   STATUS    RESTARTS   AGE
busybox-enforce-restrict   1/1     Running   0          13s
```

As we can see that after fixing the security context, the pod is able to run without errors.

Practice Question 1: Create a new namespace called **secure-app**; within the namespace, all pods must adhere to the **restricted** PSS. Once you have the namespace, try deploying a new pod with **allowPrivilegeEscalation: true.** Verify the behaviour and fix the deployment error.

Practice Question 2: Create a new namespace called **dev-test**, and apply the **baseline** standard in **audit** mode. After the namespace has been created, try to deploy a new pod with security context **runAsUser: 0** in the same namespace. Validate the behaviour of the deployment. Also, confirm that the pod has been created with the audit **annotation** matching the PSS profile and mode.

Practice Question 3: Create a new namespace called **migration-test.** Apply the PSS policy and PSA mode on the namespace which will **warn** the users when they deploy a mode which is violating the **baseline** Pod Security Standard.

Practical Considerations

- **Gradual Implementation:** When working with policies, make sure you start with the warn or audit mode before moving to the enforce mode. This will allow you to test the behaviour without impacting the deployments.
- **Modes and Policies:** Before the exam, make sure to get familiar with different policies and modes and how they behave when grouped together.
- **Namespace Labels**: Get yourself familiar with the namespace labels to quickly update/apply the policies and modes.
- **Audit Logs and Warnings**: Make sure you can quickly understand the audit logs and warnings related to PSS and PSA.

Manage Kubernetes Secrets

When you have a large application running in Kubernetes, the microservices making up the application will often require access to sensitive information such as passwords, API keys, certificates, and other confidential data. One option to provide this information to the application is to directly embed this into the pod specification or container environment. However, that poses a significant security risk and is also hard to manage. To provide a secure and flexible mechanism to manage sensitive data, Kubernetes uses Secrets, ensuring that no sensitive data is exposed in plain text and is only accessible to authorized pods.

Kubernetes secrets work as a secure vault within the cluster, designed to store and distribute sensitive information with utmost care. With secrets, you can decouple sensitive data from the application code and configuration files, enhancing the overall security posture of the workloads.

Kubernetes secrets are essential for workload security and have many benefits over traditional configuration files. Some of the benefits are:

- **Security:** K8s secrets are stored in the etcd database, these can be encrypted at rest and are not exposed as text in the pod specification files or container images. Secrets can be mounted as volumes or environment variables allowing the pods to securely access the sensitive information.
- **Separation of Concerns:** Secrets allow you to separate the sensitive data from the application code and configuration, which simplifies the application management and reduces the risk of accidental exposure.
- **Centralized Management:** Secrets provide a centralized mechanism to store all sensitive content for all the workloads running in the cluster. This helps in simplified updates, rotations, and management of the details.
- **Access Control:** Secrets are subject to Kubernetes RBAC and access to the secrets can be controlled using policies. This gives us granular control over which pod and user can access the information from the secrets.

Kubernetes has several types of secrets and unique ways of creating secrets, such as imperative commands and definition files. Working with secrets is already a large part of the CKA exam, and given that CKA is a prerequisite for the CKS exam, you should already be familiar with the basics of working with Kubernetes secrets. In these sections, let us dive right into an example to see secrets in action. We will then follow it up with encrypting the secrets at rest by updating the etcd configuration.

Let us start by creating a generic sample secret.

```
$ kubectl create secret generic cks-test --from-literal=username=my-
user --from-literal=password=mypassword
secret/cks-test created
$ kubectl get secret cks-test
NAME       TYPE     DATA   AGE
cks-test   Opaque   2      10s
```

If you want to use a definition file, here is the YAML for the same secret.

```
apiVersion: v1
kind: Secret
metadata:
  name: cks-test
type: Opaque
data:
  username: $(echo -n 'myuser' | base64)
  password: $(echo -n 'mypassword' | base64)
```

Let us mount the secret in a pod as a volume and validate that it is accessible inside the pod. Use the following definition to create the pod:

```
apiVersion: v1
kind: Pod
metadata:
  name: busybox-secret
spec:
  containers:
  - name: busybox-secret
    image: busybox:latest
    command: ["sh", "-c", "sleep 3600"]
    volumeMounts:
    - name: secret-volume
      mountPath: "/etc/secrets"
      readOnly: true
  volumes:
  - name: secret-volume
    secret:
      secretName: cks-test

$ kubectl apply -f busybox-secret.yaml
pod/busybox-secret created
$ kubectl get pods
NAME             READY   STATUS    RESTARTS         AGE
busybox-secret   1/1     Running   0                3s
hello-apparmor   1/1     Running   262 (13m ago)    10d
$ kubectl exec -it busybox-secret -- /bin/sh
/# cat /etc/secrets/username
myuser
/ # cat /etc/secrets/password
mypassword
```

We can see that the secret has been mounted in the pod and is accessible as files inside the pod.

Practice Question 3: Create a new pod with **`busybox:latest`** image, mount the **`cks-test`** secret inside the pod using two **environment variables** named **`USERNAME`** and **`PASSWORD`**, respectively. Open a shell to the pod and print the environment variable on the screen.

Practice Question 4: Create a new **image pull secret** to pull images from the docker registry using your own credentials, use the **`imagepullsecret`** and create a new pod with the **`nginx:latest`** image.

Now that we have refreshed our understanding of the secrets and how the secrets are injected into the pods, let us look at how the secrets can be directly accessed from the **etcd** store if the store is not properly secured.

Note: *To follow the next procedure, you will have to install etcdctl on the node where you are running the commands from, search for the procedure to install* **etcdctl** *based on your Operating System, and then move to the next step.*

Use the following command to retrieve the secret that we had created in the last section:

```
$ export ETCDCTL_API=3
$ cd /etc/kubernetes/pki/etcd/
$ etcdctl --cacert=ca.crt --key=server.key --cert=server.crt --endpoints
"https://<K8s API endpoint>:2379" get /registry/secrets/default/cks-test |
hexdump -C
00000000  2f 72 65 67 69 73 74 72  79 2f 73 65 63 72 65 74  |/registry/secret|
00000010  73 2f 64 65 66 61 75 6c  74 2f 63 6b 73 2d 74 65  |s/default/cks-te|
00000020  73 74 0a 6b 38 73 00 0a  0c 0a 02 76 31 12 06 53  |st.k8s.....v1..S|
00000030  65 63 72 65 74 12 fa 01  0a c3 01 0a 08 63 6b 73  |ecret........cks|
00000040  2d 74 65 73 74 12 00 1a  07 64 65 66 61 75 6c 74  |-test....default|
00000050  22 00 2a 24 36 32 62 66  65 35 33 66 2d 33 36 34  |".*$62bfe53f-364|
00000060  33 2d 34 63 33 64 2d 39  33 35 65 2d 62 32 62 61  |3-4c3d-935e-b2ba|
00000070  64 31 63 33 38 63 65 31  32 00 38 00 42 08 08 ce  |d1c38ce12.8.B...|
00000080  d9 ff be 06 10 00 8a 01  75 0a 0e 6b 75 62 65 63  |........u..kubec|
00000090  74 6c 2d 63 72 65 61 74  65 12 06 55 70 64 61 74  |tl-create..Updat|
000000a0  65 1a 02 76 31 22 08 08  ce d9 ff be 06 10 00 32  |e..v1"........2|
000000b0  08 46 69 65 6c 64 73 56  31 3a 41 0a 3f 7b 22 66  |.FieldsV1:A.?{"f|
000000c0  3a 64 61 74 61 22 3a 7b  22 2e 22 3a 7b 7d 2c 22  |:data":{".":{},"|
000000d0  66 3a 70 61 73 73 77 6f  72 64 22 3a 7b 7d 2c 22  |f:password":{},"|
000000e0  66 3a 75 73 65 72 6e 61  6d 65 22 3a 7b 7d 7d 2c  |f:username":{}},|
000000f0  22 66 3a 74 79 70 65 22  3a 7b 7d 7d 42 00 12 16  |"f:type":{}}B...|
00000100  0a 08 70 61 73 73 77 6f  72 64 12 0a 6d 79 70 61  |..password..mypa|
00000110  73 73 77 6f 72 64 12 12  0a 08 75 73 65 72 6e 61  |ssword....userna|
00000120  6d 65 12 06 6d 79 75 73  65 72 1a 06 4f 70 61 71  |me..myuser..Opaq|
00000130  75 65 1a 00 22 00 0a                              |ue.."..|
00000137
```

From the above, you can see that the secret details are available in plain text, so any vector who gains access to the node can read all the secrets, which is not ideal.

To deal with this, we need to configure the kube-apiserver to include an encryption provider. The encryption provider is defined in a config file. You can read about the encryption config file in detail at https://kubernetes.io/docs/tasks/administer-cluster/encrypt-data/. For example, we will stick with a simple config file. Follow the steps below to configure the kube-apiserver for encryption at rest.

Generate a 32-byte base64 key for the configuration file.

```
$ head -c 32 /dev/urandom | base64
RwXjFAqbeHF/U7Oz/T11Qr6215QjiUeARqUCWRcBKZ8=
```

Take the generated key and update it in the following file:

```
apiVersion: apiserver.config.k8s.io/v1
kind: EncryptionConfiguration
resources:
  - resources:
      - secrets
    providers:
      - aescbc:
          keys:
            - name: aescbc-key
              secret: RwXjFAqbeHF/U7Oz/T11Qr6215QjiUeARqUCWRcBKZ8=
      - identity: {}
```

Save this file with the name **ear-aescbc.yaml**

Once you have the file, you need to update the kube-apiserver manifest. The file is typically located at **/etc/Kubernetes/manifest/kube-apiserver.yaml**. In the manifest file, you need to add a new volume, volume mount, and container spec pointing to the new encryption config file that we have created. Following is a snippet from the configured file:

```
  labels:
    component: kube-apiserver
    tier: control-plane
  name: kube-apiserver
  namespace: kube-system
spec:
  containers:
  - command:
    - kube-apiserver
    - --advertise-address=192.168.49.2
    - --allow-privileged=true
…

    - --encryption-provider-config=/etc/kubernetes/ear/ear-aescbc.yaml
…
    volumeMounts:
    - mountPath: /etc/kubernetes/ear
      name: ear-aescbc
      readOnly: true
    - mountPath: /etc/ssl/certs
      name: ca-certs
      readOnly: true
…
  volumes:
  - hostpath:
      path: /etc/kubernetes/ear-aescbc
```

```
      type: DirectoryOrCreate
    name: ear-aescbc
...
```

After you update the static manifest file, the apiserver will restart; wait for it to become available again. After making changes to the configuration, any new secret that you create will be encrypted by default; however, existing secrets will have to be recreated. Use the following command to replace all secrets in place:

```
$ kubectl get secrets --all-namespaces -o json | kubectl replace -f -
...
secret/cks-test replaced
...
...
```

Once the secret is replaced, you can pull the secret again from etcd using etcdctl. This time, you should not see the password and username in plain text.

Practice Question 5: After you have updated the kube-apiserver configuration, use the following command to read the secret from the etcd store and validate that the information is not listed in plain text.

```
$ export ETCDCTL_API=3
$ cd /etc/kubernetes/pki/etcd/
$ etcdctl --cacert=ca.crt --key=server.key --cert=server.crt --end-
points "https://<K8s API endpoint>:2379" get /registry/secrets/de-
fault/cks-test | hexdump -C
```

Practice Question 6: Create a new secret name **`db_creds`**, the secret should have two values, **`DB_USER=mydbuser`** and **`DB_PASSWORD=mydbpassword`**. After creating the secret, mount the secret in a new **busybox** pod, and use the **`sleep`** command to keep the pod from exiting. After the pod is ready, read the secret directly from the **etcd** store and validate that the new secret is not stored in plaintext.

In this section, we saw how to use secrets to store sensitive information and encrypt it to avoid exposing the information in plain text when stored in the etcd store as well.

Practical Considerations for Secrets

- **Base64 Encoding:** Kubernetes secrets are base64 encoded by default and not encrypted. Do not mistake base64 encoding for secure encryption.
- **Immutable Secrets:** Secrets by default are mutable; use immutable secrets whenever possible.
- **Imperative**: Get yourself familiar with imperative commands to create secrets to save time during the exam.
- **RBAC:** Secrets also fall under the purview of the RBAC policies, ensuring you have the right policies in place to avoid unwanted exposure.

Isolation Techniques

Kubernetes clusters and workloads have been growing at a breakneck speed; this growth has led to a lot of complexities with shared clusters hosting diverse workloads. When the clusters are shared by different workloads or teams or even LoBs, then it becomes paramount to ensure that the pods hosting one workload do not interfere or interact with other workloads running in the same cluster. This isolation ensures that there is no data breach and resources are only accessible by the pods or services that need them.

In this section, we will explore two critical isolation techniques: multitenancy and sandboxed containers. The CKS handbook's current version does not list any technique for sandboxed containers; however, older versions had traditionally focused on gVisor and Kata containers for workload isolation, so we will cover both in the upcoming sections.

Multitenancy

Multitenancy in terms of a Kubernetes cluster refers to the practice where a single cluster can be shared among multiple, potentially completely independent, untrusted workloads. These workloads, though individually trusted, might not be meant to share information. For example, the payroll system for the organization should be completely independent of the IT asset management subsystem.

Throughout the chapters, we have been working with parts of the multitenancy model. This is the time to bring all basic components together and understand how the basic Kubernetes constructs can be used to build a rudimentary multi-tenant mode.

Key Concepts

The basis of multitenancy in the Kubernetes clusters is resource, roles and access separation. All the key concepts described below are already a large part of the CKA exam and we would use the points as refreshers.

- **Namespaces:** Namespaces provide a logical separation of resources within the cluster. They allow you to partition the cluster in virtual clusters, with each namespace getting their own set of resources. Namespaces serve as the foundation for multitenancy in the Kubernetes cluster.
- **Resource Quota:** Resource quotas are used to limit the number of resources, CPU, Memory, and Storage, that a namespace can consume. This prevents a single namespace/tenant from monopolizing the cluster resources.
- **Role-Based Access Control (RBAC):** RBAC policies are used to control who can access which resources within a namespace. This allows us to control

permissions at a granular level for users and well as service accounts. A robust RBAC framework ensures that the tenants can only access their own resources.

- **Network Policies:** Once you have the resources divided among the namespaces and have controlled access to these resources with RBAC, you can control network traffic between pods and namespaces using the Network Policies. This will allow you to isolate workloads and prevent unauthorized communication between services and workloads.

Sandboxed Containers

In the last section, we saw how we can use the Kubernetes primitives to implement a simple multi-tenancy model. However, the resource sharing is being limited by the Kubernetes constructs, and this does nothing to address the concerns raised by the shared host OS kernel.

In a Kubernetes cluster, even the pods that are isolated in their own namespaces and have the most robust RBAC and Network Security policies still share the same underlying host operating system and kernel. The shared kernel model presents a potential vulnerability; a compromised container can potentially exploit kernel vulnerabilities to gain access to sensitive host resources and even other containers.

One way to address this security concern is by implementing sandboxes. A sandbox refers to an independent, completely isolated and impenetrable barrier between containers and host OS. The sandboxes are highly restricted with significant limitations which greatly reduces the possibility and impact of a security breach.

Sandboxed containers achieve this isolation by leveraging virtualization or specialized user-space kernels. They introduce an abstraction layer between the container and the host kernel, preventing direct system call access and mitigating the risk of kernel-level exploits. This approach is particularly valuable in multi-tenant environments or when running untrusted workloads, where the potential for malicious activity is higher.

In this section, we will look at two prominent sandboxed container technologies: gVisor and Kata Containers. Both gVisor and Kata take different approaches to how they implement the sandboxes. While gVisor relies on a user-space kernel approach, Kata runs containers within lightweight virtual machines. Let us look at how to use both to secure and isolate the Kubernetes workloads.

Isolating Containers with gVisor

gVisor is a user-space kernel which is written in Go. gVisor provides a strong security boundary between containers and the host OS. Unlike traditional container runtimes that rely on the host kernel, gVisor intercepts system calls and emulates the Linux kernel in user space. This effectively isolates containers from the host kernel, preventing them from directly accessing sensitive resources.

At a high level, gVisor works in three stages.

- **System Call Interception:** gVisor intercepts system calls made by containers and routes them to its user-space kernel.
- **Kernel Emulation:** gVisor emulates the Linux kernel, providing a subset of the kernel's functionality in user space.
- **Resource Isolation:** gVisor manages resources, such as memory and file systems, in user space, preventing containers from directly accessing host resources.

In a production or test environment, you need to install and configure gVisor on all the Kubernetes worker nodes. However, during the exam, you will not be asked to install and configure the sandbox environment. The required sandbox environment will be available during the exam in the right context.

Installing gVisor

The first step in using gVisor is to install it on all the worker nodes. The installation instructions differ based on Operating System, Linux Distro, and the package manager that you are using. In the lab that we have used so far, we have been running the cluster on Ubuntu, so the following instructions are based on Ubuntu with the default apt package manager.

If you are using a different operating system or package manager, you can find the installation instructions on the gVisor documentation page https://gvisor.dev/docs/user_guide/install/

Follow the succeeding instructions to install gVisor on the worker node.

```
$ sudo su -
$ sudo apt-get update && \
sudo apt-get install -y \
    apt-transport-https \
    ca-certificates \
    curl \
    gnupg

Hit:1 https://download.docker.com/linux/ubuntu focal InRelease
Get:2 http://clouds.archive.ubuntu.com/ubuntu noble InRelease [256
kB]
Get:3 http://security.ubuntu.com/ubuntu noble-security InRelease [126
kB]
Get:4 http://clouds.archive.ubuntu.com/ubuntu noble-updates InRelease
[126 kB]
```

```
…
Fetched 2162 kB in 1s (1531 kB/s)
Reading package lists... Done
W: https://download.docker.com/linux/ubuntu/dists/focal/InRelease:
Key is stored in legacy trusted.gpg keyring (/etc/apt/trusted.gpg),
see the DEPRECATION section in apt-key (8) for details.
Reading package lists... Done
Building dependency tree... Done
Reading state information... Done
apt-transport-https is already the newest version (2.7.14build2).
ca-certificates is already the newest version (20240203).
curl is already the newest version (8.5.0-2ubuntu10.6).
gnupg is already the newest version (2.4.4-2ubuntu17).
gnupg set to manually installed.
0 upgraded, 0 newly installed, 0 to remove and 135 not upgraded.

$ curl -fsSL https://gvisor.dev/archive.key | sudo gpg --dearmor -o /
usr/share/keyrings/gvisor-archive-keyring.gpg
echo "deb [arch=$(dpkg --print-architecture) signed-by=/usr/share/
keyrings/gvisor-archive-keyring.gpg] https://storage.googleapis.com/
gvisor/releases release main" | sudo tee /etc/apt/sources.list.d/gvi-
sor.list > /dev/null

$ sudo apt-get update && sudo apt-get install -y runsc
Hit:1 https://download.docker.com/linux/ubuntu focal InRelease
Get:2 https://storage.googleapis.com/gvisor/releases release InRe-
lease [4132 B]
…
Fetched 260 kB in 1s (309 kB/s)
Reading package lists... Done
W: https://download.docker.com/linux/ubuntu/dists/focal/InRelease:
Key is stored in legacy trusted.gpg keyring (/etc/apt/trusted.gpg),
see the DEPRECATION section in apt-key (8) for details.
Reading package lists... Done
…

Restarting services...
Service restarts being deferred:
 /etc/needrestart/restart.d/dbus.service
 systemctl restart docker.service
 systemctl restart getty@tty1.service
 systemctl restart serial-getty@ttyS0.service
 systemctl restart systemd-logind.service
 systemctl restart unattended-upgrades.service
…
```

Once you have gVisor installed, the next step is to restart docker.

```
$ systemctl restart docker.service
```

Note: *If you are using a different container runtime engine, follow the steps on the gVisor installation page based on your runtime.*

Once you have gVisor installed and have restarted the container runtime engine, the next step is to define a runtime class. Runtime class is a Kubernetes resource; you can find detailed instructions about the runtime class at https://kubernetes.io/docs/concepts/containers/runtime-class/. However, during the exam, you will be provided with the runtime class, and you will only have to use it with a container.

Use the following definition file to create a basic runtime class to use with gVisor. You can find the definition file at https://gvisor.dev/docs/user_guide/containerd/quick_start/.

```
apiVersion: node.k8s.io/v1
kind: RuntimeClass
metadata:
  name: gvisor
handler: runsc
```

Create the runtime class using the above file.

```
$ kubectl apply -f gvisorclass.yaml
runtimeClass/gvisor created

$ kubectl get runtimeclass
NAME     HANDLER   AGE
gvisor   runsc     6s
```

After creating the runtime class, we can use it in the pod definitions. Use the following pod definition to create the pod with the gVisor runtimeclass:

```
apiVersion: v1
kind: Pod
metadata:
  name: busybox-gvisor
spec:
  runtimeClassName: gvisor
  containers:
  - name: busybox-gvisor
    image: busybox:latest
    command: ["sh", "-c", "sleep 3600"]

$ kubectl apply -f gvisor-pod.yaml
pod/busybox-gvisor created
```

```
$ kubectl get pods
NAME              READY   STATUS    RESTARTS   AGE
busybox-gvisor    1/1     Running   0          7s
```

Once the pod is running, you can validate that gVisor had interrupted the system call and ran the pod in user space.

```
$ kubectl exec busybox-gvisor - dmesg
[    0.000000] Starting gVisor...
[    0.551121] Digging up root...
[    0.985448] Singleplexing /dev/ptmx...
[    1.351071] Feeding the init monster...
[    1.728568] Synthesizing system calls...
[    1.947574] Moving files to filing cabinet...
[    2.373802] Conjuring /dev/null black hole...
[    2.815994] Checking naughty and nice process list...
[    3.213821] Verifying that no non-zero bytes made their way into
/dev/zero...
[    3.323984] Constructing home...
[    3.718733] Forking spaghetti code...
[    3.837647] Setting up VFS...
[    4.181889] Setting up FUSE...
[    4.601043] Ready!
```

Sandboxing with Kata Containers

Kata Containers take a different approach when building the sandboxes for the pods. Kata creates lightweight virtual machines to run the pods; these virtual machines provide hardware-level isolation. Unlike gVisor, instead of emulating the kernel, Kata leverages virtualization technology to create a separate execution environment for each container.

Kata Containers' high-level working flow involves the following:

- **Lightweight VMs:** Kata Containers uses lightweight VMs such as QEMU or Firecracker to run containers.
- **Hardware Virtualization:** One prerequisite for Kata Containers is that it relies on hardware virtualization extensions such as Intel VT-x and AMD-V to provide strong isolation.
- **Container Runtime Integration:** Kata Containers are integrated with the container runtimes, such as CRI-O and containerd, to provide a seamless container experience.

Just like gVisor, you will not need to install and configure Kata Containers in the exam environment, as installing and configuring Kata involves installing a new package as well as modifying the kubelet configuration.

You can find the instructions to install Kata Containers in your existing Kubernetes cluster at https://github.com/kata-containers/documentation/tree/master/install. Note that the instructions will differ based on the Linux Distro and even the cloud provider that you are using. Make sure to install and configure Kata Containers as per your environment.

The following section assumes that Kata Container has been installed and configured for Kubernetes. In this section, we will briefly touch upon the Kata runtimeclass and pod definition.

Use the following section to create a new runtimeClass based on Kata Container and use it in a pod definition:

```
apiVersion: node.k8s.io/v1
kind: RuntimeClass
metadata:
  name: kata
handler: kata

$ kubectl apply -f kata-sc.yaml
runtimeClass/kata created
```

Next, just like gVisor uses the runtimeclass in the pod definition.

```
apiVersion: v1
kind: Pod
metadata:
  name: busybox-kata
spec:
  runtimeClassName: kata
  containers:
  - name: busybox-kata
    image: busybox:latest
    command: ["sh", "-c", "sleep 3600"]

$ kubectl apply -f kdata-pod.yaml
pod/busybox-kata created

$ kubectl get pods
NAME              READY    STATUS     RESTARTS    AGE
busybox-kata    1/1      Running    0           8s
```

Practice Question 7: Now that we have the pod running with Kata Container, you need to verify that the pod is running in a lightweight VM. One way to do this is to look at the kernel version of the container by running the uname command.

Your task is to confirm that the worker node kernel version and the kernel version seen by the container are different.

Practical Considerations for Isolation

- **Security vs. Performance:** When implementing multitenancy architecture, carefully consider the security and performance requirements for the application workload.
- **Runtime Classes:** Leverage runtime classes to selectively apply sandboxed containers to specific workload; having different runtime classes allows you granular control over the sandboxing.
- **Pod Specifications:** During the exam, you will be asked to apply different runtimeClasses to different pods. Make sure you are familiar with the pod definition file and can quickly update the existing definition to apply the `runtimeClass`.
- **Validation**: Make sure you are familiar with how to validate the runtime class and whether the pod is correctly deployed. For gVisor, it means checking the **dmsgs**, while for Kata Containers, it requires either the kernel versions of the node and container or checking that the lightweight VM is running as a Linux process.

Securing Inter Pod Communication

So far, in the previous chapters and sections, we have diligently fortified the host OS, secured the workloads with Pod Security Standards, and isolated the pods using sandboxed environments. However, the internal network communication between the pods is still a critical area of concern.

The default Kubernetes network model, while functional, often lacks the fine-grained control required to create robust security policies. Without proper network segmentation and access control, pods can potentially communicate with each other without restrictions leading to lateral movement of data and data breaches.

In this section, we will briefly look at the basics of inter-pod communications, focusing on the fundamentals of pod-to-pod networking, and explore the use of advanced tools such as Cilium.

Pod to Pod Communication Basics

In a Kubernetes cluster, pods are designed to be ephemeral. These are dynamically scheduled, this flexibility requires a robust and flexible networking model that enables pods to communicate with each other, regardless of their location within the cluster, for example a pod can communicate with another pod whether it is running in the same namespace or a different namespace.

Pod to Pod communication is a major focus area of both CKA and CKAD exams, and it is assumed that you are familiar with the inner workings of the communication. We will use this section to briefly touch upon the P2P Communication basics and inner workings.

- **Pod IP Addresses:** Every pod that runs in the cluster is assigned a unique IP address within the cluster's internal network. The IP address is used for communication between pods. This IP address is assigned from a private IP range, which is configured during the cluster setup.
- **Cluster Network:** Kubernetes relies on a cluster network to provide connectivity between pods. This network is typically implemented using an overlay network, such as Flannel, Calico, or Weave Net. Overlay networks create a virtual network on top of the existing physical network, enabling pods to communicate across different nodes.
- **CNI (Container Network Interface):** CNI is a standard for configuring container networking. Kubernetes uses CNI plugins to configure the cluster network. CNI plugins are responsible for assigning IP addresses to pods, creating network interfaces, and configuring routing rules.
- **kube-proxy:** kube-proxy is a network proxy that runs on each node. It maintains network rules that forward traffic to the appropriate pods. kube-proxy can operate in different modes, such as iptables, IPVS, or eBPF.
- **Service Discovery:** Kubernetes Services provide a stable endpoint for accessing pods. Services use DNS to resolve service names to pod IP addresses. When a pod needs to communicate with another pod, it typically uses the service name, which is then resolved to the pod's IP address.
- **ClusterIP:** A virtual IP address assigned to a Service. Used for internal communication within the cluster.
- **NodePort:** Exposes a Service on a specific port on each node's IP address. Used for external access to Services.
- **LoadBalancer:** Provisions an external load balancer to expose a Service to the internet. Used for external access to Services.
- **DNS:** Kubernetes uses **CoreDNS** or **kube-dns** for service discovery. Pods can resolve service names to IP addresses.
- **Network Policies:** These policies control the traffic flow between pods. They are essential for securing inter-pod communication.

Securing P2P Communication with Cilium

The default P2P communication method, while easy to implement, is not secure, and although we can leverage network policies to control which pods can communicate with each other, it does not account for the unencrypted traffic.

For example, you have a 3-tier application running in app, web, and db pods. You have set up the network policy, which only allows traffic between the app and db pod and blocks all communication between the web and db pod. The policies make sure that the traffic originates from the right location and gets to the right destination, but the traffic is still unencrypted, and an attacker who has gained access to the P2P communication can simply listen to the traffic between the app and db pod without much difficulty.

This concern can be resolved by encrypting the Pod-to-Pod Communication. While the older versions of the CKS exams simply mentioned mTLS adoption to secure communication between pods. The latest version specifically calls out using Cilium to implement pod-to-pod encryption. So, we will focus on Cilium implementation.

Cilium is a CNI plugin that goes beyond the basic networking and provides many advanced security features such as:

- **eBPF (Extended Berkeley Packet Filter):** eBPF is a powerful kernel technology that allows you to run sandboxed programs within the Linux kernel. Cilium uses eBPF to perform network filtering, routing and security enforcement at the kernel level which lead to high performance network processing and security.
- **Identify Based Policies:** Cilium assigns service identities to pods based on their Kubernetes metadata. Network Policies are defined using service identities ensuring that only authorized services can communicate with each other. This provides significant improvements over traditional IP based policies which are less flexible and harder to manage in a dynamic environment.
- **L7 Visibility and Control:** Cilium can inspect and filter network traffic at the application layer. This allows you to define network policies based on HTTP headers, gRPC methods, and other application-level attributes.
- **Encryption:** Cilium can be used to configure pod to pod traffic encryption, this will protect sensitive data from eavesdropping. In the following steps we will look at how to implement encryption using Cilium for P2P communication.

From the latest exam curriculum, the extent of configuration required is not clear. However, given that it is a time-based practice exam, it is safe to assume that we will not be asked to install and configure Cilium from scratch in a brand-new cluster. So, we will limit our test to a small cluster installation using Kind. It is assumed that you have a working Kubernetes cluster before you move to the next step.

If you are using a different cluster, such as kubeadm or kind, or EKS, and so on, follow the instructions listed in https://docs.cilium.io/en/stable/gettingstarted/k8s-install-default/ to install Cilium and Cilium CLI.

Save the following cluster definition file to deploy the cluster with kind.

```
kind: Cluster
apiVersion: kind.x-k8s.io/v1alpha4
nodes:
- role: control-plane
- role: worker
- role: worker
- role: worker
networking:
  disableDefaultCNI: true
```

create the cluster with kind.

```
$ kind create cluster --config cluster.yaml
Creating cluster "kind" ...
 ✓ Ensuring node image (kindest/node:v1.32.2) 🖼
 ✓ Preparing nodes 📦 📦 📦 📦
 ✓ Writing configuration 📜
 ✓ Starting control-plane 🕹️
 ✓ Installing StorageClass 💾
 ✓ Joining worker nodes 🚜
Set kubectl context to "kind-kind"
You can now use your cluster with:
kubectl cluster-info --context kind-kind
Have a question, bug, or feature request? Let us know! https://
kind.sigs.k8s.io/#community 🙂
```

Once we have the kind cluster running. Run the following command to install Cilium CLI. We will use the Cilium CLI to install Cilium later.

```
$ CILIUM_CLI_VERSION=$(curl -s https://raw.githubusercontent.com/cilium/cili-
um-cli/main/stable.txt)
CLI_ARCH=amd64
if [ "$(uname -m)" = "aarch64" ]; then CLI_ARCH=arm64; fi
curl -L --fail --remote-name-all https://github.com/cilium/cilium-cli/releases/
download/${CILIUM_CLI_VERSION}/cilium-linux-${CLI_ARCH}.tar.gz{,.sha256sum}
sha256sum --check cilium-linux-${CLI_ARCH}.tar.gz.sha256sum
sudo tar xzvfC cilium-linux-${CLI_ARCH}.tar.gz /usr/local/bin
rm cilium-linux-${CLI_ARCH}.tar.gz{,.sha256sum}
  % Total    % Received % Xferd  Average Speed   Time    Time     Time  Current
                                 Dload  Upload   Total   Spent    Left  Speed
  0     0    0     0    0     0      0      0 --:--:-- --:--:-- --:--:--     0
100 54.1M  100 54.1M    0     0  50.0M      0  0:00:01  0:00:01 --:--:--  114M
  % Total    % Received % Xferd  Average Speed   Time    Time     Time  Current
                                 Dload  Upload   Total   Spent    Left  Speed
```

```
  0      0    0      0    0      0      0         0 --:--:-- --:--:-- --:--:--      0
100     92  100     92    0      0    186         0 --:--:-- --:--:-- --:--:--      0
cilium-linux-amd64.tar.gz: OK
cilium
```

Once you have the cluster setup ready, it's time to enable pod-to-pod encryption. Cilium provides two ways to configure encryption between pods: IPSec and WireGuard. In the next section, we will cover both.

Enabling Transparent Encryption with IPSec

Before starting with IPSec encryption, we need to create a random Pre-Shared Key. This key will be used by Cilium to encrypt the traffic and will be distributed among all cluster nodes using a Kubernetes secret.

Run the following command to generate the key:

```
$ CILIUM_KEY=($(dd if=/dev/urandom count=20 bs=1 2>/dev/null |
xxd -p -c 64))

$ echo $CILIUM_KEY
8a03ad942c12ed88cf5270f4abe65accdc12f809
```

Once we have the key, it needs to be stored in a secret named cilium-ipsec-keys, the keys will be picked by Cilium automatically based on the secret name during encryption.

```
$ kubectl create -n kube-system secret generic cilium-ipsec-keys
--from-literal=keys="3 rfc4106(gcm(aes)) $CILIUM_KEY 128"
secret/cilium-ipsec-keys created
```

Once the secret is ready, installing Cilium with ipsec is easy. Just run the following command to install Cilium with IPSec encryption:

```
$ cilium install  --set encryption.enabled=true --set encryption.
type=ipsec
 Auto-detected Kubernetes kind: kind
  Using Cilium version 1.17.0
 Auto-detected cluster name: kind-kind
 Auto-detected kube-proxy has been installed
```

After the installation, the cilium pods will take a couple of minutes to get to Running state. Wait for the pods to start successfully and check the node and pods status to validate.

```
$ kubectl get pods -A
NAMESPACE          NAME                                              READY   STATUS
RESTARTS    AGE
kube-system        cilium-24gss                                      1/1     Running   0
2m38s
```

```
kube-system          cilium-8pxk8                                 1/1     Running   0
2m38s
kube-system          cilium-cvvfs                                 1/1     Running   0
2m38s
kube-system          cilium-envoy-45hwn                           1/1     Running   0
2m38s
kube-system          cilium-envoy-5xwtt                           1/1     Running   0
2m38s
kube-system          cilium-envoy-gr6n4                           1/1     Running   0
2m38s
kube-system          cilium-envoy-rhp8j                           1/1     Running   0
2m38s
kube-system          cilium-operator-7b8b6b6fc-4mvbq              1/1     Running   0
2m38s
kube-system          cilium-q8hg5                                 1/1     Running   0
2m38s
kube-system          coredns-668d6bf9bc-4cphv                     1/1     Running   0
7m5s
kube-system          coredns-668d6bf9bc-b4bx4                     1/1     Running   0
7m5s
kube-system          etcd-kind-control-plane                      1/1     Running   0
7m16s
kube-system          kube-apiserver-kind-control-plane            1/1     Running   0
7m14s
kube-system          kube-controller-manager-kind-control-plane   1/1     Running   0
7m15s
kube-system          kube-proxy-7wc96                             1/1     Running   0
7m1s
kube-system          kube-proxy-889xm                             1/1     Running   0
7m6s
kube-system          kube-proxy-lbdxp                             1/1     Running   0
7m1s
kube-system          kube-proxy-wvbtb                             1/1     Running   0
7m1s
kube-system          kube-scheduler-kind-control-plane            1/1     Running   0
7m14s
local-path-storage   local-path-provisioner-7dc846544d-4rxfg      1/1     Running   0
7m5s

$ kubectl get nodes
NAME                 STATUS   ROLES           AGE     VERSION
kind-control-plane   Ready    control-plane   7m39s   v1.32.2
kind-worker          Ready    <none>          7m23s   v1.32.2
kind-worker2         Ready    <none>          7m23s   v1.32.2
kind-worker3         Ready    <none>          7m23s   v1.32.2
```

Verify that the encryption is ready by running the following command:

```
$ kubectl -n kube-system exec -it ds/cilium -- cilium encrypt status
Defaulted container "cilium-agent" out of cilium-agent, config (init),
mount-cgroup (init), apply-sysctl-overwrites (init), mount-bpf-fs
(init), clean-cilium-state (init), install-cni-binaries (init)
Encryption: IPsec
Decryption interface(s):
Keys in use: 12
Max Seq. Number: N/A
Errors: 0
```

You can also validate the cilium installation status by running the following command:

```
$ cilium status --wait
    /¯¯\
 /¯¯\__/¯¯\    Cilium:             OK
 \__/¯¯\__/    Operator:           OK
 /¯¯\__/¯¯\    Envoy DaemonSet:    OK
 \__/¯¯\__/    Hubble Relay:       disabled
    \__/       ClusterMesh:        disabled

DaemonSet              cilium                   Desired: 4, Ready: 4/4,
Available: 4/4
DaemonSet              cilium-envoy             Desired: 4, Ready: 4/4,
Available: 4/4
Deployment             cilium-operator          Desired: 1, Ready: 1/1,
Available: 1/1
Containers:            cilium                   Running: 4
                       cilium-envoy             Running: 4
                       cilium-operator          Running: 1
                       clustermesh-apiserver
                       hubble-relay
Cluster Pods:          3/3 managed by Cilium
Helm chart version:    1.17.0
Image versions         cilium             quay.io/cilium/cilium:v1.17.0@
sha256:51f21bdd003c3975b5aaaf41bd21aee23cc08f44efaa27effc91c621bc9d8b1d: 4
                       cilium-envoy       quay.io/cilium/cilium-en-
voy:v1.31.5-1737535524-fe8efeb16a7d233bffd05af9ea53599340d3f18e@
sha256:57a3aa6355a3223da360395e3a109802867ff635cb852aa0afe03ec7bf04e545: 4
                       cilium-operator    quay.io/cilium/operator-gener-
ic:v1.17.0@sha256:1ce5a5a287166fc70b6a5ced3990aaa442496242d1d4930b5a3125e44c-
ccdca8: 1
Warnings:              cilium             cilium-24gss    Hubble: Server not
initialized
```

Enabling Transparent Encryption with WireGuard

As seen in the last section, setting up transparent encryption was relatively easy; however, we still had to create the pre-shared key as well as create the secret. This involves the added operational overhead of maintaining and rotating the shared key to avoid risks associated with stale keys.

With WireGuard, setting up encryption for pods communication is further simplified. Instead of us manually managing the key, the encryption key pair for each node is generated and managed by Cilium automatically.

To enable P2P encryption with WireGuard, we must follow the same steps as listed in the above section, but we do not need to create the key or store it as a secret manually.

After creating the kind cluster with no default CNI, we can simply run the following command to install Cilium with WireGuard encryption.

```
$ kind create cluster --config cluster.yaml
Creating cluster "kind" ...
 ✓ Ensuring node image (kindest/node:v1.32.2)
 ✓ Preparing nodes
 ✓ Writing configuration
 ✓ Starting control-plane
 ✓ Installing StorageClass
 ✓ Joining worker nodes
Set kubectl context to "kind-kind"
You can now use your cluster with:
kubectl cluster-info --context kind-kind
Not sure what to do next? Check out https://kind.sigs.k8s.io/docs/user/quick-start/

$ cilium install  --set encryption.enabled=true --set encryption.type=wireguard
 Auto-detected Kubernetes kind: kind
  Using Cilium version 1.17.0
 Auto-detected cluster name: kind-kind
 Auto-detected kube-proxy has been installed

$ kubectl get nodes
NAME                 STATUS   ROLES           AGE     VERSION
kind-control-plane   Ready    control-plane   4m22s   v1.32.2
kind-worker          Ready    <none>          4m6s    v1.32.2
kind-worker2         Ready    <none>          4m6s    v1.32.2
kind-worker3         Ready    <none>          4m6s    v1.32.2

$ kubectl get pods -A
NAMESPACE            NAME                                                 READY   STATUS
```

```
RESTARTS   AGE
kube-system          cilium-4jvtq                                    1/1     Running   0
3m56s
kube-system          cilium-6l5g4                                    1/1     Running   0
3m56s
kube-system          cilium-envoy-jbh8t                              1/1     Running   0
3m56s
kube-system          cilium-envoy-lg5fx                              1/1     Running   0
3m56s
kube-system          cilium-envoy-rmrd2                              1/1     Running   0
3m56s
kube-system          cilium-envoy-rs9bh                              1/1     Running   0
3m56s
kube-system          cilium-mf8ff                                    1/1     Running   0
3m56s
kube-system          cilium-ndxk9                                    1/1     Running   0
3m56s
kube-system          cilium-operator-7b8b6b6fc-mxvgj                 1/1     Running   0
3m56s
kube-system          coredns-668d6bf9bc-kdgw5                        1/1     Running   0
4m16s
kube-system          coredns-668d6bf9bc-twfqg                        1/1     Running   0
4m16s
kube-system          etcd-kind-control-plane                         1/1     Running   0
4m25s
kube-system          kube-apiserver-kind-control-plane               1/1     Running   0
4m25s
kube-system          kube-controller-manager-kind-control-plane      1/1     Running   0
4m25s
kube-system          kube-proxy-d88s7                                1/1     Running   0
4m12s
kube-system          kube-proxy-m8s9x                                1/1     Running   0
4m12s
kube-system          kube-proxy-mhfrf                                1/1     Running   0
4m12s
kube-system          kube-proxy-wk922                                1/1     Running   0
4m17s
kube-system          kube-scheduler-kind-control-plane               1/1     Running   0
4m25s
local-path-storage   local-path-provisioner-7dc846544d-z7gpq         1/1     Running   0
4m16s

$ kubectl -n kube-system exec -it ds/cilium -- cilium encrypt status
Defaulted container "cilium-agent" out of cilium-agent, config (init), mount-cgroup (init),
apply-sysctl-overwrites (init), mount-bpf-fs (init), clean-cilium-state (init), in-
stall-cni-binaries (init)
Encryption: Wireguard
```

```
Interface: cilium_wg0
        Public key: r7M2jdqt/tR+gfsNyeEQDnaat6bF6FdvqqxUsOO6F1A=
        Number of peers: 3
```

Conclusion

In this chapter, we covered the critical practice of minimizing the microservices vulnerability within the Kubernetes cluster. Building upon the secure foundation that we had established in the previous chapter, we transitioned from securing the host OS and network perimeter to fortifying the workloads themselves. We explored the Pod Security Standards and Pod Security Admission. We also tackled the sensitive data with Kubernetes Secrets and explored how Secrets provide a secure mechanism for storing and distributing confidential information. We also looked at different isolation techniques focused on multi-tenancy and sandboxing. We also addressed inter-pod communication security with third-party tools such as Cilium.

In the next chapter, we will cover the fifth pillar of the CKS exam, which deals with Supply chain security. We will look at how to reduce the base image footprint to shrink the attack surface. We will also cover the basics of supply chain and how to secure the components and applications involved in the supply chain. We will also look at tools that can be used to perform static analysis of user workloads and container images.

CHAPTER 6
Supply Chain Security

Introduction

In the previous chapters, we have focused on building and securing the Kubernetes cluster including all the cluster components as well as the pods, services and containers running the application workload in the cluster. Those chapters focused mainly on securing an existing application based on existing image.

However, the applications do not just materialize out of thin air. The application code is written by developers based on a particular framework and environment. Securing a Kubernetes environment is more than just implementing perimeter security and securing the Kubernetes bits. We need to take a comprehensive approach to Kubernetes security and address the entire lifecycle of the application, starting right from the application development to the final runtime.

Application code development, image building, registry storage, deployment, execution, and upgrades are collectively called the supply chain. Vulnerability introduced in any stage of the supply chain can have a domino effect and compromise the security of the whole cluster.

In this chapter, we will work through the essentials to secure the Kubernetes supply chain. Although there are a lot of steps and stages involved in the whole application supply chain, we will focus on the topics that are covered in the Certified Kubernetes Security (CKS) Specialist exam. We will start the chapter by exploring the techniques to reduce the image size, thus reducing the overall attack surface of the image.

Next, we will dive into the broader supply chain and focus on how to establish trust and maintain security throughout the development process. This includes understanding and implementing Software Bill of Material (SBoM) to track all the components that are part of the application, securing CI/CD pipelines to prevent unauthorized modifications, and utilizing trusted private repositories to control image sources. We will also cover ways to sign images and validate image signatures to avoid image tampering.

In the last section, we will explore the use of static analysis tools such as **Kubesec** and **KubeLinter** to identify misconfigurations and potential security risks in the

Kubernetes manifests and images before the deployment. These tools serve as crucial checkpoints and prevent vulnerabilities in the Kubernetes environment.

Structure

At an elevated level, this chapter covers the following concepts:

- Securing Base Image
  - Reduce Image Footprint
  - Reduce Layers
  - Multi-Stage Build
  - Image Scanning
  - Practical Considerations
- Understand and Secure Supply Chain
  - Introduction to SBoM, CI/CD, and Repositories
  - Controlling Access to Registries
  - Sign Images and Validate Signatures
- Static Analysis of Workload and Images
  - Kubesec
  - KubeLinter
  - Practical Considerations

Securing Base Image

Container images are the fundamental building blocks for any application built to run in a Kubernetes environment. You can think of the images as the blueprint and raw material for the application; the image defines the application runtime, code, as well as its dependencies. This ultimately defines the security posture for the application. Therefore, securing the base image is not just a best practice, but it is a highly critical necessity for maintaining the integrity and security of the overall application and the Kubernetes environment.

If the image is not properly secured, it can introduce a multitude of risks. For example, if an image contains unnecessary tools such as shell or outdated libraries, it can expand the attack surface. If a vulnerability is discovered in one of the components that is not necessary for the application, it can be exploited to gain unauthorized access to the container and potentially the entire cluster.

Every container image is built in multiple layers, and every new utility or execution will add another layer to the image. For example, let us consider an image that contains the application code and runtime along with all the operating system packages, development tools, and libraries. While this might be a convenient way to simplify the application development process, this will significantly increase the size and complexity of the image. This will also add many layers to the image, with every layer being an additional point of attack. If a security vulnerability is fixed in one of the components of a large image, patching and updating the whole image becomes a cumbersome and time-consuming process, increasing the window of vulnerability.

Furthermore, without proper image scanning, you are essentially deploying applications with unknown security risks. A base image might contain known vulnerabilities that could be exploited by the attacker.

To avoid all these pitfalls, we must adopt a proactive approach to securing the base image. In this section, we will delve into the best practices for minimizing the base image footprint, reduce the image size by reducing the layers in the image, and we will also implement a robust image scanning practice. Let us look at these one by one in the following sections.

Reduce Image Footprint

The size of a container image directly impacts its security and performance. Larger images tend to have a larger attack surface due to the addition of additional packages and libraries.

When building an application using a base image, we need to understand that not all images with the same name or even from the same vendor are created equally. Even base images from reputable sources can vary significantly in size, depending on the included packages and libraries. For example, a standard Ubuntu image might include a full operating system complete with package managers, system utilities, and development tools. While this provides flexibility, it also results in a large image size.

Most applications do not need the full array of features and packages that the full image provides and only require a minimal runtime with select packages and libraries. If you choose a large base image, such as the full Ubuntu image, you are essentially carrying unnecessary baggage. This not only makes the application bulky, but it also means that you are carrying unnecessary baggage that can be exploited. Furthermore, larger images consume more network bandwidth, storage, and compute, which slows down the deployment as well as application scaling.

Alpine Images

Alpine Linux is a lightweight Linux distribution which has been specifically designed for container environments. It uses `musl libc` and `BusyBoxy`, this results in a significantly smaller image compared to the traditional distributions such as Ubutntu or Debian.

Let us compare the sizes of a base Ubuntu image with the base Alpine image.

```
$ docker image pull ubuntu:latest
latest: Pulling from library/ubuntu
5a7813e071bf: Pull complete
Digest: sha256:72297848456d5d37d1262630108ab308d3e9ec7ed1c3286a32fe09856619a782
Status: Downloaded newer image for ubuntu:latest
docker.io/library/ubuntu:latest
$ docker image pull alpine:latest
latest: Pulling from library/alpine
f18232174bc9: Pull complete
Digest: sha256:a8560b36e8b8210634f77d9f7f9efd7ffa463e380b75e2e74aff4511df3ef88c
Status: Downloaded newer image for alpine:latest
docker.io/library/alpine:latest
$ docker images
REPOSITORY                    TAG       IMAGE ID       CREATED         SIZE
alpine                        latest    aded1e1a5b37   7 weeks ago     7.83MB
ubuntu                        latest    a04dc4851cbc   2 months ago    78.1MB
```

From the preceding output, you can see that while the Ubuntu image is ~78MB, the Alpine image is just ~7.8MB. That is a 90% reduction in size.

One thing to note is that it is the size of only the base image without the libraries and the application package. When you build your application with the Alpine image, you can add only the application package and libraries that are absolutely necessary, without any fluff packages. This will ensure that the image has the smallest possible footprint.

Alpine images are pretty small to start with, but they still have some operating system packages, such as **shell**. It gives you the flexibility to secure the application while still being able to troubleshoot the application in case something breaks.

Distroless Images

While the Alpine images are a great starting point in the right direction, your application will still not need all the packages provided by the images. For a highly secure and sensitive application, you might want to use an image that has no operating system packages at all.

This is where the distroless images can be utilized, Distroless images have no operating system components. These images contain only the application and its runtime dependencies.

Let us compare a distroless image with the Ubuntu and Alpine images that we pulled in the last section.

```
$ docker pull gcr.io/distroless/static-debian12
Using default tag: latest
latest: Pulling from distroless/static-debian12
```

```
3d78e577de35: Pull complete
bfb59b82a9b6: Pull complete
4eff9a62d888: Pull complete
a62778643d56: Pull complete
...
Digest: sha256:3d0f463de06b7ddff27684ec3bfd0b54a425149d0f8685308b1fdf297b0265e9
Status: Downloaded newer image for gcr.io/distroless/static-debian12:latest
gcr.io/distroless/static-debian12:latest
$ docker pull gcr.io/distroless/java-base-debian12
Using default tag: latest
latest: Pulling from distroless/java-base-debian12
3d78e577de35: Already exists
df4a74163d8a: Pull complete
5ef042acb7ea: Pull complete
538dbdaf1872: Pull complete
...
Digest: sha256:7c89e3f11a39a1f54aced0e94c5e21fb10e305b163313fa0815c12a75eb2e941
Status: Downloaded newer image for gcr.io/distroless/java-base-debian12:latest
gcr.io/distroless/java-base-debian12:latest

$ docker images
REPOSITORY                  TAG        IMAGE ID       CREATED        SIZE
alpine                      latest     aded1e1a5b37   7 weeks ago    7.83MB
ubuntu                      latest     a04dc4851cbc   2 months ago   78.1MB
gcr.io/distroless/static-debian12 latest     2e67dcc920d0   N/A           1.99MB
gcr.io/distroless/java-base-debian12 latest       3b8191667922   N/A          33.4MB
```

As we can see, the static Debian image is just **1.99 MB**, and even the distroless Java base Debian image is just **33.4 MB**.

From the preceding examples, we can see that not all images are created equally, and we must select the appropriate image based on our application requirements. During the image-building process, start with the smallest possible image and only install the necessary packages to keep the image size in check.

Reduce Layers

Container images are constructed using a layered file system. Certain instructions in a Docker file create a new layer while others create temporary images. Layers capture the changes made to the file system at that step. While layering provides benefits such as caching and efficient image distribution, excessive layers can lead to increased image size and introduce security challenges.

When a dockerfile is built, instructions such as RUN, COPY, FROM, and so on, create a new layer in the image. Layers are point-in-time snapshots of the file system; every new layer that you add to the container increases the size of the image. Layers are stacked on top of each other, forming the final layer. Each layer contributes to the overall image size. Even if a file is deleted in the subsequent layer, it still exists in the previous layer, adding to the image's size. For example, if you install a large package, use it, and then delete it. The package will remain in the layer where it was installed, even though it is not present in the final image.

More layers can also increase the attack surface. Debugging and auditing become more complex with excessive layers, making it harder to identify and address security vulnerabilities. Larger images also take longer to download and deploy, impacting application startup times and scaling.

The most effective way to reduce the layers in an image is to combine multiple RUN commands into a single command using **&&**. Let us look at this with an example.

Example Dockerfile with multiple RUN commands on separate lines:

```
FROM ubuntu:latest
RUN apt-get update -y
RUN apt-get upgrade -y
RUN apt-get install nginx -y
```

Save the preceding file as dockerfile in an empty directory and use the following command to build the image:

```
$ docker build .
[+] Building 16.2s (7/7) FINISHED
docker:default
 => [internal] load build definition from dockerfile
0.0s
 => => transferring dockerfile: 130B
0.0s
 => [internal] load metadata for docker.io/library/ubuntu:latest
0.0s
 => [internal] load .dockerignore
0.0s
 => => transferring context: 2B
0.0s
 => [1/4] FROM docker.io/library/ubuntu:latest
0.0s
 => [2/4] RUN apt-get update -y
4.9s
 => [3/4] RUN apt-get upgrade -y
=> [4/4] RUN apt-get install nginx -y
3.9s
 => exporting to image
0.3s
 => => exporting layers
0.3s
 => => writing image sha256:8407da2f5cb970f15695390b9ba6903adcb1b16f4ed53e6ce9f4571820
```

```
e52f4c                                                  0.0s
=> => naming to docker.io/library/ubuntu_nginx:local
0.0s
$ docker images
REPOSITORY                          TAG         IMAGE ID       CREATED          SIZE
ubuntu_nginx                        local       8407da2f5cb9   2 minutes ago    173MB
```

Each RUN statement in the image definition will create a new layer, increasing the size and complexity of the image. Let us rebuild the image by putting all the RUN commands in a single line.

```
FROM ubuntu:latest
RUN apt-get update -y && apt-get upgrade -y && apt-get install nginx -y

# docker build -t ubuntu_nginx_efficient:local .
[+] Building 17.7s (6/6) FINISHED
docker:default
 => [internal] load build definition from dockerfile
0.0s
 => => transferring dockerfile: 128B
0.0s
 => [internal] load metadata for docker.io/library/ubuntu:latest
0.0s
 => [internal] load .dockerignore
0.0s
 => => transferring context: 2B
0.0s
 => CACHED [1/2] FROM docker.io/library/ubuntu:latest
0.0s
 => [2/2] RUN apt-get update -y && apt-get upgrade -y && apt-get install nginx -y
17.2s
 => exporting to image
0.4s
 => => exporting layers
0.4s
 => => writing image sha256:9c1993aade1c95bcd5ebc085e2f984c017ca8a77bf39810225264c761f519
af9                                             0.0s
 => => naming to docker.io/library/ubuntu_nginx_efficient:local
$ docker images
REPOSITORY                 TAG          IMAGE ID       CREATED           SIZE
ubuntu_nginx_efficient    local        9c1993aade1c   24 seconds ago   172MB
ubuntu_nginx               local         8407da2f5cb9   8 minutes ago    173MB
```

In the preceding example, we can see that all the package installation and cleanup were done in a single layer. Similarly, you can club other commands, such as COPY and ADD, in a single string to reduce the number of layers.

If possible, download and extract archives within the same RUN command, instead of using a separate ADD instruction.

After installing packages or performing other operations, clean up temporary files and caches to reduce the layer size. For example, use the following command to clean up the apt-cache after the package installation:

```
RUN apt-get update && apt-get install -y nginx && rm -rf /var/lib/
apt/lists/*
```

Multi-Stage Build

Traditional dockerfiles include build dependencies as well as some intermediate files which are not required in the fine runtime image. These unnecessary components contribute to the image size and increase the attack surface. Multi-stage builds address this issue by allowing you to use a larger build image with all the necessary tools and dependencies in the initial image and then copy only the required artifacts to a smaller runtime image.

Multi-Stage build essentially breaks the build and deployment process in two separate stages, you build the application within one container and then copy the resulting compiled application into a second much smaller container with only the required binaries and dependencies. This prevents the large build tools, features and binaries from being included in the final image.

Let us demonstrate this with a simple go application. Copy the following code in a file called main.go:

```
package main
import "fmt"
func main() {
    fmt.Println("Hello, Multi-Stage Build Tests!")
}
```

In the same directory, build the **go.mod** file with the following content:

```
module myapp
go 1.24.2
```

Next, build the container image; copy the following Dockerfile:

```
FROM golang:1.24.2-alpine
WORKDIR /app
COPY go.mod ./
RUN go mod download
COPY . .
RUN go build -o myapp
CMD ["/app/myapp"]
```

```
$ docker build -t goapp_singlebuild:latest .
[+] Building 9.8s (11/11) FINISHED
docker:default
 => [internal] load build definition from dockerfile
0.0s
 => => transferring dockerfile: 162B
0.0s
 => [internal] load metadata for docker.io/library/golang:1.24.2-alpine
0.3s
 => [internal] load .dockerignore
0.0s
 => => transferring context: 2B
0.0s
 => [1/6] FROM docker.io/library/golang:1.24.2-alpine@sha256:7772cb-
5322baa875edd74705556d08f0eeca7b9c4b5367754ce3f2f00041ccee            0.0s
 => [internal] load build context
0.0s
 => => transferring context: 213B
0.0s
 => CACHED [2/6] WORKDIR /app
0.0s
 => [3/6] COPY go.mod ./
0.0s
 => [4/6] RUN go mod download
0.2s
 => [5/6] COPY . .
0.1s
 => [6/6] RUN go build -o myapp
8.9s
 => exporting to image
0.2s
 => => exporting layers
0.2s
 => => writing image sha256:40f0752d7ec9f7a8ec1d7246be6c37af812c0e29830e8bf90f20688efb55
791d                                          0.0s
 => => naming to docker.io/library/goapp_singlebuild:latest

$ docker images
REPOSITORY                      TAG         IMAGE ID       CREATED           SIZE
goapp_singlebuild               latest      40f0752d7ec9   59 seconds ago    296MB
```

Let us build the same image with the multistage process. We will keep the same files for now, but update the dockerfile to the following.

```
# Stage 1: Build the Go application
FROM golang:1.24.2-alpine AS builder
WORKDIR /app
COPY go.mod ./
```

```
RUN go mod download
COPY . .
RUN go build -o myapp

# Stage 2: Create the runtime image
FROM alpine:latest
WORKDIR /app
COPY --from=builder /app/myapp /app/myapp
CMD ["/app/myapp"]

# docker build -t goapp_multibuild:latest .
[+] Building 9.5s (15/15) FINISHED
docker:default
 => [internal] load build definition from dockerfile
0.0s
 => => transferring dockerfile: 321B
0.0s
 => [internal] load metadata for docker.io/library/golang:1.24.2-alpine
0.5s
 => [internal] load metadata for docker.io/library/alpine:latest
0.0s
 => [internal] load .dockerignore
0.0s
 => => transferring context: 2B
0.0s
...
 => => naming to docker.io/library/goapp_multibuild:latest
0.0s
root@terrapyauto-ubuntu:~/golang# docker images
REPOSITORY                      TAG           IMAGE ID       CREATED             SIZE
goapp_multibuild                latest        ff3819d45686   4 seconds ago       10MB
goapp_singlebuild               latest        40f0752d7ec9   6 minutes ago       296MB
```

From the preceding output, we can see that while the image built with a regular docker file is **296MB**, the multi-stage build image is just **10MB**.

Image Scanning

So far, we understand that container images are made up of many layers with multiple OS and application packages, as well as their dependency. Every new package added to the image is a potential gateway and can pose significant security risks. Image scanning is a process of analyzing container images for known vulnerabilities, misconfigurations, and other security issues. It is a critical practice to ensure the security and integrity of the Kubernetes deployments. Image scanning allows us to:

- **Detecting Vulnerabilities:** Container images often include third-party libraries, which can contain known vulnerabilities. Image scanning tools such as **Trivy** analyse the image's contents and compare them against the CVE database.

- **Identify Misconfigurations:** Images can contain misconfigurations such as exposed secrets, insecure file permissions or unnecessary services which can be exploited by the attackers. Scanning tools can help identify these misconfigurations in the images.

CKS curriculum explicitly mentions Trivy, which is an open-source tool to scan images for vulnerabilities. Trivy can be easily installed on many platforms and can also integrate with the CI/CD pipeline. During the exam, you will not be asked to install Trivy on the workstation. However, you should be familiar with how to use Trivy to scan images, how to interpret the results, and how to fix the identified vulnerabilities. You can find detailed documentation on Trivy at https://trivy.dev/latest/docs/.

Once you have Trivy installed, you can scan a container image by running the following command:

```
$ trivy image ubuntu:latest
2025-04-06T08:43:05Z    INFO    [vuln] Vulnerability scanning is enabled
2025-04-06T08:43:05Z    INFO    [secret] Secret scanning is enabled
2025-04-06T08:43:05Z    INFO    [secret] If your scanning is slow, please try
'--scanners vuln' to disable secret scanning
2025-04-06T08:43:05Z    INFO    [secret] Please see also https://trivy.dev/
v0.61/docs/scanner/secret#recommendation for faster secret detection
2025-04-06T08:43:08Z    INFO    Detected OS     family="ubuntu" version="24.04"
2025-04-06T08:43:08Z    INFO    [ubuntu] Detecting vulnerabilities...   os_ver-
sion="24.04" pkg_num=92
2025-04-06T08:43:08Z    INFO    Number of language-specific files       num=0

Report Summary

┌─────────────────────────────┬────────┬─────────────────┬─────────┐
│           Target            │  Type  │ Vulnerabilities │ Secrets │
├─────────────────────────────┼────────┼─────────────────┼─────────┤
│ ubuntu:latest (ubuntu 24.04) │ ubuntu │       25        │    -    │
└─────────────────────────────┴────────┴─────────────────┴─────────┘
Legend:
- '-': Not scanned
- '0': Clean (no security findings detected)


ubuntu:latest (ubuntu 24.04)

Total: 25 (UNKNOWN: 0, LOW: 10, MEDIUM: 15, HIGH: 0, CRITICAL: 0)
```

NOTE: The command output has been redacted to fit the page length.

With the preceding command, trivy will generate a detailed list of known vulnerabilities in the image along with their CVE number, Severity, Status, and fixed versions. The following are a couple of examples of how you can work with Trivy results:

Filter based on severity:

```
# trivy image ubuntu:latest --severity MEDIUM
2025-04-06T08:46:24Z    INFO    [vuln] Vulnerability scanning is enabled
2025-04-06T08:46:24Z    INFO    [secret] Secret scanning is enabled
2025-04-06T08:46:24Z    INFO    [secret] If your scanning is slow, please try '--scanners vuln' to disable secret scanning
2025-04-06T08:46:24Z    INFO    [secret] Please see also https://trivy.dev/v0.61/docs/scanner/secret#recommendation for faster secret detection
2025-04-06T08:46:24Z    INFO    Detected OS    family="ubuntu" version="24.04"
2025-04-06T08:46:24Z    INFO    [ubuntu] Detecting vulnerabilities...    os_version="24.04" pkg_num=92
2025-04-06T08:46:24Z    INFO    Number of language-specific files    num=0

Report Summary

┌─────────────────────────────┬────────┬─────────────────┬─────────┐
│           Target            │  Type  │ Vulnerabilities │ Secrets │
├─────────────────────────────┼────────┼─────────────────┼─────────┤
│ ubuntu:latest (ubuntu 24.04)│ ubuntu │       15        │    -    │
└─────────────────────────────┴────────┴─────────────────┴─────────┘
Legend:
- '-': Not scanned
- '0': Clean (no security findings detected)


ubuntu:latest (ubuntu 24.04)

Total: 15 (MEDIUM: 15)

┌──────────────┬────────────────┬──────────┬────────┬───────────────────┬
──────────────────────────────────────────────────────────────────┐
│   Library    │ Vulnerability  │ Severity │ Status │ Installed Version │
Fixed Version │                           Title                         │
├──────────────┼────────────────┼──────────┼────────┼───────────────────┼
──────────────────────────────────────────────────────────────────┤
│ gpgv         │ CVE-2025-30258 │ MEDIUM   │ fixed  │ 2.4.4-2ubuntu17   │
2.4.4-2ubuntu17.2         │ gnupg: verification DoS due to a malicious subkey in the │
│              │                │          │        │                   │
│ keyring                                                 │
│              │                │          │        │                   │
│ https://avd.aquasec.com/nvd/cve-2025-30258              │
├──────────────┼────────────────┤          │        ├───────────────────┼
```

```
...
| libtasn1-6          | CVE-2024-12133 |          | fixed     | 4.19.0-3build1          |
4.19.0-3ubuntu0.24.04.1        | libtasn1: Inefficient DER Decoding in libtasn1 Leading to |
|                     |                |          |           |                         |
| Potential Remote DoS                                              |
|                     |                |          |           |                         |
| https://avd.aquasec.com/nvd/cve-2024-12133                        |
```

Output the result in JSON:

```
$ trivy image ubuntu:latest --severity MEDIUM --format json > results.json
2025-04-06T08:50:25Z    INFO    [vuln] Vulnerability scanning is enabled
2025-04-06T08:50:25Z    INFO    [secret] Secret scanning is enabled
2025-04-06T08:50:25Z    INFO    [secret] If your scanning is slow, please try
'--scanners vuln' to disable secret scanning
2025-04-06T08:50:25Z    INFO    [secret] Please see also https://trivy.dev/
v0.61/docs/scanner/secret#recommendation for faster secret detection
2025-04-06T08:50:25Z    INFO    Detected OS     family="ubuntu" version="24.04"
2025-04-06T08:50:25Z    INFO    [ubuntu] Detecting vulnerabilities...   os_version
="24.04" pkg_num=92
2025-04-06T08:50:25Z    INFO    Number of language-specific files       num=0
```

Practical Considerations

When preparing for the CKS exam and also when working with a production Kubernetes environment or application, it is paramount that you get yourself familiar with the Command Line Interface (CLI) as well as file formats for dockerfile, docker CLI, Trivy, and so on. Some of the key things to keep in mind are:

- Practice working with the Alpine Linux image as well as the apk package manager.
- Practice writing Dockerfile for small containers using Alpine images.
- Practice combining the RUN commands to minimize the number of layers in the image.
- Understand how to clean up temporary files and caches to reduce the layer size.
- Get proficient with Trivy CLI, you should be comfortable running a new scan, filtering the results based on severity or any other factor. You should also be able to read the result and understand the steps to fix a particular vulnerability.

Understand and Secure Supply Chain

In the previous sections and chapters, we have been focusing on securing the cluster, network access, and application images. However, the application code and images do not live in a vacuum; in most cases, the application development, testing, and deployment are part of an automated process that allows the developers to quickly develop the code, test it in a test environment, and make it production-ready before putting it on a production cluster. This process of taking the application from coding all the way to the production deployment is called a Supply Chain.

Securing the Kubernetes setup is not just about locking the containers and cluster down; we need to keep the whole process safe, from the movement a developer starts writing the code to when it is actually running in the cluster. In this section, we will dive into the security threats and best practices of how to secure your application from its inception to deployment.

Let us take an example: someone sneaks into the code repository and slips in some bad code. If the repository is not properly protected and scanned, the code can end up in the container image, making its way to the registry and finally to the production.

Another scenario is if the CI/CD pipeline, used to build the artifacts, is not secured properly, someone will tweak the repository, and you end up with application images with security holes.

The supply chain is a complex ecosystem with numerous potential security weaknesses. Any vulnerability introduced in any part of the supply chain can end up compromising the whole application and the Kubernetes platform itself.

We will start this section by building a basic understanding of the supply chain and focus on Software Bill of Material, CI/CD pipeline, and repositories, which have been explicitly called out as part of the CKS curriculum. Then we will move to the next section dealing with restricting access to repositories and whitelisting only approved repositories. In the last sub-section, we will focus on container image signatures and ways to validate the signatures to ensure that the image has not been tampered with.

Introduction to SBoM, CI/CD, and Repositories

Let us start this section with an overview of some of the key components of the software lifecycle, namely SBoM, CI/CD, and Repositories.

Software Bill of Material (SBoM)

Modern applications are complex ecosystems of a multitude of components that are stitched to work together in a cohesive manner. Applications can include open-source libraries, third-party dependencies, and custom code. Tracking these components and their associated vulnerabilities is crucial for the security and compliance of the whole application. This is where the Software Bill of Materials (SBoM) comes into play. Think of SBoM as an inventory of all the software components used in the application.

SBoM provides a comprehensive list of ingredients that make up the application software. It is a machine-readable document that lists all the software components, including the libraries, modules, and dependencies, and captures detailed information about every part. The following is the high-level information that is captured in the SBoM:

- **Component Name and Version:** Identifies the specific components and their version.
- **Supplier Information:** Provides the details about the component's supplier or creator. This could be an OEM, developer, or Open-Source project.
- **License Information:** Lists the details of the license under which the component is distributed.
- **Dependency Relationships:** This is probably one of the most vital details captured in the SBoM. It shows the relationship between components, indicating which components depend on others.
- **Download locations:** This is the location from which the package can be obtained.

Now that we know what an SBoM is, let us understand how SBoM can help enhance the security posture of the application as well as the cluster.

- **Vulnerability Management:** SBoMs enable you to quickly identify the components and track vulnerabilities associated with the components. When new vulnerabilities are reported, you can quickly refer to the SBoM to identify whether the application will be impacted by the vulnerability or not. This helps in faster remediation by prioritizing the efforts based on the impact area.
- **Supply Chain Transparency:** SBoM helps in maintaining transparency in the software supply chain. They allow you to understand the origin and dependencies of the application components. This transparency is crucial in identifying and mitigating risks associated with compromised or malicious components.
- **Compliance and Auditing:** SBoM can help an organisation to comply with the security and regulatory requirements by providing an audit trail of the software components used in the application. This audit trail can be used for faster security audits, change tracking and speedy security posture assessments.

The following is an example of a small SBoM in CycloneDX format.


```
{
  "bomFormat": "CycloneDX",
  "specVersion": "1.3",
  "components": [
    {
      "type": "library",
      "name": "express",
      "version": "4.17.1",
      "purl": "pkg:npm/express@4.17.1",
      "licenses": [
        {
          "license": {
            "id": "MIT"
          }
        }
      ]
    },
    {
      "type": "library",
      "name": "lodash",
      "version": "4.17.21",
      "purl": "pkg:npm/lodash@4.17.21",
      "licenses": [
        {
          "license": {
            "id": "MIT"
          }
        }
      ]
    },
    {
      "type": "application",
      "name": "my-application",
      "version": "1.0.0"
    }
  ]
}
```


Continuous Integration/Continuous Deployment (CI/CD)

Over the last few years, CI/CD pipelines have revolutionized software development by automating the build, test, and deployment process. However, this automation can also introduce significant security risks if the overall pipeline is not properly secured. Given how important role these pipelines play in the software supply chain, a compromised pipeline can spell disaster for the application and even the underlying Kubernetes cluster.

CI/CD pipelines automate the process of building, testing, and deploying the software changes. They often involve multiple stages. Some of the most common stages in a CI/CD pipeline are:

1. **Code Retrieval:** This stage involves retrieving the application source code from version control systems such as GitHub or Gitlab.
2. **Build**: The code is compiled, dependencies are packaged, and a container image is generated as part of the build process. The generated image is then pushed to a test registry, which is often separated from the production registry for security purposes.
3. **Test**: Unit tests, integration tests, and security scans can be performed in the test stage. This stage ensures that there are no gaping holes in the application functionality of the security stance.
4. **Deployment**: Once the application tests are successful, it can be deployed in the staging or production area for further testing and production release.

A working CI/CD pipeline relies on multiple applications and automation frameworks to work together. Every component in the pipeline is a potential attack surface. Below are some of the most common security exploits, along with the security measures to avoid them.

- **Unauthorized access:** If access to the pipeline is not properly controlled, malicious actors can modify the build and deployment process, leading to a compromised application package or image. We need to implement strong access controls and authentication mechanisms for all the components involved in the pipeline. RBAC should be used to govern access to the sensitive pipeline operations. We can also implement Multi-Factor Authentication (MFA) for all users.
- **Secrets Exposure:** Pipelines, during the build and deployment phase, require access to sensitive information such as API Keys, database credentials, and certificates. If these secrets are not securely stored and managed, they can be exposed and used by malicious actors. To secure the sensitive information, make use of secret vaults or secret management systems such as HashiCorp Vault, AWS Secret Manager. You should also avoid injecting these secrets directly into the configuration files and dynamically inject the secrets into the build process. The secrets should also be rotated regularly to avoid the impact of compromised secrets.

- **Pipeline Tampering:** If a malicious actor gains access to the pipeline management tool, they can modify the configuration or scripts to inject malicious code into the software build. To avoid pipeline tampering, you can treat the pipeline configuration as code and store that in a version control system. You can apply Infrastructure-as-Code (IaC) principles to ensure consistency and reproducibility.

CKS curriculum does not go into the details of what is covered as part of the exam; however, you will not be asked to build or troubleshoot the pipeline, as that does not fall in the purview of the Kubernetes Operators or administrators.

Repositories

In the context of Software lifecycle, repositories play a vital role. These serve as the bedrock of the software development cycle. These repositories can hold the instructions that control the behavior and the security posture of the application. Securing these repositories is one of the key tenets of application security. The repositories can hold the application source code, configuration files, and even the application artifacts such as container images.

Repositories, whether they are Git repositories or container registries, can be targeted by malicious actors. Some of the most common assets are:

- **Source Code:** This is the blueprint for the application. This is the most critical component of the application and also most sensitive as this will mostly be the internal property of the organization.
- **Configuration Files:** Configuration files can include a wide range of files such as Kubernetes manifests, application configuration files, Helm Charts, Dockerfiles, and so on. The configuration files define the behavior of the application as well as the overall software lifecycle including the Kuberentes cluster.
- **Container Images:** Images are packaged applications ready for deployment. These are generally generated as part of the CI/CD pipeline and stored in a registry such as Docker Registry, GCR, or internal registries.

Just like any other IT system that is part of any large system, Repositories also have inherent security risks associated with them. Some of the security risks are common with other IT systems and share the same remediation, such as Access Control, Compromised Credentials, and Tampering. The following are a couple of mitigation steps that you can take to ensure the security of the repositories:

- **Access Control and Authentication:** Just like the Kubernetes environment, we need to implement strong access controls using Role-Based Access Control (RBAC). We can also enforce MFA for all users to avoid malicious access to the system. Regular maintenance and review of permissions is also critical and makes sure that there are no stale entries in the RBAC system for users who have either moved to a different role or are no longer part of the team.

- **Branch Protection:** To protect against unintentional or malicious code commits, make sure you have a branch protection policy to prevent direct commits to critical branches such as **main** and **release**. Every commit to these branches should go through a code review process and require approvals before merging the commit.
- **Code Reviews and Auditing:** To quickly identify and prevent malicious or vulnerable code from being merged, we should implement a mandatory code review. We should also maintain an audit trail of all the code changes and access logs.
- **Secrets Management:** Secret should never be a part of the repository and should be installed in a separate secrets management system. You should also avoid direct injection of secrets in the code, requiring automated secrets retrieval only when needed by the system.
- **Container Registry Security:** You should avoid using public container registries and build and use private container registries with strong access control systems. Even with the private registries, ensure that you have implemented vulnerability scanning for the images. You should also enable policies that prevent the use of public repositories and define a list of registries that can be used for the application images. Enable image signing and signature checks to ensure that the image content is trusted and not tampered with.
- **Repository Scanning:** You should use tools to scan the repositories for vulnerabilities, secret exposure, and misconfigurations. You should also automate the scan and integrate these into the CI/CD pipelines.
- **Updates and Patching:** It is essential to ensure that the repository software and its dependencies are up-to-date and have the latest security patches. Implementing automated updates whenever possible is recommended.

Controlling Access to Registries

As discussed in the last section, in a Kubernetes environment, controlling access to the source of container images is a fundamental supply chain security aspect. All the examples that we have built in the previous chapter have relied on images from public registries such as `gcr.io` and `docker.io`. However, this exposes the cluster to potential risks including the deployment of vulnerable or malicious images.

Let us take an example where the access to the public repository has been compromised by a malicious actor. The attacker can log in to the public repository and upload a compromised image in the public registry with the same tag using the compromised credentials. Any container that you deploy using that image will run the malicious code in the application, and you will have no way or control to stop that unless you move to a completely different image.

That is why using only trusted repositories, whether public or private, is a must for most production applications. For most enterprise customers, it is recommended to set up a private registry on the internal network that is controlled and managed by in-house teams with no access or interference from external vectors. You can then set up policies in the Kubernetes environment restricting which registries are allowed and which are denied, effectively ensuring that all the images that the team is using are coming from a trusted source, helping minimize the risk of deploying compromised images in the environment. There are two main ways that you can control access to the repositories.

- Open Policy Agent (OPA) Gatekeeper
- ImagePolicyWebhook Admission Controller Plugin

Using OPA Gatekeeper to Whitelist Allowed Image Registries

Open Policy Agent (OPA) is an open-source, general-purpose policy engine. OPA allows you to enforce rules across different technologies. OPA allows you to unify the enforcement as it is not specific to Kubernetes and can work across different technologies in the stack.

OPA is very flexible with its policy definition. OPA uses a high-level declarative language called **Rego,** to define the policies. OPA decouples the policy decision making from the policy enforcement, policy rules define if the object is accepted or not, this decoupling allows you to enforce policies across different systems including but not limited to Kubernetes, Microservices and CI/CD pipelines.

Gatekeeper is what allows us to define policies for Kubernetes primitives, Gatekeeper is a Kuberentes extension similar to an admission controller, it integrates OPA with the Kubernetes API Server. Gatekeeper uses Custom Resource Definitions (CRDs) to define constraint templates (Rego Policies) and constraints (policy instance). It allows a central and declarative way to manage and enforce policies in the Kubernetes cluster.

Installing Gatekeeper

Getting started with Gatekeeper is simple and is extensively documented at https://github.com/open-policy-agent/gatekeeper. Although as part of the CKS exam, you will not be asked to install Gatekeeper from scratch, you should still be familiar with the procedure.

Run the following command to install Gatekeeper in an existing cluster:

```
$ kubectl apply -f https://raw.githubusercontent.com/open-poli-
cy-agent/gatekeeper/v3.18.2/deploy/gatekeeper.yaml
namespace/gatekeeper-system created
resourcequota/gatekeeper-critical-pods created
```

```
customresourcedefinition.apiextensions.k8s.io/assign.mutations.gate-
keeper.sh created
customresourcedefinition.apiextensions.k8s.io/assignimage.mutations.
gatekeeper.sh created
customresourcedefinition.apiextensions.k8s.io/assignmetadata.muta-
tions.gatekeeper.sh created
customresourcedefinition.apiextensions.k8s.io/configpodstatuses.status.
gatekeeper.sh created
customresourcedefinition.apiextensions.k8s.io/configs.config.gatekeeper.
sh created
customresourcedefinition.apiextensions.k8s.io/constraintpodstatuses.
status.gatekeeper.sh created
customresourcedefinition.apiextensions.k8s.io/constrainttemplatepod-
statuses.status.gatekeeper.sh created
customresourcedefinition.apiextensions.k8s.io/constrainttemplates.tem-
plates.gatekeeper.sh created
customresourcedefinition.apiextensions.k8s.io/expansiontemplate.expan-
sion.gatekeeper.sh created
customresourcedefinition.apiextensions.k8s.io/expansiontemplatepodsta-
tuses.status.gatekeeper.sh created
customresourcedefinition.apiextensions.k8s.io/modifyset.mutations.
gatekeeper.sh created
customresourcedefinition.apiextensions.k8s.io/mutatorpodstatuses.sta-
tus.gatekeeper.sh created
customresourcedefinition.apiextensions.k8s.io/providers.externaldata.
gatekeeper.sh created
customresourcedefinition.apiextensions.k8s.io/syncsets.syncset.gate-
keeper.sh created
serviceaccount/gatekeeper-admin created
role.rbac.authorization.k8s.io/gatekeeper-manager-role created
clusterrole.rbac.authorization.k8s.io/gatekeeper-manager-role created
rolebinding.rbac.authorization.k8s.io/gatekeeper-manager-rolebinding
created
clusterrolebinding.rbac.authorization.k8s.io/gatekeeper-manag-
er-rolebinding created
secret/gatekeeper-webhook-server-cert created
service/gatekeeper-webhook-service created
deployment.apps/gatekeeper-audit created
deployment.apps/gatekeeper-controller-manager created
poddisruptionbudget.policy/gatekeeper-controller-manager created
mutatingwebhookconfiguration.admissionregistration.k8s.io/gatekeep-
er-mutating-webhook-configuration created
validatingwebhookconfiguration.admissionregistration.k8s.io/gatekeep-
er-validating-webhook-configuration created
```

You can view the details of the deployed resources by listing components in the gatekeeper-system compartment.

```
$ kubectl get all -n gatekeeper-system
NAME                                              READY   STATUS    RESTARTS      AGE
pod/gatekeeper-audit-dd5bdff99-r7fpr              1/1     Running   1 (21s ago)   31s
pod/gatekeeper-controller-manager-77dd8d9cf6-47cv8   1/1     Running   0             30s
pod/gatekeeper-controller-manager-77dd8d9cf6-qmrrg   1/1     Running   0             30s
pod/gatekeeper-controller-manager-77dd8d9cf6-sfpm8   1/1     Running   0             31s

NAME                                 TYPE        CLUSTER-IP      EXTERNAL-IP   PORT(S)
AGE
service/gatekeeper-webhook-service   ClusterIP   10.96.245.164   <none>        443/TCP
31s

NAME                                            READY   UP-TO-DATE   AVAILABLE   AGE
deployment.apps/gatekeeper-audit                1/1     1            1           31s
deployment.apps/gatekeeper-controller-manager   3/3     3            3           31s

NAME                                                       DESIRED   CURRENT   READY   AGE
replicaset.apps/gatekeeper-audit-dd5bdff99                 1         1         1       31s
replicaset.apps/gatekeeper-controller-manager-77dd8d9cf6   3         3         3       31s
```

Defining Constraint Template (Rego Policy)

Once we have Gatekeeper installed and running, the next step is to define the constraint template. A constraint template is what defines the rules with Rego. The template also defines the schema for the constraint.

The following is an example constraint template that will limit which registries can be used to pull the images when deploying the pod:

```
apiVersion: templates.gatekeeper.sh/v1beta1
kind: ConstraintTemplate
metadata:
  name: k8sallowedrepos
spec:
  crd:
    spec:
      names:
        kind: K8sAllowedRepos
      validation:
        openAPIV3Schema:
          properties:
            allowedRegistries:
              type: array
              items:
                type: string
```

```
targets:
  - target: admission.k8s.gatekeeper.sh
    rego: |
      package K8sAllowedRepos

      violation[{"msg": msg}] {
        container := input.review.object.spec.containers[_]
        image := container.image
        result := startswith(image, input.parameters.repos[_])
        not result
        msg := sprintf("container <%v> has an invalid image repo
<%v>, allowed repos are %v", [container.name, container.image, input.
parameters.repos])
      }
```

```
Use the file to deploy the constraint template in the Kubernetes cluster.
# kubectl apply -f opa-template.yaml
constrainttemplate.templates.gatekeeper.sh/k8sallowedrepos created
```

Defining Constraint

Once the constraint template has been created, the next step is to create the constraint. Use the following definition to create the policy instance:

```
apiVersion: constraints.gatekeeper.sh/v1beta1
kind: K8sAllowedRepos
metadata:
  name: repo-is-gcr
spec:
  match:
    kinds:
      - apiGroups: [""]
        kinds: ["Pod"]
  parameters:
    repos:
      - "gcr.io/"
```

Create the policy by running the following command.

```
$ kubectl apply -f opa-constraint.yaml
k8sallowedrepos.constraints.gatekeeper.sh/repo-is-gcr created
```

Validating the Policy

Once the constraint template and constraint have been created, we can test them by running the following commands. Any pod that does not use an image from gcr.io must be forbidden.

```
$ kubectl run nginx --image=nginx:latest
Error from server (Forbidden): admission webhook "validation.
```

```
gatekeeper.sh" denied the request: [repo-is-gcr] container <ng-
inx> has an invalid image repo <nginx:latest>, allowed repos are
["gcr.io/"]
```

Let us try to run another pod with an image from Google Container Registry.

```
$ kubectl run test --image=gcr.io/distroless/java-base-debian12
pod/test created
```

As seen in the preceding example, we cannot deploy a pod from the docker.io registry as it is being blocked by OPA; however, images from gcr.io can be pulled successfully.

ImagePolicyWebhook Admission Controller Plugin

Another method of ensuring that the image being used is from an approved image registry is to use an Admission Controller. As part of the CKA exam curriculum, you should already be familiar with what an Admission Controller is and how it works. You can get more details about the Admission Controller at https://kubernetes.io/docs/reference/access-authn-authz/admission-controllers/.

In essence, Admission controllers are plugins that can intercept API calls coming from the API server and can approve, deny, or mutate the request before it has been executed, but after it has been authenticated and authorized.

ImagePolicyWebhook admission controller defines image policies based on which an image can be allowed or restricted. As the name suggests, this admission controller relies on an external HTTPS application, Webhook, to make decisions about the image admission and provide a response to the admission controller.

At a high level, the process of configuring the image policies with ImagePolicyWebhook works as follows:

1. **Deploy Webhook Server:** Building and implementing the external application is out of scope for the CKS exam. During the exam, you will be provided with the application endpoint that you can configure the admission controller with.

2. **Create `KubeConfig` File:** The admission controller relies on a **`kubeconfig`** file to work with the Kubernetes API server. The following is an example configuration file. You can update the endpoint, certificate path, and CA certificate location based on your cluster.

```
$ cat <<EOF >/etc/kubernetes/imagepolicy-webhook/webhook.yaml
apiVersion: v1
kind: Config
clusters:
- cluster:
    certificate-authority: /etc/kubernetes/imagepolicy-webhook/
server.crt
```

```
    server: https://<External Server IP>:<PORT>
  name: webhook
users:
- name: webhook-user
  user:
    client-certificate: /etc/kubernetes/pki/apiserver.crt
    client-key: /etc/kubernetes/pki/apiserver.key
contexts:
- context:
    cluster: webhook
    user: webhook-user
  name: webhook
current-context: webhook

EOF
```

3. **Create `AdmissionConfiguration` File:** Once you have the **`KubeConfig`** file, you can use it to configure the **`AdmissionConfiguration`** file. Use the following format for the file.

```
$cat <<EOF >/etc/kubernetes/image policy-webhook/admissionConfig.
yaml
apiVersion: apiserver.config.k8s.io/v1
kind: AdmissionConfiguration
plugins:
  - name: ImagePolicyWebhook
    configuration:
      imagePolicy:
        kubeConfigFile: /etc/kubernetes/imagepolicy-webhook/
webhook.yaml
        allowTTL: 50
        denyTTL: 50
        retryBackoff: 500
        defaultAllow: true
EOF
```

4. **Update the API Server Manifest:** Once you have the aforementioned files ready, the last step is to update the API Server manifest to enable the **`ImagePolicyWebhook`**. The following is an excerpt from the updated API Server manifest.

```
…
spec:
  containers:
  - command:
    - kube-apiserver
    - --enable-admission-plugins=ImagePolicyWebhook
```

```
    - --admission-control-config-file=/etc/kubernetes/imagepolicy
-webhook/admissionConfig.yaml

    volumeMounts:
    - mountPath: /etc/kubernetes/imagepolicy-webhook
      name: webhook
      readOnly: true

  - hostPath:
      path: /etc/kubernetes/imagepolicy-webhook/
      type: DirectoryOrCreate
    name: webhook
```

Once you update the **kube-apiserver** manifest file, the kube-apiserver pod will restart. After the server is up and running, you can test the policies by deploying new pods with allowed and restricted image registries.

Sign Images and Validate Signatures

In the last section, we saw how to ensure that the image we are using is coming from a trusted source. However, consider a scenario where the registry itself has been compromised and the attacker has tampered with the image and reuploaded the image with the same name and tag but with application code allowing him/her remote access to the application.

When it comes to software supply chain security, ensuring the image authenticity and integrity is just as important, if not more so. Just like a legally signed document ensures the document's origin and integrity, signing a container image generates a cryptographic guarantee that it is not only coming from the same source but has also not been modified.

Let us look at how to sign the image and how to validate the signature.

1. **Signing the image**

   Before you can sign the image, you will need to create a new registry in **docker.io** to store your custom image.

   Log in to your registry using the following command.

   ```
   # docker login

   USING WEB-BASED LOGIN

   i Info → To sign in with credentials on the command line, use
   'docker login -u <username>'
   ```

```
Your one-time device confirmation code is: XXXX-XXXX
Press ENTER to open your browser or submit your device code here:
https://login.docker.com/activate

Waiting for authentication in the browser…

WARNING! Your credentials are stored unencrypted in '/root/.dock-
er/config.json'.
Configure a credential helper to remove this warning. See
https://docs.docker.com/go/credential-store/

Login Succeeded
```

After the login, you can tag a local image and push it to the repository. For example, we will use the **goapp_multibuild** image that we created in the previous section.

```
$ docker tag goapp_multibuild:latest kumarvijay/cksdemorepo:-
signed
$ docker push kumarvijay/cksdemorepo:signed
The push refers to repository [docker.io/kumarvijay/cksdemorepo]
f78d43e5042e: Pushed
1205e8132ffe: Pushed
08000c18d16d: Pushed
signed: digest: sha256:22190e137d627a8b1e9721fc38d3d0c4861edd-
39b209636640e076e5725f57bc size: 945
```

Once the image is pushed to the registry, you can use the following command to sign the image. If this is the first time you are signing the image in the repository, you might be asked to create a passphrase for the repository.

```
$ docker trust sign kumarvijay/cksdemorepo:signed
You are about to create a new root signing key passphrase. This
passphrase
will be used to protect the most sensitive key in your signing
system. Please
choose a long, complex passphrase and be careful to keep the
password and the
key file itself secure and backed up. It is highly recommended
that you use a
password manager to generate the passphrase and keep it safe.
There will be no
way to recover this key. You can find the key in your config direc-
tory.
Enter passphrase for new kumarvijay key with ID 1578d9a:
Repeat passphrase for new kumarvijay key with ID 1578d9a:
Created signer: kumarvijay
Finished initializing signed repository for kumarvijay/cksdemore-
po:signed
```

```
Signing and pushing trust data for local image kumarvijay/cksde-
morepo:signed, may overwrite remote trust data
The push refers to repository [docker.io/kumarvijay/cksdemorepo]
f78d43e5042e: Layer already exists
1205e8132ffe: Layer already exists
08000c18d16d: Layer already exists
signed: digest: sha256:22190e137d627a8b1e9721fc38d3d0c4861edd39b2
09636640e076e5725f57bc size: 945
Signing and pushing trust metadata
Enter passphrase for kumarvijay key with ID 1578d9a:
Successfully signed docker.io/kumarvijay/cksdemorepo:signed
```

You can validate the digest by logging in to your private registry and viewing the image details.

Figure 6.1 shows the digest of an image in Docker registry.

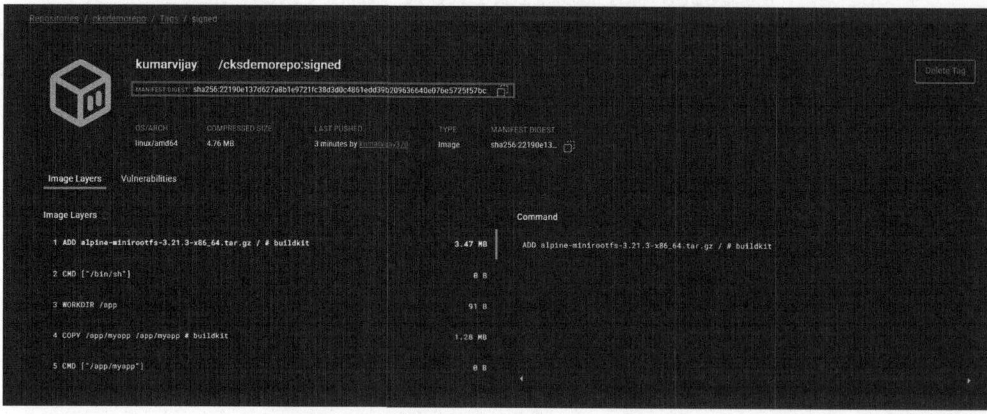

Figure 6.1: *Image Digest in Docker Registry*

2. **Using the digest in the pod definition**

   When defining the Pod manifest, you can add the image digest details in the image configuration. Adding the digest details with the image config ensures that when building the pod, the actual image digest will be compared against the defined digest, and the pod will only be created if the digests match.

   Use the following file to deploy the pod with the wrong digest information. Note that the digest only differs by 1 character at the end. We are using 'd' instead of 'c' in the actual digest.

```
apiVersion: v1
kind: Pod
metadata:
  labels:
    run: digest-test
  name: digest-test
```

```
spec:
  containers:
  - image: kumarvijay/cksdemorepo@sha256:22190e137d627a8b1e9721f-
c38d3d0c4861edd39b209636640e076e5725f57bd
    name: digest-test
```

Deploy the pod using the file and view the pod description.

```
$ kubectl apply -f digest-test.yaml
pod/digest-test created

$ kubectl describe pod digest-test
Name:             digest-test
Namespace:        default
Priority:         0
Service Account:  default
…
    State:          Waiting
      Reason:       ErrImagePull
    Ready:          False
    Restart Count:  0
    Environment:    <none>
…
Events:
  Type     Reason     Age   From               Message
  ----     ------     ----  ----               -------
  Normal   Scheduled  10s   default-scheduler  Successfully assigned default/di-
gest-test to kind-worker
  Normal   Pulling    10s   kubelet            Pulling image "kumarvijay/cksdemore-
po@sha256:22190e137d627a8b1e9721fc38d3d0c4861edd39b209636640e076e5725f57bd"
  Warning  Failed     9s    kubelet            Failed to pull im-
age "kumarvijay/cksdemorepo@sha256:22190e137d627a8b1e9721fc38d3d0c4861edd-
39b209636640e076e5725f57bd": rpc error: code = NotFound desc = failed to pull and
unpack image docker.io/kumarvijay/cksdemorepo@sha256:22190e137d627a8b1e9721fc38d-
3d0c4861edd39b209636640e076e5725f57bd
…
```

As you can see, the pod is failing with an image pull error.

Practice Question 1: Follow the steps mentioned in the last section and update the pod definition with the correct image digest from your registry. Test and validate that the pod is able to run successfully.

Static Analysis of Workload and Images

When it comes to security of any kind, being proactive is the key to a robust environment. Rather than solely relying on monitoring and reactive responses, identifying potential security vulnerabilities and misconfigurations before deployment has significant advantages. This is where static analysis can assist.

Static analysis involves examining the code, configuration files and container images without executing them. Doing this means that we can identify a wide range of security issues early in the development process, preventing them from getting to the running clusters.

In this section, we will focus on the application of static analysis in two key areas as defined by the CKS curriculum: User Workload (Defined by the Kubernetes manifests) and Container images. There are many specialized tools that can automatically scan these artifacts for security flaws and provide corrective measures as well as best practices.

User workloads are typically defined in the YAML manifests for Pods, Deployments, Services, and so on. Static scanning tools can help identify misconfigurations such as open permissions, missing security contexts, exposed common ports and improper resource limits.

Similarly, static analysis of container images goes beyond scanning for known vulnerabilities and CVEs. It involves examining the image configuration, file-system permissions, and presence of sensitive information.

CKS exam curriculum prominently mentions **`Kubesec`** and **`KubeLinter`** as the tools for static analysis. Though there are many tools with similar or better functionality, for the sake of this book, we will focus on **`Kubesec`** and **`KubeLinter`** for static analysis.

Kubesec

`Kubesec` focuses primarily on evaluating the security posture of Kubernetes resource manifests based on a set of predefined security risks. It is an open-source static analysis tool specifically designed to evaluate the security posture of Kubernetes resource manifests written in YAML.

`Kubesec` can help in identifying potential security risks and misconfigurations. **`Kubesect`** analyzes the file for specific settings and configurations that deviate from security best practices. You can find detailed information on **`Kubesec`** scans at https://kubesec.io/.

`Kubesec` can run as a container, installed as a binary, as a Kubernetes Admission Controller, and even as a **`Kubectl`** plugin. This flexibility allows us to integrate **`Kubesec`** directly into the software life cycle. During the exam, you are not expected to install **`Kubesec`** from scratch, but you should be familiar with how to use **`Kubesec`** and how to interpret and fix the observations from the scan result. You can find the **`Kubesec`**

installation instructions at https://github.com/controlplaneio/kubesec?tab=readme-ov-file#download-kubesec

Once you have **Kubesec** installed, you can use it to scan Kubernetes manifests. Let us create a sample deployment YAML file and scan it with **Kubesec**. Use the following definition and save it in a YAML file.

```
apiVersion: apps/v1
kind: Deployment
metadata:
  name: insecure-app
spec:
  replicas: 1
  selector:
    matchLabels:
      app: insecure-app
  template:
    metadata:
      labels:
        app: insecure-app
    spec:
      containers:
        - name: insecure-container
          image: nginx:latest
          securityContext:
            privileged: true
            allowPrivilegeEscalation: true
          ports:
            - containerPort: 80
              hostPort: 8080
          resources:
            limits:
              cpu: "1"
              memory: "1Gi"
            requests:
              cpu: "500m"
              memory: "512Mi"
```

Scan the YAML file with **Kubesec** by running the scan command.

```
$ kubesec scan insecure-deployment.yaml
[
  {
    "object": "Deployment/insecure-app.default",
    "valid": true,
    "fileName": "insecure-deployment.yaml",
    "message": "Failed with a score of -33 points",
    "score": -33,
```

```
    "scoring": {
      "critical": [
        {
          "id": "Privileged",
          "selector": "containers[] .securityContext .privileged
== true",
          "reason": "Privileged containers can allow almost
completely unrestricted host access",
          "points": -30
        },
        {
          "id": "AllowPrivilegeEscalation",
          "selector": "containers[] .securityContext
.allowPrivilegeEscalation == true",
          "reason": "Ensure a non-root process can not gain more
privileges",
          "points": -7
        }
      ],
      "passed": [
        {
          "id": "LimitsCPU",
          "selector": "containers[] .resources .limits .cpu",
          "reason": "Enforcing CPU limits prevents DOS via re-
source exhaustion",
          "points": 1
        },
…
      "advise": [
        {
          "id": "ApparmorAny",
          "selector": ".metadata .annotations .\"container.apparmor
.security.beta.kubernetes.io/nginx\"",
          "reason": "Well defined AppArmor policies may provide
greater protection from unknown threats. WARNING: NOT PRODUCTION
READY",
          "points": 3
        },
        {
          "id": "ServiceAccountName",
          "selector": ".spec .serviceAccountName",
          "reason": "Service accounts restrict Kubernetes API ac-
cess and should be configured with least privilege",
          "points": 3
        },
…
```

The output has three main sections that we need to focus on.

Score: This is the overall score assigned to the manifest. A higher score means better protection. In our sample, the overall score is -33.

Scoring: Critical: This section lists the critical configuration issues along with their score. These configurations must be fixed to ensure that the manifest follows the security best practices. In our example, running a privileged container and also allowing privilege escalation has resulted in -30 and -7 score respectively.

Advise: The advice section lists security best practices that can be incorporated in the manifest to increase the score and closely match the laid out security guidelines.

Practical Question 2: Update the YAML manifest from the last example, use the **`Kubesec`** output, and fix all the critical observations. Scan the new YAML file with **`Kubesec`** and ensure that it passes with a positive scan score.

KubeLinter

`KubeLinter` is an open-source static analysis tool that checks Kubernetes YAML files and Helm charts against a variety of best practices, with a strong focus on security, correctness, and operational efficiency. Unlike **`Kubesec`**, which primarily focuses on identifying specific security risks, **`KubeLinter`** takes a broader approach, aiming to ensure that your Kubernetes configurations adhere to recommended guidelines that indirectly and directly contribute to a more secure and stable environment.

`KubeLinter` examines the structure and settings within the manifest and applies predefined 'linters' or checks that look for deviations from established best practices. **`KubeLinter`** is highly customizable and can be configured to go beyond the basic security scanning. You can find detailed information about **`KubeLinter`** at https://docs.kubelinter.io/#/.

Once you have **`KubeLinter`** installed, we can use it to scan the Deployment yaml. We will use the following yaml manifest.

```
apiVersion: apps/v1
kind: Deployment
metadata:
  name: insecure-app
spec:
  replicas: 1
  selector:
    matchLabels:
      app: insecure-app
  template:
    metadata:
      labels:
```

```
        app: insecure-app
    spec:
      containers:
        - name: insecure-container
          image: nginx:latest
          securityContext:
            privileged: true
            allowPrivilegeEscalation: true
          ports:
            - containerPort: 80
              hostPort: 8080
          resources:
            limits:
              cpu: "1"
              memory: "1Gi"
            requests:
              cpu: "500m"
              memory: "512Mi"
```

Run the following command to scan the manifest.

```
# kube-linter lint insecure-deployment.yaml
KubeLinter 0.7.2

/root/insecure-deployment.yaml: (object: <no namespace>/insecure-app
apps/v1, Kind=Deployment) The container "insecure-container" is us-
ing an invalid container image, "nginx:latest". Please use images
that are not blocked by the `BlockList` criteria : [".*:(latest)$"
"^[^:]*$" "(.*/[^:]+)$"] (check: latest-tag, remediation: Use a con-
tainer image with a specific tag other than latest.)

/root/insecure-deployment.yaml: (object: <no namespace>/inse-
cure-app apps/v1, Kind=Deployment) container "insecure-container"
does not have a read-only root file system (check: no-read-only-
root-fs, remediation: Set readOnlyRootFilesystem to true in the
container securityContext.)

/root/insecure-deployment.yaml: (object: <no namespace>/insecure-app
apps/v1, Kind=Deployment) container "insecure-container" has Allow-
PrivilegeEscalation set to true. (check: privilege-escalation-con-
tainer, remediation: Ensure containers do not allow privilege esca-
lation by setting allowPrivilegeEscalation=false, privileged=false
and removing CAP_SYS_ADMIN capability. See https://kubernetes.io/
docs/tasks/configure-pod-container/security-context/ for more de-
tails.)

/root/insecure-deployment.yaml: (object: <no namespace>/inse-
cure-app apps/v1, Kind=Deployment) container "insecure-container"
```

```
is privileged (check: privileged-container, remediation: Do not
run your container as privileged unless it is required.)

/root/insecure-deployment.yaml: (object: <no namespace>/inse-
cure-app apps/v1, Kind=Deployment) container "insecure-container"
is not set to runAsNonRoot (check: run-as-non-root, remediation:
Set runAsUser to a non-zero number and runAsNonRoot to true in
your pod or container securityContext. Refer to https://kuberne-
tes.io/docs/tasks/configure-pod-container/security-context/ for
details.)

Error: found 5 lint errors
```

As per the output, **`KubeLinter`** has found 5 errors in the manifest. The linter output provides the details of the identified security misconfiguration as well as remediation steps.

Practical Question 3: Use the above **`KubeLinter`** output and apply the provided remediation steps to the deployment manifest file. Re-run the lint operations and ensure that the result does not have any errors.

Practical Considerations

In this chapter, we looked at ways to secure the complete software supply chain, starting with the image footprint and going all the way to static analysis of the manifest files. The following are some of the things that you should keep in mind when preparing for the CKS exam:

- **Reducing Image Footprint:** Make yourself familiar with different ways in which you can reduce the image size. Research and practice ways to shrink the image without impacting the core functionality. You should also be able to look at the image definition file and identify possible enhancements in the definition file.
- **Image Signature:** Practice working with image digests, signing images, and validating the image digests before deploying containers with that image. Also practices Linux CLI commands to compare the provided digest and the actual image digest.
- **Working with Registries:** Practice using OPA Gatekeeper and **`ImagePolicyWebhook`** admission controller to restrict the registries from which you can pull images in the cluster. You should also be familiar with different error messages generated by the Pods to quickly identify the issues with using unauthorized registries.
- **Image Scanning:** Although you will not be asked to install scanning tools such as **`Trivy`**, **`KubeSec`**, and **`KubeLinter`**, you should be familiar with how to scan

images with these tools as well as how to read the scan results and quickly apply the provided recommendations.

Conclusion

Securing the Kubernetes supply chain is not a singular task but rather an ongoing activity that spans the entire lifecycle of the application and the cluster. In this chapter, we looked at how to secure the entire supply chain, starting from the application development, CI/CD pipeline, and going all the way to scanning the images for known vulnerabilities.

We understood the security best practices around minimizing image footprints, reducing layers, implementing robust image scanning, leveraging SBOMs, securing CI/CD pipelines and repositories, enforcing permitted registries, signing and validating images, and employing static analysis tools such as **`Kubesec`**, **`Trivy`**, and **`KubeLinter`**.

In the next chapter, we will move to post deployment monitoring of the cluster and application. We will focus on collecting and analysing behavioral patterns, explore ways to ensure container immutability and implement logging, monitoring and auditing systems for the Kubernetes environment.

CHAPTER 7

Monitoring, Logging, and Runtime Security

Introduction

All the security pillars that we have covered so far have focused on building a secure Kubernetes environment by locking the environment down against unauthorized application, cluster, and even network access. We have even secured the underlying Operating System and the software development life cycle, including the CI/CD pipeline and repositories. However, even the most secure environment can be broken into and compromised during runtime. That is why we need to ensure that we can monitor when things do not behave the way they are supposed to. Real-time threat detection can help identify the bad actors in a system and reduce their impact on the environment.

The last vertical of the CKS exam focuses on the runtime security of the Kubernetes environment as well as the application hosted on the platform. We will kick off this chapter with an understanding of behavioral analysis. Think of behavioral analysis as monitoring what is "normal" in the cluster and detecting any deviations from the expected behavior. We will look at Falco, which is an open-source tool that can keep an eye on system calls and Kubernetes events to catch unexpected activities.

The next section will deal with detecting threats that can pop up in different places in the Kubernetes environment. We will start by looking into the actual hardware that the cluster runs on, the network that enables seamless connection between the nodes, pods, and services, then we will shift our focus to the data that you are storing and generating as part of the day-to-day operations of the application and the cluster. Next, we will shift our focus to the users and figure out what they are doing and what they are allowed to do, and lastly, we will also cover the workloads that run in the cluster.

After that, we will also break down the typical stages of an attack in Kubernetes and how to recognize the bad actors by understanding what they are doing. Understanding the steps and methods that the attacker usually takes, from getting a foothold in the system to moving around and grabbing sensitive data, will help us catch them earlier and reduce the impact that they have on the system.

In all the chapters focusing on container security, we have said that the containers hosting the application are ephemeral and generally do not retain any data. However, in some cases, if the container has not been properly deployed or secured, it is possible to change the container behavior and use it for nefarious purposes. We will talk about container immutability in a dedicated section to ensure that the containers cannot be changed or updated during runtime.

In the last section, we will dig into Kubernetes audit logs. These are dedicated records of everything that happens in the cluster's control plane. We will dive into how to set up audit logs, how to collect the logs, and read them to find suspicious API calls and potential security challenges.

Structure

- Behavioral Analysis
  - Falco
- Detecting threats in Kubernetes Environment
  - Physical Infrastructure
  - Network
  - Data
  - User
  - Applications
- Identifying Phases of Attack and Bad Actors
- Ensure Container Immutability
- Using Kubernetes Audit Logs

Behavioral Analysis

Traditional security measures such as firewalls, RBAC, IPC, and so on focus on preventing outsiders from getting into the system. However, they do not provide any protection against attack vectors which are already in the system or the application. These methods do not even raise any alarm or notification if the attacker changes something from the inside, that is where behavioral analysis comes in.

In the context of Kubernetes security, behavioral analysis is about understanding what is "normal" for the cluster and the application. Behavioral analysis focuses on establishing a baseline of activities within the cluster, the applications that the cluster interacts with, the method of interaction, different system calls made by the cluster, and the APIs that are generally used by the applications. Once you have this baseline, you can start looking for things that deviate from this baseline – anything that creates unusual spikes, makes unnecessary or unwanted system calls, or creates strange communication patterns can indicate security threats.

Legacy security systems rely on signatures of known attacks; on the other hand, behavioral analysis focuses on the actions being performed. Let us take an example: if a container that only connects to an internal application suddenly starts outbound network connections to unfamiliar IP addresses, or a user who is supposed to have limited permissions on the cluster suddenly starts trying to access sensitive resources via the API. All these could point towards a potential malicious activity, even if they do not match a predefined attack pattern.

In this section, we will introduce the core concepts of behavioral analysis at a high level for Kubernetes systems. We will also cover the importance of detecting threats that might otherwise go unnoticed. By understanding what "normal" looks like, you can easily spot the "abnormal" behavior and take timely actions to protect the Kubernetes environment both against internal as well as external threats.

Within a Kubernetes environment, behavioral analysis focuses on observing and understanding the typical interactions or actions of various Kubernetes entities. Some of the most important entities and their tracked behaviors are listed as follows:

- **Container Behavior:** To set up a baseline normal behavior, it is important to track the system calls made by the processes in the container, their network activities, file system access patterns, and resource consumption. Any deviation from the established norms for a specific container image or application can signal a compromised container or system.
- **Kubernetes API interactions:** Kubernetes API is the main gateway to the cluster and is used by human users, applications, and machines. It is imperative to understand how users and applications interact with the Kubernetes API. Unexpected API calls, unauthorized access or modification attempts, or unusual sequences of API calls can indicate malicious activity or policy violation.
- **Network Flows:** Almost every application pod, service, and external endpoints are built with expected network patterns and flows. Unusual connection attempts, excessive traffic to unknown or unwanted destinations, or changes in the communication protocols can be indicators of a compromised or misconfigured system.
- **User and Role Activity:** Users in the Kubernetes system or application tend to have defined roles and responsibilities. Attempts to escalate privileges, accessing resources beyond assigned roles, or unusual login patterns can be flagged and investigated.
- **Resource Consumption:** Observing the typical compute, network, and storage usage of pods and nodes to detect sudden spikes and unusual patterns of

resource consumption could indicate resource hijacking or denial-of-service attempts.

CKS curriculum mentions **"Falco"** specifically as the go-to tool for behavior analysis. Although there are other tools that can do what Falco does, those are not part of the curriculum, so we will only focus on Falco as part of this chapter.

Falco

Falco is a powerful, open-source runtime security tool designed specifically for cloud-native environments, including Kubernetes, containers, and Linux hosts. It was created by Sysdig and operates by continuously monitoring system calls at the OS kernel level as well as monitoring Kubernetes API Server events in real-time. It has a customizable rule engine that can detect abnormal and potentially malicious behavior. Falco has some predefined security rules, and you can define your own rules and policies. When an event is detected that violates a rule, Falco generates alerts which provides immediate visibility into suspicious activity within the Kubernetes cluster.

Falco Architecture

Falco's high-level architecture is based on the following key components.

- **Driver:** Falco can interpret Linux system calls during runtime by rebuilding the kernel state in memory. To do this, the Falco engine depends on a driver, the driver helps Falco consume the raw stream that contains system call information. Currently Falco supports three different drivers depending on specific environmental constraints and requirements.
    - **Kernel Module**: The Falco kernel module is the traditional way of working with stream data. The kernel module depends on the linux-headers package in order to compile and must be loaded in order to work.
    - **Extended Berkeley Packet Filter (eBPF)**: **eBPF** is a more modern and often preferred method due to its safety and flexibility. This low-level access provides a comprehensive view of process behavior.
    - **pDig**: **pdig** binary is the latest and most viable path when using the Kernel or **eBPF** module is not an option. **Pdig** is built on **ptrace(2)**

Kubernetes Audit Log Monitoring: Falco can also consume and analyze events from the Kubernetes Audit Log. This allows it to detect suspicious API activity, such as unauthorized resource modifications, attempts to escalate privileges, or the creation of risky resources.

Rules Engine: The heart of Falco is its rules engine. Rules are written in a declarative YAML format and define specific conditions or patterns of behavior that are considered suspicious. These rules can be based on system call arguments (for example, a container executing a shell with root privileges), Kubernetes API events (for example, a secret being created in a public namespace), or a combination of both.

Alerting Mechanism: When a rule is triggered by a monitored event, Falco generates an alert. These alerts can be outputted in various formats (for example, stdout, syslog, JSON) and can be integrated with other security tools and alerting systems (for example, Slack, Elasticsearch, SIEM).

Falco Installation

Falco is quite versatile when it comes to installation and consumption. It can run as a Docker container, a Kubernetes Pod, or as a binary on the host operating system, depending on different Linux distributions. Falco, being an open source project, you can even compile it yourself from the Falco source. Detailed installation instructions for Falco are available at https://falco.org/docs/setup/.

As part of the CKS exam questions, you will not be asked to install Falco from scratch and can assume that it will be available in the exam environment whenever needed. As part of the exercise, you can follow the following steps to install Falco on a **kind** cluster using Helm. For any other environment, follow the setup steps available on the Falco docs page at https://falco.org/docs/.

Create a kind configuration file with the following content.

```
kind: Cluster
apiVersion: kind.x-k8s.io/v1alpha4
nodes:
- role: control-plane
  extraMounts:
    # allow Falco to use devices provided by the kernel module
  - hostPath: /dev
    containerPath: /dev
    # allow Falco to use the Docker unix socket
  - hostPath: /var/run/docker.sock
    containerPath: /var/run/docker.sock
- role: worker
  extraMounts:
    # allow Falco to use devices provided by the kernel module
  - hostPath: /dev
    containerPath: /dev
    # allow Falco to use the Docker unix socket
  - hostPath: /var/run/docker.sock
    containerPath: /var/run/docker.sock
- role: worker
  extraMounts:
    # allow Falco to use devices provided by the kernel module
  - hostPath: /dev
```

```
      containerPath: /dev
      # allow Falco to use the Docker unix socket
    - hostPath: /var/run/docker.sock
      containerPath: /var/run/docker.sock
  - role: worker
    extraMounts:
      # allow Falco to use devices provided by the kernel module
    - hostPath: /dev
      containerPath: /dev
      # allow Falco to use the Docker unix socket
    - hostPath: /var/run/docker.sock
      containerPath: /var/run/docker.sock
```

Create the kind cluster by running the following command.

```
$ kind create cluster --config=./cluster.yaml
Creating cluster "kind" ...
 ✓ Ensuring node image (kindest/node:v1.32.2) 🖼
 ✓ Preparing nodes 📦 📦 📦 📦
 ✓ Writing configuration 📜
 ✓ Starting control-plane 🕹️
 ✓ Installing CNI 🔌
 ✓ Installing StorageClass 💾
 ✓ Joining worker nodes 🚜
Set kubectl context to "kind-kind"
You can now use your cluster with:

kubectl cluster-info --context kind-kind

Thanks for using kind! 😊
```

Once the cluster nodes are ready, you can use Helm to deploy Falco. If you are not familiar with Helm, please follow the instructions at https://helm.sh/docs/intro/quickstart/.

```
$ helm repo add falcosecurity https://falcosecurity.github.io/charts
helm repo update
"falcosecurity" has been added to your repositories
Hang tight while we grab the latest from your chart repositories...
...Successfully got an update from the "falcosecurity" chart
repository
Update Complete. ⎈Happy Helming!⎈
$ helm install --replace falco --namespace falco --create-namespace
--set tty=true falcosecurity/falco
NAME: falco
LAST DEPLOYED: Sun Apr 13 09:33:48 2025
NAMESPACE: falco
STATUS: deployed
```

```
REVISION: 1
TEST SUITE: None
NOTES:
Falco agents are spinning up on each node in your cluster. After a
few
seconds, they are going to start monitoring your containers looking
for
security issues.

No further action should be required.

Tip:
You can easily forward Falco events to Slack, Kafka, AWS Lambda and
more with falcosidekick.
Full list of outputs: https://github.com/falcosecurity/charts/tree/
master/charts/falcosidekick.
You can enable its deployment with `--set falcosidekick.enabled
=true` or in your values.yaml.
See: https://github.com/falcosecurity/charts/blob/master/charts/
falcosidekick/values.yaml for configuration values.
```

Validate that the Falco pods are running.

```
# kubectl get pods -n falco
NAME          READY   STATUS                 RESTARTS          AGE
falco-gtt84   2/2     Running                0                 4m52s
falco-h9v8p   2/2     Running                1 (2m38s ago)     4m52s
falco-mmcs8   2/2     Running          1 (2m28s ago)      4m52s
falco-qhmzb   2/2     Running                0                 4m52s
```

Falco File Structure

The main Falco configuration files are typically located in the **/etc/falco/** directory, irrespective of how Falco is deployed. Falco configurations and rules are managed by the following config files.

- **`falco.yaml`:** This is the primary configuration file for Falco. It controls various aspects of Falco's behavior, including:
  - **`load_rules`:** Specifies the rule files to load.
  - **`rules_directories`:** Defines directories where Falco looks for rule files.
  - **`grpc_server`:** Configuration for Falco's gRPC server (used by falcoctl and other integrations).
  - **`outputs`:** Defines where and how Falco alerts are sent (for example, stdout, syslog, file, program, gRPC).

  - **tags:** Global tags that can be used in rules.
  - **k8s_audit_log:** Configuration for consuming Kubernetes audit logs.
  - **syscall_event_buffering:** Settings related to syscall event processing.
- **falco_rules.yaml:** This file contains the default set of Falco rules provided by the Falco project. These rules cover a wide range of common security threats and best practices for Linux systems and containers. It is generally recommended not to modify this file directly.
- **falco_rules.local.yaml (or other files specified in falco.yaml):** This is where you should define your custom Falco rules or override settings from the default rules. Keeping your custom rules separate makes it easier to manage and update Falco.
- **rules.d/ (directory):** You can organize your custom rules into separate files within this directory, and then include this directory in the **load_rules** or **rules_directories** section of **falco.yaml**.

Falco Rules

Falco rules define the conditions that need to be monitored by the engine and the respective output string that will be generated if the rule is triggered. Falco rules are segregated into two categories.

- **Default Rules**

  Falco installations come pre-configured with some default rules. These rules are stored in the falco_rules.yaml file that contains a comprehensive set of rules that cover many common security scenarios. Some of these scenarios are:

  - **Shell activity in containers:** Detecting the execution of shell commands (for example, **sh**, **bash**) inside containers.
  - **Privileged containers:** Alerting on the creation or running of privileged containers.
  - **Access to sensitive files:** Monitoring attempts to read or write sensitive host files from within containers.
  - **Unexpected network connections:** Detecting containers making outbound connections to unusual ports or IP addresses.
  - **Changes to security-related binaries:** Monitoring modifications to important system binaries.
  - **Kubernetes API activity:** Detecting suspicious API calls such as the creation of privileged pods or the modification of security-sensitive resources.

Let us look at the default rule in action.

Here is a rule from the **falco_rules.yaml** file. This rule states that any attempt to read a sensitive file, defined as a list, will result in a warning. One such file is **/etc/shadow**.

```
- rule: Read sensitive file untrusted
  desc: >
    An attempt to read any sensitive file (e.g. files containing user/
password/authentication
   ...
  condition: >
    open_read
    and sensitive_files
    and proc_name_exists
    and not proc.name in (user_mgmt_binaries, userexec_binaries,
package_mgmt_binaries,
...
    and not user_read_sensitive_file_containers
  output: Sensitive file opened for reading by non-trusted program
 (file=%fd.name gparent=%proc.aname[2] ggparent=%proc.aname[3] ggg-
parent=%proc.aname[4] evt_type=%evt.type user=%user.name user_uid
=%user.uid user_loginuid=%user.loginuid process=%proc.name proc_
exepath=%proc.exepath parent=%proc.pname command=%proc.cmdline
terminal=%proc.tty %container.info)
  priority: WARNING
...
- list: sensitive_file_names
  items: [/etc/shadow, /etc/sudoers, /etc/pam.conf, /etc/security
/pwquality.conf]
```

Let us create a new nginx pod and try to open the shadow file inside the pod.

```
$ kubectl run nginx --image=nginx
pod/nginx created
# kubectl exec -it nginx -- cat /etc/shadow
root:*:20185:0:99999:7:::
daemon:*:20185:0:99999:7:::
bin:*:20185:0:99999:7:::
sys:*:20185:0:99999:7:::
...
$ kubectl logs -l app.kubernetes.io/name=falco -n falco -c falco |
grep Warning
12:24:53.055405394: Warning Sensitive file opened for reading by
non-trusted program (file=/etc/shadow gparent=<NA> ggparent=<NA>
gggparent=<NA> evt_type=openat user=root user_uid=0 user_loginuid=-1
process=cat proc_exepath=/usr/bin/cat parent=containerd-shim com-
mand=cat /etc/shadow terminal=34816 container_id=4320507cbe4f con-
tainer_image=<NA> container_image_tag=<NA> container_name=<NA> k8s_
ns=<NA> k8s_pod_name=<NA>)
```

Note: *Falco messages are outputted based on the output configuration in the* **falco.yaml** *config file. For example, if you are using Falco local installation on the Kubernetes nodes. You can view the messages generated by Falco in the OS Journal. Use the following command to list all messages generated by Falco.*

```
$ sudo journalctl -u falco
```

- **Custom Rules**

  With custom rules, you can modify Falco's detection capabilities to specify security requirements closely matching your security requirements, the behavior of your Kubernetes environment, and application. Falco rules follow a user-readable YAML format and consist of the following parts.

  - **rule:** The name of the rule (must be unique).
  - **desc:** A human-readable description of what the rule detects.
  - **condition:** A boolean expression that defines when the rule should trigger. This condition can involve system call arguments, Kubernetes API object fields, and other Falco event data.
  - **output:** The message to be included in the alert when the rule is triggered. You can use format specifiers to include relevant event data in the message.
  - **priority:** The severity level of the alert (for example, INFO, NOTICE, WARNING, ERROR, CRITICAL).
  - **tags (optional):** Labels that can be used to categorize and filter rules.

Apart from these necessary fields, you can also have one or more of the following as part of the rule definition.

- **Macros:** Macros can be defined in the custom rules file. These are reusable rule conditions that can be reused inside other rules and even other macros. Macros allow you to name common patterns, and you can avoid rewriting the same code again and again.
- **Lists:** Lists are a collection of items that can be included in other rules, macros, or even other lists. Unlike other rules and macros, lists are not parsed as filtering expressions.

Let us create a sample rule that will generate a warning for any pod that has hostNetwork set to true. Save the following rule in a file called **falco_custom_rule_cm.yaml**

```
customRules:
  custom-rules.yaml: |-
    - rule: Host Network Used Outside Allowed Namespace
        desc: Detects the creation of a Pod with hostNetwork: true
outside of the allowed kube-system namespace.
        condition: >
```

```
          k8s.pod.host_network and
          not k8s.pod.namespace = "kube-system" and
          k8s.audit.verb = "create" and
          k8s.audit.resource.resource = "pods"
      output: >
          A Pod with hostNetwork: true was created in a disallowed
namespace
          (pod=%k8s.pod.name namespace=%k8s.pod.namespace us-
er=%k8s.user.name).
      priority: WARNING
      tags: [kubernetes, hostnetwork, security]
```

Load the rule in Falco. As we are running Falco as a pod, we will update the pod definition using Helm. However, if you are using the binary, you can save the rule in a file, update the file location in the **falco.yaml** file, and reload the Falco application.

```
$ helm upgrade --namespace falco falco falcosecurity/falco --set
tty=true -f falco_custom_rule_cm.yaml
Release "falco" has been upgraded. Happy Helming!
NAME: falco
LAST DEPLOYED: Sun Apr 13 12:54:19 2025
NAMESPACE: falco
STATUS: deployed
REVISION: 2
TEST SUITE: None
NOTES:
Falco agents are spinning up on each node in your cluster. After a few
seconds, they are going to start monitoring your containers looking
for
security issues.
No further action should be required.
Tip:
You can easily forward Falco events to Slack, Kafka, AWS Lambda and
more with falcosidekick.
Full list of outputs: https://github.com/falcosecurity/charts/tree/
master/charts/falcosidekick.
You can enable its deployment with `--set falcosidekick.enabled
=true` or in your values.yaml.
See: https://github.com/falcosecurity/charts/blob/master/charts/fal-
cosidekick/values.yaml for configuration values.
```

Let us create a pod with the following definition, where we have set the **hostNetwork** switch to true.

```
apiVersion: v1
kind: Pod
metadata:
  name: host-network-pod
```

```
  namespace: default
spec:
  hostNetwork: true
  containers:
    - name: nginx
      image: nginx:latest
      ports:
        - containerPort: 8080
          hostPort: 8080

$ kubectl apply -f hostpod.yaml
pod/host-network-pod created
$ kubectl logs -l app.kubernetes.io/name=falco -n falco -c falco |
grep Warning
12:59:47.067267102:Warning Warning A Pod with hostNetwork: true
was created in a disallowed namespace (pod=host-network-pod name-
space=default user=kubectl).
```

Detecting Threats in Kubernetes Environment

Kubernetes security goes beyond individual components and requires a holistic approach. Threats can manifest at various layers of the system, and a robust security strategy must ensure that it covers detection and prevention at each level. The latest CKS curriculum defines the levels that should be protected to build a secure Kubernetes environment. In this section, we will explore the importance of this layered approach and outline the methods for identifying malicious activities targeting physical infrastructure, network, data, user, and application behavior.

In a complex distributed environment such as Kubernetes, relying on a single layer of security is inefficient, as attackers can find ways to bypass certain controls. A layered approach to security ensures that even if one of the layers fails, other layers are in place to detect and respond to threats. By implementing separate detection and prevention systems, we can increase the visibility into potential malicious activity, improve the chances of early detection, and enhance the overall security posture.

CKS curriculum does not specify any monitoring tools or prevention methods as part of this pillar, so it is assumed that having a general idea of different security best practices for different parts of the system, clubbed with the security fundamentals and tools covered so far in the previous chapters, will be sufficient. Let us take a brief look at different layers of a Kubernetes system, along with the best practices for these components.

Physical Infrastructure

The underlying physical infrastructure, servers, storage, networking hardware, and so on, is the foundation for any IT application including the Kubernetes cluster. While Kubernetes will abstract a lot of the underlying infrastructure, its security is still tied to the data center facilities availability, integrity and confidentiality. Compromise at the physical level can have disastrous consequences, potentially bypassing any higher-level security controls. Therefore, having a robust detection system for the physical layer is paramount.

Threats in the physical infrastructure can range from unauthorized physical access to hardware tampering and network attacks, which are specifically targeted at the management plane. Environmental disruptions, such as natural disasters, can also wreak havoc on the physical system. Let us look at some of the best practices when it comes to securing the physical infrastructure.

- **Hardware Monitoring:** Networking devices, servers, and storage systems make up the majority of the physical infrastructure on which all IT applications are dependent. Most modern systems these days are equipped with a Baseboard Management Controller (BMC) such as iLO, iDRAC, and IPMI. These systems provide out-of-band management capabilities. Monitoring the BMC logs for unusual login attempts, configuration changes, and firmware updates can indicate potential tampering with the system. System Event Logs (SEL) also allow us to monitor hardware errors, temperature anomalies, and unexpected reboots. These can signify a physical issue or manipulation.
- **Network Infrastructure Monitoring:** Network traffic destined for the management interfaces of the devices should also be monitored for unusual protocols, source IPs, and excessive failed login attempts. You can utilize SNMP to collect performance metrics and status information from the devices, establish a baseline, and alert on deviations that might indicate unauthorized access or denial-of-service attempts.
- **Physical Security:** Protecting the physical infrastructure also involves ensuring that only authorized actors have access to the physical hardware and data centers. Ensure that the datacenter, racks, and system access logs are regularly reviewed in the Physical Security Access Control system. Correlating these with the server access logs can form a complete picture.

CCTVs also play a vital role in securing the server roles and DC floor access. These can help identify any signs of unauthorized physical access or tampering. Automated video analytics can help identify any suspicious activity.

Network

Network is the most critical layer when it comes to distributed systems such as

Kubernetes, as these systems heavily rely on the underlying network layer for the smooth functioning of the whole system, as well as the applications hosted on these systems. If the network layer is not properly secured and monitored, it can be exploited for lateral movement, data exfiltration, and DoS attacks. Network security measures such as Network Policies, service meshes, and IDS/IPS systems can help build a robust networking layer for Kubernetes systems. Let us look at network security best practices briefly in the following sections.

- **Network Policy Monitoring and Auditing:** In the previous chapters, we had discussed how network policies can help in ensuring that the traffic flow is limited to intended audiences. However, only building the right network policies is not sufficient. We should regularly audit and verify that the network policies are correctly implemented and are restricting traffic as intended.

  We also need to ensure that any attempt by the pods to establish connections that are explicitly denied by network policies. Any unwanted network traffic can point toward a compromised container or pod. Network policy changes should also be tracked using Kubernetes audit logs to identify any unauthorized modifications.

- **Intrusion Detection Systems (IDS) and Intrusion Prevention Systems (IPS):** Although not explicitly mentioned in the exam curriculum, you can employ IDS/IPS solutions within the Kubernetes cluster network to inspect traffic between pods and services for known attack signatures and malicious patterns.

  You can also employ external IDS/IPS systems to monitor the cluster's egress points and control outbound traffic. With an external system, you can detect attempts to communicate with the cluster with known malicious command and control servers or any attempt to exfiltrate data from the cluster.

- **Network Flow Monitoring (NetFlow, IPFIX):** You can collect and analyze network flow data from the Kubernetes nodes and network infrastructure to identify unusual traffic volumes, protocols, unknown traffic destinations, or IP addresses within the cluster. Anomaly detection systems such as Falco can help you identify deviations from baseline patterns.

- **Kubernetes Audit Logs:** Kubernetes audit logs can be used to monitor for unauthorized creation and modification of services and endpoints. These endpoints can be used to redirect traffic by malicious actors. Audit logs can also help you track changes in the network policies.

Data

Almost every malicious access attempt in an IT system or application is focused on retrieving the data, this is true for Kubernetes environments as well. Data residing in the Kubernetes environment is the primary target for attackers be it from outside or within the system.

Within a Kubernetes environment, this data can reside in persistent volumes, databases running in the cluster, secrets, and even configuration maps. Data can also be in transit between applications. Threats to this data can come from unauthorized access, modification, deletion, or exfiltration. This can potentially lead to significant business and service impact. Let us look at some ways to protect data within the Kubernetes cluster.

- **Monitor Access Patterns:** Monitoring access patterns to persistent volumes is a key aspect of threat detection. You need to understand how these applications interact with the volumes and build a baseline for these access patterns. Once you have the baseline, you can identify unusual read and write activity, access from unexpected pods or users, or any attempt to modify the file permissions in a suspicious manner. Implementing file integrity monitoring (FIM) that can track changes to critical data directories within persistent volumes using Falco rules can also help detect unauthorized changes to the files.

  If you have databases running in the cluster, then enabling and actively monitoring database access logs is essential. These logs can provide insight into who is accessing the database, what queries are being executed, and whether any administrative actions are being performed that deviate from the norm. Database monitoring methods and tools will differ based on the database being used in the application, and are out of the scope of the exam.

- **Protecting Secrets and Configuration Maps:** While secrets and config maps do not contain traditional data, these often hold sensitive information such as API keys, passwords, and configuration details that could be valuable to an attacker. Kubernetes audit logs can be used to monitor access to these resources. Audit logs can help detect frequent access to the secrets by unauthorized pods and users or unexpected modification to the secrets or config maps data. These access patterns can indicate a compromised system.
- **Encryption at Rest and in-transit:** Encrypting data at rest and in-transit helps protect the data even if it is compromised, as the encrypted data is hard to decrypt without getting the right private encryption key. Monitoring the network traffic for unencrypted sensitive data or attempts to intercept encrypted communication can serve as a detection mechanism. Finally, implementing data loss prevention (DLP) tools within the Kubernetes environment can help identify and potentially block the unauthorized transfer of sensitive data, both within the cluster and to external destinations. These tools can analyze data content and context to detect policy violations and prevent data leakage.

User

Kubernetes users, including human users, service accounts and even external systems with access to the environment represent a large attack vector. Unauthorized or malicious user actions can lead to severe consequences, including data breaches, service disruption, and the compromise of the entire cluster. Weak authentication, overly permissive authorizations, and a lack of monitoring of user activities can create opportunities for attackers to gain a foothold, escalate privileges, and perform malicious actions.

Therefore, establishing robust mechanisms for authenticating, authorizing, and monitoring user interactions with the Kubernetes API and related resources is crucial for maintaining the security and integrity of the environment. Detecting threats targeting user security involves identifying anomalous or unauthorized actions performed by individuals interacting with the cluster. Following are some of the best practices that need to be implemented in order to safeguard the Kuberentes environment against malicious actors and compromised users.

- **Kubernetes Audit Log Analysis:** Kuberentes audit logs allows us to monitor all kinds of user activities, such as tracking failed login attempts, tracking successful logins coming from unusual IP addresses and outside of regular working hours. Audit logs also keep a track of users attempting to access resources which are beyond their assigned role.

  You can also use audit logs to detect attempts to modify critical RBAC objects such as `roles`, `rolebindings`, `clusterroles`, and `clusterrolebindings`. All these changes can be tracked in the logs and alerts can be configured to notify of such changes by or to the user account.

- **RBAC Monitoring and Enforcement:** In the previous chapters, we have seen that a robust RBAC mechanism can help implement the principle of least privilege. However, we still need to monitor the RBAC controls and track any and all changes to the policies. Create maps that can help track RBAC bindings and identify potential overly permissive configurations.
- **User Behavior Analytics:** Use behavioral analysis tools to create a baseline for typical user activity patterns including but not limited to the resources that they access and the type of API calls that they generally make. Use tools to track deviations from these baselines which can indicate compromised accounts or malicious insiders.

Applications

Applications tend to be the primary targets of attacks in a Kuberentes environment as these often have public endpoints which expose the application to the world either within the organization or outside. Vulnerabilities in application code or misconfigurations in the container image or runtime can be exploited to allow attacker unauthorized access to the system. This access can be used to manipulate the application data and/or disrupt services.

Since applications are the core value providers in most Kubernetes deployments, ensuring their security and implementing robust detection mechanisms for application-level threats is paramount to protecting the overall environment and the data it processes. Let us briefly look at the detection methods for application threats in Kubernetes.

- **Application Log Analysis:** Application logs can help reveal suspicious activities, errors, and even deviations from normal application behavior. Use the application logs to look for patterns such as excessive error rates, unusual HTTP status codes, unexpected user agent strings, or attempts to access sensitive endpoints.
- **Performance Monitoring:** Applications generally have predictable performance and resource usage metrics. Application monitoring tools can help gain insight into application performance metrics, transaction traces, and service dependencies. Anomalies in response times, error rates, or resource consumption for specific application components can indicate a potential attack or system compromise. Tracing requests can also help identify unusual pathways or interactions.
- **Web Application Firewalls:** For web-facing applications exposed through Kubernetes Services (such as LoadBalancer or Ingress), WAFs analyze HTTP and HTTPS traffic at the application layer. They can identify and block known web attack patterns, malicious payloads, and attempts to exploit application vulnerabilities before they reach the application.
- **Container Runtime Security:** As discussed previously, tools such as Falco monitor system calls made by processes within containers. Unusual or unexpected system call patterns originating from application containers (for example, a web server suddenly spawning shell processes or accessing sensitive host files) can indicate a compromise or malicious activity.
- **Vulnerability Scanning:** Regularly scanning running container images for known vulnerabilities (CVEs) is crucial. While static image scanning during build time is important, continuous scanning in the runtime environment can detect newly discovered vulnerabilities in already deployed images.
- **Anomaly Detection on Application Behavior:** Employing anomaly detection techniques on various application metrics (for example, request rates, user activity, data access patterns) can help identify deviations from normal behavior that might indicate an attack or a compromised application component.

Identifying Phases of Attack and Bad Actors

Effective threat detection and response to these threats in Kubernetes needs a thorough understanding of not just **what** suspicious activity is occurring but also **how** an attacker might operate and **who** the potential bad actor could be. In this section, we will dive into the typical stages of an attack within a Kubernetes environment. We will map these stages to the well-established MITRE ATT&CK framework for Kubernetes. By understanding the tactics and techniques employed by the attacker at each stage, security teams can develop more targeted detection strategies, prioritize alerts based on the overall impact, and respond more effectively to security incidents.

The MITRE ATT&CK framework provides a structured knowledge base of tactics used by attackers based on real-world observations. These behaviors are then categorized into distinct phases. These phases build the complete lifecycle of the attack from initial reconnaissance to finally achieving their objective. Aligning Kubernetes-specific attack scenarios with this framework will allow us to leverage a common language and understanding of attack behavior in cloud-native environments. You can get more details about the MITRE ATT&CK Container Matrix that covers containerized applications as well as container orchestration frameworks such as Kubernetes at https://attack.mitre.org/matrices/enterprise/containers/.

In this section, we will explore the typical attack lifecycle in Kubernetes by breaking it into phases, discussing potential attacker objectives and common techniques employed in every phase by the attacker. Let us look at the phases mentioned in the MITRE ATT&CK Containers Matrix along with the techniques used by the attacker in every phase.

Initial Access

The initial access phase describes how an attacker gains initial access in the containerized environment. The focus in this stage is on the initial intrusion that allows the attacker to execute code or gain access to the resources. An Attacker can use one or more of the following techniques in the initial stage.

- **Compromised Credentials:** An attacker may get access to valid user credentials either by social engineering, phishing, exposure through public repositories, credential theft, or interruptions. In a Kubernetes environment, this could involve stolen Kubernetes API server credentials, kubeconfig files, service account tokens, or credentials for container registries.
- **Exploit Public-Facing Application:** If applications running in containers are exposed to the internet or internal networks, vulnerabilities in these

applications (for example, web application vulnerabilities such as SQL injection or remote code execution) can be exploited to gain initial access to a container or the underlying node.

- **External Remote Services:** Adversaries might leverage vulnerabilities or misconfigurations in externally accessible services that interact with the Kubernetes environment (for example, CI/CD systems, monitoring dashboards) to pivot into the cluster.

You can employ the following prevention methods to detect and protect against initial access attempts.

- **Strong Authentication and Authorization:** A robust authentication mechanism that employs multi-factor authentication for users and service accounts and also enforces principles of least privilege with granular RBAC policies can help prevent attacks arising from compromised valid credentials.
- **Secure Credential Management:** Employ secure storage solutions for kubeconfig files and Kubernetes Secrets. Rotate API tokens and avoid embedding sensitive credentials in container images or application code.
- **Network Segmentation and Policies:** Implement Kubernetes Network Policies to restrict network access to the API server and other critical control plane components. Limit external access to application services to only necessary ports and protocols.
- **Vulnerability Management:** Establish a comprehensive vulnerability scanning program for container images throughout the CI/CD pipeline and in the runtime environment. Patch applications and underlying OS packages promptly.
- **Supply Chain Security Measures:** Implement image signing and verification, utilize trusted container registries, and generate and analyze Software Bill of Materials (SBOMs) to ensure the integrity of the software supply chain.
- **Secure Configuration of External Services:** Harden the security of any external services that interact with the Kubernetes environment and monitor their access logs for suspicious activity.

Execution

Once the attacker has gained access to the environment using the techniques mentioned in the last section, they can use any or all of the following techniques to execute malicious code in the Kubernetes environment, further cementing their access to the system and application.

- **Container Execution:** Once inside a container or with sufficient Kubernetes API access, an attacker can execute arbitrary commands within a running container using tools such as kubectl exec or by exploiting application vulnerabilities. This allows them to perform further reconnaissance, establish persistence, or execute malicious payloads.

- **Deploy Container:** Attackers with sufficient permissions can deploy new, malicious containers within the Kubernetes cluster. These containers might be designed for cryptojacking, network scanning, or establishing command and control.
- **Serverless Execution:** If the Kubernetes environment integrates with serverless platforms (for example, Knative), adversaries might leverage compromised credentials or vulnerabilities to execute malicious code within serverless functions.
- **Scheduled Task/Job:** Attackers can also leverage the task scheduler or jobs for initial and recurring attacks. These jobs or tasks can be scheduled to run on container or node startup ensuring that every new workload or node has built in access for the attacker.

Use one or more of the following prevention methods to limit the attack surface and attacker access in this phase.

- **Strict RBAC Controls:** Ability to execute commands in a container and deploy new pods/containers should be restricted to certain users, and strict RBAC should be employed for every user, and audits should be done at regular intervals to ensure that RBAC is working as expected and has not been tampered with.
- **Admission Controllers:** Implement admission controllers to enforce security policies that prevent the deployment of risky container configurations, such as privileged containers or those with excessive resource requests.
- **Network Policies:** Restrict network connections originating from newly deployed or potentially compromised containers to limit their ability to spread within the cluster.
- **Container Runtime Security:** Deploy runtime security tools such as Falco to detect unexpected process execution, system calls, or file system modifications within containers.
- **Immutable Container Design:** Architect applications to run in immutable containers, making it harder for attackers to execute persistent malicious code within them. We will be covering immutable containers in the upcoming section.
- **Security Contexts:** Enforce restrictive security contexts on pods and containers, limiting their privileges and capabilities.

Persistence

Once the attacker has gained access to the system, they would want to maintain that access. They would use the following techniques to ensure that they do not lose access across restarts, credential changes, and other disruptions. This will ensure that they can return to the system later to continue with their objectives.

- **Create Account:** Attackers with sufficient Kubernetes API privileges may create new, malicious service accounts or manipulate existing ones to maintain persistent access. These accounts can be granted broad permission to facilitate future malicious activities.
- **Modify Kubelet Configuration:** If attackers gain access to the underlying nodes and can modify the Kubelet configuration, they might be able to execute arbitrary commands on the nodes or compromise the container runtime, leading to persistent control over the worker nodes.
- **Scheduled Job/Cron Job:** Attackers can create or modify Kubernetes CronJobs to schedule the periodic execution of malicious containers or commands, ensuring that they do not lose access to the system.
- **Compromise Kube-Proxy:** By compromising the kube-proxy component, adversaries might be able to manipulate network traffic routing within the cluster, potentially redirecting sensitive data or intercepting communications for persistent control.
- **Modify Admission Controller:** If attackers can compromise or modify admission controllers, they can bypass security policies and deploy malicious resources or alter existing ones for persistent access.

You can apply the following Kubernetes best practices to prevent an attacker from gaining persistent access to the environment.

- **Strict RBAC and Auditing:** Enforce the principle of least privilege for all users and service accounts and rigorously audit all modifications to RBAC objects (**Roles**, **RoleBindings**, **ClusterRoles**, **ClusterRoleBindings**).
- **Immutable Infrastructure Practices:** Treat Kubernetes infrastructure components (including node configurations) as immutable and automate their provisioning to prevent unauthorized modifications.
- **Secure Access to Kubelet:** Restrict access to Kubelet configuration files and the Kubelet API to only authorized components. Implement strong authentication and authorization for Kubelet access.
- **Admission Controller Enforcement:** Utilize admission controllers to prevent the creation or modification of risky persistent mechanisms such as overly permissive **CronJobs** or the alteration of critical system components.
- **Regular Security Audits:** Conduct frequent security audits of Kubernetes configurations, including RBAC policies, CronJobs, and admission controller settings, to identify and remediate potential persistence mechanisms.

- **Network Segmentation:** Implement network policies to restrict access to critical control plane components such as the Kubelet and kube-proxy.

Privilege Escalation

This phase involves techniques that adversaries use to gain higher-level permissions within the Kubernetes environment, allowing them to perform actions they were not initially authorized to do.

- **Exploit Container Escape:** Attackers might exploit vulnerabilities in the container runtime (for example, Docker, containerd), the underlying kernel, or misconfigurations to escape the confines of a container and gain access to the host operating system.
- **Abuse Mounts:** Misconfigured volume mounts, particularly hostPath mounts, can allow containers to access files and directories on the underlying node. Adversaries can leverage this access to escalate privileges by modifying sensitive system files or executing commands on the host.
- **Container Service Account Token Abuse:** If a compromised container has a service account with overly permissive roles, attackers can use the container's service account token to interact with the Kubernetes API and potentially escalate their privileges within the cluster.
- **RBAC Abuse:** Attackers who have gained some level of access might leverage existing permissions to create new, more powerful RBAC roles or role bindings, effectively granting themselves higher privileges.

You can use the following prevention methods in this phase of the attack.

- **Secure Container Runtime and Kernel:** Keep the container runtime and the underlying operating system kernel up to date with the latest security patches. Implement kernel hardening measures.
- **Restrict `HostPath` Mounts:** Minimize or completely disallow the use of **`hostPath`** volumes. If necessary, restrict their usage to specific, well-understood use cases with strict access controls.
- **Principle of Least Privilege for Service Accounts:** Grant service accounts only the absolute minimum permissions required for their intended function. Regularly review and refine service account roles.
- **Robust RBAC Policies:** Implement strict RBAC policies that adhere to the principle of least privilege. Regularly audit and review RBAC configurations to identify and remediate any overly permissive roles or bindings.
- **Security Contexts:** Enforce restrictive security contexts on pods and containers, including setting **`runAsNonRoot`**, **`readOnlyRootFilesystem`**, and explicitly setting **`allowPrivilegeEscalation: false`**.

- **Admission Controllers:** Utilize admission controllers to prevent the creation of pods with risky mount configurations or security contexts.

Defense Evasion

This phase encompasses techniques that adversaries may use to avoid detection by security controls or to hinder defensive measures within the containerized environment.

- **Container Capabilities Modification:** Attackers who have compromised a container might attempt to add or remove Linux capabilities at runtime to gain additional privileges or evade security restrictions.
- **Impair Container Logs:** Adversaries may try to tamper with or delete container logs to hide their activity and hinder forensic analysis.
- **Hide Artifacts:** Attackers might attempt to delete or modify malicious containers, pods, or other Kubernetes objects to remove evidence of their presence and actions.
- **Masquerading:** Adversaries might try to blend in with legitimate activity by impersonating legitimate users, service accounts, or processes within the containerized environment.

The following are some of the prevention methods that you can employ to prevent defense evasions.

- **Immutable Containers:** Design and enforce the use of immutable containers, preventing runtime modifications to their filesystem or configuration.
- **Centralized and Secure Logging:** Forward all Kubernetes control plane logs, node logs, and container logs to a secure, centralized logging system with strong access controls and integrity checks.
- **Comprehensive Audit Logging:** Ensure that Kubernetes audit logging is enabled at an appropriate level to capture security-relevant events. Securely store and monitor these audit logs.
- **RBAC Restrictions:** Limit the ability of users and service accounts to modify container configurations or delete logs and resources.
- **File Integrity Monitoring (FIM):**Implement FIM on critical files within containers and on nodes to detect unauthorized modifications.
- **Network Policies:** Restrict network access to logging and monitoring infrastructure to prevent tampering.
- **Credential Access:** This phase focuses on techniques that might be used to steal or obtain credentials that can be used to gain further access to the Kubernetes environment, its components, or the applications running within it.

- **Container Service Account Token Stealing:** Attackers who have compromised a pod or have sufficient API access may attempt to access and exfiltrate the service account token associated with that pod. These tokens can grant access to the Kubernetes API and other resources based on the service account's RBAC roles.
- **Kubeconfig File Access:** Kubeconfig files contain credentials for accessing the Kubernetes API server. Adversaries may attempt to obtain these files from compromised developer workstations, insecure storage locations, or through social engineering.
- **Secret Extraction:** Kubernetes Secrets store sensitive information such as API keys, passwords, and TLS certificates. Attackers may target Secrets through API access or by accessing them from within compromised containers that have permission to mount them.
- **Node Credential Harvesting:** If attackers gain access to the underlying nodes, they might attempt to harvest credentials stored on the node, such as cloud provider API keys, SSH keys, or other sensitive information that could grant access to the Kubernetes environment or related infrastructure.

Here are some of the prevention methods that can be employed in this phase.

- **Principle of Least Privilege for Service Accounts:** Grant service accounts only the minimum necessary permissions required for their tasks. Avoid granting cluster-admin privileges unnecessarily.
- **Secure Secret Management:** Utilize Kubernetes Secrets securely. Consider using external secret management solutions (for example, HashiCorp Vault, AWS Secrets Manager) integrated with Kubernetes. Implement RBAC to restrict access to Secrets.
- **Restrict Access to Kubeconfig Files:** Limit access to kubeconfig files to authorized users and store them securely. Educate users on the risks of sharing or storing kubeconfig files insecurely.
- **Node Security Hardening:** Harden the security of the underlying Kubernetes nodes by limiting access, patching regularly, and removing unnecessary services. Securely manage credentials stored on the nodes.
- **Audit Logging for Credential Access:** Monitor Kubernetes audit logs for suspicious access attempts or modifications to Secrets and ServiceAccounts.
- **Network Policies:** Restrict network access from pods to the kubelet API and other node services that might expose credentials.

Discovery

This phase involves techniques that can be used to gather information about the

Kubernetes environment, its configuration, and the resources it contains. This information helps the attackers plan and execute subsequent attack phases.

- **Cluster Discovery:** Bad actors may use `kubectl` commands or the Kubernetes API to enumerate cluster resources such as pods, services, namespaces, nodes, and deployments. This helps them understand the environment's layout and identify potential targets.
- **Container Discovery:** Once inside a node or with container execution capabilities, attackers might list running containers to identify potential targets for lateral movement or further exploitation.
- **Node Discovery:** Attackers may gather information about the Kubernetes nodes, including their operating systems, kernel versions, and network configurations, to identify potential vulnerabilities or misconfigurations.
- **Service Account Discovery:** Adversaries might attempt to identify available service accounts and their associated RBAC permissions to find accounts with elevated privileges that can be abused.
- **Network Configuration Discovery:** Attackers may try to map the Kubernetes network configuration, including network policies, service IPs, and pod networking, to understand how different components communicate and identify potential pathways for lateral movement.

Use the following prevention methods against discovery phase techniques.

- **Principle of Least Privilege for RBAC:** Implement granular RBAC policies to limit the information that users and service accounts can access through the Kubernetes API. Avoid granting broad get, list, or watch permissions unnecessarily.
- **Network Policies:** Restrict network access to internal services and metadata endpoints that could reveal information about the cluster's configuration.
- **Secure Configuration of Metadata API:** If the Kubernetes metadata API is exposed, ensure appropriate authorization controls are in place to limit the information that can be accessed.
- **Limit Information Exposure:** Avoid exposing unnecessary internal details through application interfaces or error messages.
- **Audit Logging for Discovery Activities:** Monitor Kubernetes audit logs for excessive or unusual API calls related to resource enumeration.

Lateral Movement

This phase describes techniques that attackers use to move through the Kubernetes environment to gain access to other systems or resources after their initial compromise. The goal is often to reach higher-value targets or gain broader control.

- **Container Execution:** Attackers who have compromised one container might use kubectl exec or similar methods to execute commands in other containers within the same pod or different pods, potentially leveraging trust relationships or shared resources.
- **Deploy Container:** Adversaries with sufficient permission can deploy new, malicious containers in different namespaces or on different nodes to gain a foothold in other parts of the cluster.
- **SSH:** If SSH is enabled within containers or on the underlying nodes, attackers might use stolen SSH credentials or exploited vulnerabilities to move laterally between these systems.

The following are the prevention methods in this phase.

- **Strict RBAC Policies:** Implement the principle of least privilege to limit the ability of compromised entities to access resources in other namespaces or nodes. Segregate applications and workloads using namespaces and enforce strong RBAC boundaries.
- **Network Policies:** Implement strict network segmentation using Kubernetes Network Policies to prevent unauthorized communication between pods and namespaces. Follow a default-deny approach.
- **Disable Unnecessary Services:** Disable SSH and other non-essential services within containers and on the underlying nodes to reduce the attack surface.
- **Secure Container Images:** Build minimal container images that do not include unnecessary tools or services that could be leveraged for lateral movement.
- **Audit Logging for Lateral Movement:** Monitor Kubernetes audit logs for API calls indicative of lateral movement, such as executing commands in remote containers or deploying new pods in sensitive namespaces.

Impact

This phase represents the adversary's ultimate goals, such as disrupting services, destroying data, or compromising the integrity of the Kubernetes environment and its applications.

- **Denial of Service:** Attackers might attempt to disrupt the availability of applications or the Kubernetes control plane by overwhelming resources, exploiting vulnerabilities, or terminating critical components.
- **Data Destruction:** Adversaries might aim to delete or corrupt data stored within persistent volumes, databases, or other data stores accessible from the compromised environment.

- **Resource Hijacking:** Attackers could leverage compromised containers or nodes to mine cryptocurrency or perform other resource-intensive malicious activities.
- **Container Termination:** Adversaries might terminate or delete containers to disrupt services or cause instability.
- **Compromise Cloud Resources:** If the Kubernetes environment has access to underlying cloud resources, attackers might leverage compromised credentials or vulnerabilities to impact those resources.

Use the following prevention methods in this phase of the attack.

- **Resource Quotas and Limits:** Implement resource quotas and limits on namespaces and individual pods to prevent resource exhaustion and denial-of-service.
- **Network Policies for Isolation:** Use network policies to isolate critical applications and infrastructure components to limit the blast radius of a potential compromise.
- **Immutable Infrastructure:** Makes it harder for attackers to make destructive changes persist across deployments.
- **Regular Backups and Disaster Recovery:** Implement robust backup and recovery plans for critical data and Kubernetes configurations.
- **Monitoring and Alerting for Resource Usage and Availability:** Detect unusual resource consumption patterns or service disruptions that might indicate an attack.
- **Incident Response Planning:** Develop and regularly test incident response plans to effectively address and mitigate the impact of security incidents.

As evident from the above phases, techniques and prevention methods, all the topics that we have covered so far in the previous chapters such as RBAC, Network Policies, and Smaller images are aligned with the MITRE ATT&CK. Implementing these security best practices will ensure protection against different types of attacks across different attack phases.

Ensure Container Immutability

With the increasing popularity of containerized applications running in environments such as Kubernetes, the concept of immutability has gained significant traction. Immutability is a cornerstone of security and operational stability. At its core, immutability refers to the principle of "not being able to be changed after creation." When you apply this concept to containers, this means that once a container image is built and a container is built from this image, the content of this container filesystem should remain static throughout the lifecycle of this container. Any modification to the running container, especially to its core application files, libraries, or system configurations, should not be allowed and should be considered deviations from the intended state.

Container images are designed to be self-contained, reproducible units that contain the application code, dependencies, and runtime environment. This nature lends itself well to the concept of immutability. When you create a container from an image, it is created as a read-only snapshot of that image's file system along with a writable layer on top for runtime modification, such as logs and temporary files generated by the application.

This writable layer creates a potential security risk, if an attacker gains access to a running container, they can modify the files within the writable layer and even inject malicious code, alter the container and application configuration or establish persistence. These changes in the container can be difficult to track and can persist even after the container is restarted, provided the underlying writable layer persists.

While containers have a layered filesystem with a writable layer, Kubernetes provides several mechanisms and best practices to enforce and leverage immutability for enhanced security of the overall application. Let us look at some of these mechanisms.

Read-only Root Filesystem

One of the easiest and most direct methods to implement immutability at the container level is to configure the container's root filesystem to be read-only. This can be implemented through the **`securityContext`** of a pod or container specification in Kubernetes by setting the **`readOnlyRootFilesystem: true`**. When enabled, any attempt to write to the root filesystem, except predefined volumes, will result in an error. This will result in significant limitations on an attacker's ability to make persistent changes in a compromised container.

Let us build a sample pod using the **`readOnlyRootFilesystem`** and try writing a file in a volume that is not explicitly mentioned in **`volumeMounts`**. Use the following pod definition file to deploy the container.

```
apiVersion: v1
kind: Pod
metadata:
  name: readonly-nginx-pod
spec:
  containers:
    - name: nginx-container
      image: nginx:latest
      securityContext:
        readOnlyRootFilesystem: true
      ports:
```

```
          - containerPort: 80
        volumeMounts:
          - name: nginx-cache
            mountPath: /var/cache/nginx
          - name: nginx-log
            mountPath: /var/log/nginx
    volumes:
      - name: nginx-cache
        emptyDir: {}
      - name: nginx-log
        emptyDir: {}
```

```
$ kubectl apply -f readonly-nginx.yaml
pod/readonly-nginx-pod created

$ kubectl exec -it readonly-nginx-pod -- /bin/sh
# touch /var/tempfile
touch: cannot touch '/var/tempfile': Read-only file system
# touch /var/run/tempfile
#
```

As seen from the preceding example, trying to create a file in **/var/**, resulted in an error as this mountpoint was not explicitly defined. However, the same file could be created in **/var/run** as an **emptyDir** volume was mounted in that location.

When building a container with **readOnlyRootFilesystem**, make sure that you map all the requirements of the container and application to avoid application or container failures due to filesystem access issues.

Ephemeral Storage for Writes

When deploying an application in a Kubernetes pod, you might have applications that need to write temporary files or logs that are part of their lifecycle. Kubernetes provides ephemeral storage, such as **emptyDir** used in the last example. As the name suggests, ephemeral storage is temporary in nature and is tied to the pod execution; as soon as a pod is removed/deleted, any content stored in the pod is removed. You can direct any data generated during the lifecycle to ephemeral storage if it does not need to be retained past the pod lifecycle. This will ensure that the container's core filesystem remains read-only and immutable.

Let us look at the same pod that we had created in the last section. Start by listing the files in the **/var/run** location. We will also add some content to the temp file that we had created earlier.

```
$ kubectl exec -it readonly-nginx-pod -- /bin/sh
# ls /var/run
nginx.pid  secrets  tempfile
```

```
# echo "Temporary File Content" > /var/run/tempfile
# cat /var/run/tempfile
Temporary File Content
#

Now, let us delete the pod and recreate it with the same file as
earlier.
root@terrapyauto-ubuntu:~# kubectl delete -f readonly-nginx.yaml
pod "readonly-nginx-pod" deleted
root@terrapyauto-ubuntu:~# kubectl apply -f readonly-nginx.yaml
pod/readonly-nginx-pod created
root@terrapyauto-ubuntu:~# kubectl exec -it readonly-nginx-pod --
/bin/sh
# ls /var/run
nginx.pid  secrets
#
```

As we can see that after the pod was recreated, the tempfile is not retained in **/var/run**.

Using Secure Immutable Container Images

The immutability principle of container dictates that once a container image has been created and pushed to the final registry, it should never be modified. Any change that is needed in the application code, its dependencies, runtime environment, or configuration should result in the creation of a completely new image, new tag, and ideally a unique content digest.

This ensures that the image contains only the necessary components for the application. By eliminating unnecessary tools, libraries, and binaries, we can also reduce the potential attack surface.

We had also discussed the distroless images in the last chapter, distroless images also provide the basis for building immutable images and enhanced security. Distroless images do not have any shell or user interface that can be used to modify the container during runtime.

Immutable and smaller images also simplify vulnerability management. To build an immutable image, we have to have a clear understanding of software packages in the image, this will simplify the image building and scanning. If any vulnerability is detected in any of the components, we know exactly which component and image needs to be rebuilt.

Using Kubernetes Audit Logs

Kubernetes audit logs provide a chronological record of activities performed within a Kubernetes cluster. These logs meticulously document requests made to the Kubernetes API server, the responses to those requests, and the metadata associated with each event, such as the user or service account making the request, the resource being accessed or modified, and the timestamp of the action. This rich source of information is invaluable for security, compliance, operational troubleshooting, and gaining deep insights into the behavior of your Kubernetes environment. By effectively configuring, collecting, and analyzing Kubernetes audit logs, organizations can significantly enhance their security posture, improve tracking of critical events, and enable proactive monitoring for suspicious activity.

The Kubernetes API server is the central control plane component that handles all requests to interact with the cluster. The audit logging feature intercepts these requests at various stages of their processing lifecycle (for example, when the request is receaived, after the request is processed, and before the response is sent). Based on a defined audit policy, the API server generates audit events, which are then processed by an audit backend and persisted to a storage mechanism.

The audit policy dictates which events are recorded and the level of detail included in each event. This policy is highly configurable, allowing you to tailor the logging to your specific security and operational needs. You can specify rules based on users, groups, namespaces, resource types, and the verbs (actions) being performed.

Audit backends determine how the audit events are processed and stored. Kubernetes offers several built-in backends, two of the most widely used backends are:

- **log backend:** Writes audit events to a file on the API server's local filesystem. This is often used for development or smaller clusters but is not recommended for production due to scalability and reliability concerns.
- **webhook backend:** Sends audit events as HTTP POST requests to a configured external webhook endpoint. This allows for integration with centralized logging systems, SIEM platforms, or custom audit processing pipelines.

Building Custom Audit Policy

As mentioned earlier, audit policies are highly configurable and can be customized to meet your application and environment specifications. Let us build a sample audit policy file. Use the following audit file definition and save it as **`/etc/kubernetes/audit-policy.yaml`**. This path will be used in the second step when configuring the apiserver to use this policy definition.

```
apiVersion: audit.k8s.io/v1
kind: Policy
rules:
  - level: Metadata
    verbs: [ "create" ]
    resources:
```

```
      - group: ""
        resources: [ "pods" ]
  - level: Metadata
    verbs: [ "delete" ]
    resources:
      - group: ""
        resources: [ "pods" ]
```

At a high level, a policy file will have the following fields.

- **`apiVersion: audit.k8s.io/v1`**: Specifies the API version for the audit policy.
- **`kind: Policy`**: Defines this as a Kubernetes audit policy configuration.
- **`rules`**: An array of rules that define which events should be audited and at what level of detail.

Let us break down both rules from the provided audit file definition.

Rule 1: Tracking Pod Creation

- **`level: Metadata`**: This specifies the audit level for events matching this rule. Metadata level logs the request metadata (user, timestamp, resource, namespace, name) but excludes the request and response bodies. This is generally sufficient for tracking creation events without generating overly verbose logs.
- **`verbs: [ "create" ]`**: This rule will only match API requests with the verb "create".
- **`resources`**: This section specifies the Kubernetes resources that this rule applies to.
    - **`group: ""`**: An empty string indicates the core API group (for example, Pods, Services, Nodes).
    - **`resources: [ "pods" ]`**: This specifies that the rule applies specifically to "pods" resources.

Rule 2: Tracking Pod Deletion

- **`level: Metadata`**: Similar to the first rule, we are logging the metadata for pod deletion events.
- **`verbs: [ "delete" ]`**: This rule will only match API requests with the verb "delete".
- **`resources`**: This section specifies the Kubernetes resources that this rule applies to.
    - **`group: ""`**: Again, the core API group.
    - **`resources: [ "pods" ]`**: This specifies that the rule applies specifically to "pods" resources.

You can find detailed information about the audit policy and supported fields to fine-tune the policy as per your requirements at https://kubernetes.io/docs/tasks/debug/debug-cluster/audit/.

Configure Kubernetes Cluster for Audit Policy

To use a custom audit policy we need to modify the Kubernetes API server to use this audit policy. The changes are made in the kube-apiserver pod.

In a typical Kubernetes deployment, **`kube-apiserver`** is deployed as a static pod, and its manifest file is located at **`/etc/kubernetes/manifests/kube-apiserver.yaml`**. Following is a snippet of the kube-apiserver.yaml file with the added configuration parameters needed to use the defined audit policy.

```
apiVersion: v1
kind: Pod
metadata:
  annotations:
    kubeadm.kubernetes.io/kube-apiserver.advertise-address.endpoint
: 172.18.0.4:6443
  creationTimestamp: null
  labels:
    component: kube-apiserver
    tier: control-plane
  name: kube-apiserver
  namespace: kube-system
spec:
  containers:
  - command:
    - kube-apiserver
    - --allow-privileged=true
    - --authorization-mode=Node,RBAC
    - --client-ca-file=/etc/kubernetes/pki/ca.crt
    - --audit-policy-file=/etc/kubernetes/audit-policy.yaml
    - --audit-log-path=/var/log/kubernetes/kube-apiserver-audit.log
…
    volumeMounts:
      - mountPath: /etc/kubernetes/audit-policy.yaml
        name: audit
        readOnly: true
      - mountPath: /var/log/kubernetes
        name: audit-log
        readOnly: false
…
volumes:
  - name: audit
```

```
    hostPath:
      path: /etc/kubernetes/audit-policy.yaml
      type: File
  - name: audit-log
    hostPath:
      path: /var/log/kubernetes
      type: DirectoryOrCreate
...
```

Let us understand the changes made to the manifest file.

- **`--audit-policy-file`:** This switch defines the location of the audit file that we had created earlier.
- **`--audit-log-path`:** This is the location of the file where the audit logs will be saved.
- **`volume and volumemount`:** Volume and volumeMounts allow the configuration file from the control plane node to be mounted inside the kube-apiserver pod and also allow the logs to be written to a node file, which can be read from the pod itself.

After you update the file, the kube-apiserver pod will restart, wait for it to become ready, and then try creating a new pod.

```
$ kubectl run nginx –image=nginx:latest
pod/nginx created

$ less /var/log/kubernetes/kube-apiserver-audit.log
...
{"kind":"Event","apiVersion":"audit.k8s.io/v1","level":"Meta-
data","auditID":"fc11d1e5-ad1e-4251-97d6-a8ca6bb3883d","stage":
"RequestReceived","requestURI":"/api/v1/namespaces/default/
pods?fieldManager=kubectl-run","verb":"create","user":{"user-
name":"kubernetes-admin","groups":["kubeadm:cluster-admins","sys-
tem:authenticated"],"extra":{"authentication.kubernetes.io/
credential-id":["X509SHA256=a28c78e13572879c78edd4c48f17798bd4fdc-
9f39aab57552c034e2e318b1b59"]}},"sourceIPs":["172.18.0.1"],
"userAgent":"kubectl/v1.31.0 (linux/amd64) kubernetes/9edcffc",
"objectRef":{"resource":"pods","namespace":"default","apiVersion"
:"v1"},"requestReceivedTimestamp":"2025-04-14T16:55:14.694399Z",
"stageTimestamp":"2025-04-14T16:55:14.694399Z"}
{"kind":"Event","apiVersion":"audit.k8s.io/v1","level":"Meta-
data","auditID":"fc11d1e5-ad1e-4251-97d6-a8ca6bb3883d","stage":
"ResponseComplete","requestURI":"/api/v1/namespaces/default/
pods?fieldManager=kubectl-run","verb":"create","user":{"user-
name":"kubernetes-admin","groups":["kubeadm:cluster-admins","sys-
tem:authenticated"],"extra":{"authentication.kubernetes.io/cre-
dential-id":["X509SHA256=a28c78e13572879c78edd4c48f17798bd4fdc9
```

```
f39aab57552c034e2e318b1b59"]}},"sourceIPs":["172.18.0.1"],"user-
Agent":"kubectl/v1.31.0 (linux/amd64) kubernetes/9edcffc","objec-
tRef":{"resource":"pods","namespace":"default","name":"nginx","apiV-
ersion":"v1"},"responseStatus":{"metadata":{},"code":201},"reques-
tReceivedTimestamp":"2025-04-14T16:55:14.694399Z","stageTimestamp":
"2025-04-14T16:55:14.701439Z","annotations":{"authorization.k8s.io/
decision":"allow","authorization.k8s.io/reason":"RBAC: allowed by
ClusterRoleBinding \"kubeadm:cluster-admins\" of ClusterRole \"clus-
ter-admin\" to Group \"kubeadm:cluster-admins\"","pod-security.
kubernetes.io/enforce-policy":"privileged:latest"}}
```

As per the foregoing example, the pod creation log was collected in the log file stated in kube-apiserver configuration. You can define other custom audit policies and attach that by updating the kube-apiserver manifest.

Conclusion

In this chapter, we covered the critical aspects of proactively detecting threats within a Kubernetes environment. We explored the benefits of behavioral analysis using tools such as Falco and identifying anomalous activities that signature-based approaches might miss.

We also looked at the lifecycle of attacks in a Kubernetes environment, which gave us insight into various phases that an attacker might traverse and the specific best practices that we might employ to build targeted detection and prevention rules.

Finally we also got introduced to container immutability and how it can help us protect against known security threats. In the last section of the chapter, we covered how Kubernetes audit logs can help us keep track of all the activities that are happening inside the Kuberentes cluster.

This marks the end of all pillars that are covered in the CKS exam. In the next and last chapter, we will cover some practical questions to build hands-on expertise on the topics that we have covered so far.

CHAPTER 8
Practice Questions with Solutions

Introduction

In the previous chapters, we have covered all the pillars that help you secure a production-ready Kubernetes environment with a strict focus on topics included in the CKS exam curriculum.

CKS is a practical exam, and you can read as much theory on security topics as you want, but it would never be enough if you do not practice the concepts. In this chapter, we will practice what we have learned so far with practical examples. This will give you an opportunity to get hands-on experience on different security and Kubernetes topics that you are expected to encounter during the exam.

Structure

In this chapter, we will cover the following topics:

- Practice Question with Solutions
- Practice Questions

Practice Questions with Solutions

In this section, we will start by covering the practice questions that we provided in the previous chapters. In the following section, we will cover questions on every topic. There are many topics that have multiple questions on the same topic. We will not cover such questions and let you figure out the best way to solve those and practice on your own.

Question 1

Create a sample 3-tier application using the following YAML and deploy it in 3 different namespaces. Then, create a default deny network policy to restrict all traffic. Create a test pod in the backend namespace and validate that traffic from the backend to the database namespace is blocked.

Step 1. Apply the manifest file to create the namespace and sample application pods.

```
---
apiVersion: v1
kind: Namespace
metadata:
  name: frontend
  labels:
    tier: frontend
---
apiVersion: v1
kind: Namespace
metadata:
  name: backend
  labels:
    tier: backend
---
apiVersion: v1
kind: Namespace
metadata:
  name: database
  labels:
    tier: database
---
apiVersion: v1
kind: Pod
metadata:
  name: frontend-pod
  namespace: frontend
  labels:
    app: frontend
    tier: frontend
spec:
  containers:
  - name: frontend
    image: httpd:latest
    ports:
    - containerPort: 80
---
apiVersion: v1
kind: Pod
metadata:
  labels:
    app: frontend
```

```
    tier: frontend
  name: frontend-test
  namespace: frontend
spec:
  containers:
  - image: alpine:latest
    name: frontend-test
    args:
    - /bin/sh
    - -c
    - while true; do sleep 5; done;
---
apiVersion: v1
kind: Pod
metadata:
  name: backend-pod
  namespace: backend
  labels:
    app: backend
    tier: backend
spec:
  containers:
  - name: backend
    image: httpd:latest
    ports:
    - containerPort: 80
---
apiVersion: v1
kind: Pod
metadata:
  name: database-pod
  namespace: database
  labels:
    app: database
    tier: database
spec:
  containers:
  - name: database
    image: httpd:latest
    ports:
    - containerPort: 80
```

```
$ kubectl apply -f sample
namespace/frontend created
namespace/backend created
namespace/database created
```

```
pod/frontend-pod created
pod/frontend-test created
pod/backend-pod created
pod/database-pod created

% kubectl get po -n frontend -o wide
NAME            READY   STATUS    RESTARTS   AGE     IP            NODE
frontend-pod    1/1     Running   0          25m     10.0.10.114    10.0.10.14
frontend-test   1/1     Running   0          2m12s   10.0.10.117   10.0.10.238

% kubectl get po -n backend -o wide
NAME          READY   STATUS    RESTARTS   AGE   IP            NODE
backend-pod   1/1     Running   0          25m   10.0.10.148   10.0.10.194

% kubectl get po -n database -o wide
NAME           READY   STATUS    RESTARTS   AGE   IP            NODE
database-pod   1/1     Running   0          26m   10.0.10.118   10.0.10.238
```

Step 2. Create a deny-all ingress policy.

```
---
apiVersion: networking.k8s.io/v1
kind: NetworkPolicy
metadata:
  name: deny-all-ingress
  namespace: frontend
spec:
  podSelector: {}
  policyTypes:
    - Ingress
---
apiVersion: networking.k8s.io/v1
kind: NetworkPolicy
metadata:
  name: deny-all-ingress
  namespace: backend
spec:
  podSelector: {}
  policyTypes:
    - Ingress
---
apiVersion: networking.k8s.io/v1
kind: NetworkPolicy
metadata:
  name: deny-all-ingress
  namespace: database
spec:
  podSelector: {}
```

```
  policyTypes:
    - Ingress

% kubectl apply -f default-deny-np.yaml
networkpolicy.networking.k8s.io/deny-all-ingress created
networkpolicy.networking.k8s.io/deny-all-ingress created
networkpolicy.networking.k8s.io/deny-all-ingress created
```

Step 3. Create a test pod in the backend namespace.

```
apiVersion: v1
kind: Pod
metadata:
  labels:
    app: backend
    tier: backend
  name: backend-test
  namespace: backend
spec:
  containers:
  - image: alpine:latest
    name: backend-test
    args:
    - /bin/sh
    - -c
    - while true; do sleep 5; done;

$ kubectl apply -f backend-test.yaml
pod/backend-test created
```

Step 4. Test connectivity to the database pod.

```
% kubectl get po -n database -o wide
NAME          READY   STATUS    RESTARTS   AGE   IP            NODE
database-pod  1/1     Running   0          59m   10.0.10.118   10.0.10.238

% kubectl exec --stdin --tty backend-test -n backend -- /bin/sh
/ # wget --timeout=5 http://10.0.10.118
Connecting to 10.0.10.118 (10.0.10.118:80)
wget: download timed out
```

Question 2

Create a new network policy to allow traffic from pods running in the backend namespace with **tier:backend** label to the database namespace and pods with **tier:database** label. Use the backend-test pod to validate connectivity to the database pod after applying the policy.

Step 1. Create the ingress policy.

```
apiVersion: networking.k8s.io/v1
kind: NetworkPolicy
metadata:
  name: allow-frontend-to-backend
  namespace: database
spec:
  podSelector:
    matchLabels:
       tier: database
  policyTypes:
    - Ingress
  ingress:
  - from:
    - namespaceSelector:
        matchLabels:
          tier: backend
    - podSelector:
        matchLabels:
          tier: backend
    ports:
    - protocol: TCP
      port: 80

$ kubectl apply -f backend-to-database-traffic.yaml
networkpolicy.networking.k8s.io/allow-frontend-to-backend created
```

Step 2. Test the connectivity.

```
$ kubectl exec --stdin --tty backend-test -n backend -- /bin/sh
/ # wget --timeout=5 http://10.0.10.118
Connecting to 10.0.10.118 (10.0.10.118:80)
saving to 'index.html'
index.html           100% |************************************************************
***********************************************************************************
*****|    45  0:00:00 ETA
'index.html' saved
/ #
```

Question 3

In some cases, instead of blocking the ingress traffic, you might want to control the outgoing traffic. This is especially useful when you want to prevent data exfiltration. You need to use the same deployment and build the following scenario:

1. The database pod can only communicate with the backend pod; all other egress should be blocked.

2. The backend pod should only be able to communicate with the frontend pod; all other egress should be blocked.

Step 1. Create a default deny egress policy for the frontend, backend, and database namespace.

```
---
apiVersion: networking.k8s.io/v1
kind: NetworkPolicy
metadata:
  name: deny-all-egress
  namespace: frontend
spec:
  podSelector: {}
  policyTypes:
    - Egress
---
apiVersion: networking.k8s.io/v1
kind: NetworkPolicy
metadata:
  name: deny-all-egress
  namespace: backend
spec:
  podSelector: {}
  policyTypes:
    - Egress
---
apiVersion: networking.k8s.io/v1
kind: NetworkPolicy
metadata:
  name: deny-all-egress
  namespace: database
spec:
  podSelector: {}
  policyTypes:
```

- Egress

```
$ kubectl apply -f deny-egress.yaml
networkpolicy.networking.k8s.io/deny-all-egress created
networkpolicy.networking.k8s.io/deny-all-egress created
networkpolicy.networking.k8s.io/deny-all-egress created
```

Step 2: Create egress policies to allow traffic as mentioned in the question.

```
---
apiVersion: networking.k8s.io/v1
kind: NetworkPolicy
metadata:
  name: allow-database-to-backend
```

```
  namespace: database
spec:
  podSelector:
    matchLabels:
      tier: database
  policyTypes:
    - Egress
  egress:
  - to:
    - namespaceSelector:
        matchLabels:
          tier: backend
    - podSelector:
        matchLabels:
          tier: backend
---
apiVersion: networking.k8s.io/v1
kind: NetworkPolicy
metadata:
  name: allow-backend-to-frontend
  namespace: backend
spec:
  podSelector:
    matchLabels:
      tier: backend
  policyTypes:
    - Egress
  egress:
  - to:
    - namespaceSelector:
        matchLabels:
          tier: frontend
    - podSelector:
        matchLabels:
          tier: frontend
```

```
$ kubectl apply -f allow-egress.yaml
networkpolicy.networking.k8s.io/allow-database-to-backend created
networkpolicy.networking.k8s.io/allow-backend-to-frontend created
```

Step 3: Deploy a test pod in the database namespace and validate the policy.

```
apiVersion: v1
kind: Pod
metadata:
  labels:
    app: database
    tier: database
```

```
    name: database-test
    namespace: database
  spec:
    containers:
    - image: alpine:latest
      name: database-test
      args:
      - /bin/sh
      - -c
      - while true; do sleep 5; done;

$ kubectl apply -f database-sample
pod/database-test created

$ kubectl exec --stdin --tty database-test -n database -- /bin/sh
/ # wget --timeout=5 http://10.0.10.148
Connecting to 10.0.10.148 (10.0.10.148:80)
saving to 'index.html'
index.html           100% |************************************************************
***********************************|    45  0:00:00 ETA
'index.html' saved
/ # wget --timeout=5 http://10.0.10.114
Connecting to 10.0.10.114 (10.0.10.114:80)
wget: download timed out
```

Question 4

Run **kube-bench** in your Kubernetes cluster and look for the following test in the output.

```
1.1.11 Ensure that the etcd data directory permissions are set to 700 or more
restrictive (Automated)
```

Apply the accompanying recommendation for the test if the test had failed and re-run the test. Validate that the test passes.

Step 1: Run the **kube-bench** job.

```
$ kubectl apply -f https://raw.githubusercontent.com/aquasecurity/kube-bench/refs/
heads/main/job.yaml
kubectl get pods
NAME               READY   STATUS      RESTARTS   AGE
kube-bench-96d9g   0/1     Completed   0          10s
```

Step 2: Validate the test status.

```
$ kubectl logs kube-bench-96d9g | grep 1.1.11
[PASS] 1.1.11 Ensure that the etcd data directory permissions are set to 700 or more
restrictive (Automated)
```

Question 5

Following is the test result from **kube-bench** along with the recommendation to fix the warning.

```
[WARN] 1.3.1 Ensure that the --terminated-pod-gc-threshold argument is set as
appropriate (Manual)
```

Recommendation:

1.3.1 Edit the Controller Manager pod specification file **/etc/kubernetes/manifests/kube-controller-manager.yaml** on the control plane node and set the **--terminated-pod-gc-threshold** to an appropriate threshold,for example, **--terminated-pod-gc-threshold=10**

Apply the recommendation in your cluster, run **kube-bench**, and validate that the warning goes away.

Step 1. Edit the **kube-controller-manager.yaml file**.

```
$ vi /etc/kubernetes/manifests/kube-controller-manager.yaml
apiVersion: v1
kind: Pod
…
spec:
  containers:
  - command:
    - kube-controller-manager
…
    - --requestheader-client-ca-file=/etc/kubernetes/pki/front-proxy-ca.crt
    - --root-ca-file=/etc/kubernetes/pki/ca.crt
    - --service-account-private-key-file=/etc/kubernetes/pki/sa.key
    - --service-cluster-ip-range=10.96.0.0/16
    - --use-service-account-credentials=true
    - -- terminated-pod-gc-threshold=10

$ kubectl get pods -n kube-system
NAME                                        READY   STATUS    RESTARTS   AGE
coredns-668d6bf9bc-mxjv6                    1/1     Running   0          11d
coredns-668d6bf9bc-ssz9c                    1/1     Running   0          11d
etcd-kind-control-plane                     1/1     Running   0          11d
kindnet-ntzlf                               1/1     Running   0          11d
kube-apiserver-kind-control-plane           1/1     Running   0          11d
kube-controller-manager-kind-control-plane  1/1     Running   0          15s
kube-proxy-njbqd                            1/1     Running   0          11d
kube-scheduler-kind-control-plane           1/1     Running   0          11d
```

Step 2. Run **kube-bench** again and validate the result.

```
$ kubectl apply -f job.yaml
job.batch/kube-bench created
$ kubectl get pods
NAME                READY   STATUS      RESTARTS   AGE
kube-bench-28xlb    0/1     Completed   0          4s

$ kubectl logs kube-bench-28xlb   | grep 1.3.1
[PASS] 1.3.1 Ensure that the --terminated-pod-gc-threshold argument is set as
appropriate (Manual)
```

Question 6

Deploy a pod named webpage, use **httpd:latest** image. Expose this pod via a load balancer service named **webpage-service**. Create a new TLS Certificate and Key with CNAME **webpage.localhost**, and use the generated certificate and key to create a new **tls** secret using the YAML file. Create a new ingress object and use this TLS secret in the ingress. Validate the connection over https to the ingress and backend service.

Step 1: Deploy the pod and the service.

```
---
apiVersion: v1
kind: Pod
metadata:
  name: webpage
  labels:
    app: webpage
spec:
  containers:
  - name: webpage
    image: httpd:latest
    ports:
    - containerPort: 80

---
apiVersion: v1
kind: Pod
metadata:
  name: webpage
  labels:
    app: webpage
spec:
  containers:
  - name: webpage
```

```
    image: httpd:latest
    ports:
    - containerPort: 80

$ kubectl apply -f pod-service.yaml
pod/webpage created
pod/webpage created
```

Step 2: Generate certificate.

```
$ openssl req -x509 -nodes -days 365 -newkey rsa:2048 -keyout webpage.key -out
webpage.crt -subj "/CN=webpage.local/O=webpage"
```

Step 3: Create webpage-tls-secret.

```
$ kubectl create secret tls webpage-tls-secret --key=webpage.key --cert=webpage.crt
secret/webpage-tls-secret created
```

Step 4: Create ingress and test the connection.

```
apiVersion: networking.k8s.io/v1
kind: Ingress
metadata:
  name: webpage-ingress
  annotations:
    nginx.ingress.kubernetes.io/rewrite-target: /
spec:
  tls:
  - hosts:
    - webpage.localhost
    secretName: webpage-tls-secret
  rules:
  - host: webpage.localhost
    http:
      paths:
      - path: /
        pathType: Prefix
        backend:
          service:
            name: webpage-service
            port:
              number: 80

$ kubectl apply -f webpage-ingress.yaml
ingress.networking.k8s.io/webpage-ingress created

$ kubectl get ingress
NAME              CLASS   HOSTS               ADDRESS        PORTS     AGE
webpage-ingress   nginx   webpage.localhost   192.168.49.3   80, 443   72s

% curl -vvv -k https://192.168.49.3/
```

```
* Host 192.168.49.3:443 was resolved.
* Connected to 192.168.49.3 (127.0.0.1) port 443
* ALPN: curl offers h2,http/1.1
* (304) (OUT), TLS handshake, Client hello (1):
* (304) (IN), TLS handshake, Server hello (2):
* (304) (IN), TLS handshake, Unknown (8):
* (304) (IN), TLS handshake, Certificate (11):
* (304) (IN), TLS handshake, CERT verify (15):
* (304) (IN), TLS handshake, Finished (20):
* (304) (OUT), TLS handshake, Finished (20):
* SSL connection using TLSv1.3 / AEAD-CHACHA20-POLY1305-SHA256 / [blank] / UNDEF
* ALPN: server accepted h2
* Server certificate:
*  subject: CN=TRAEFIK DEFAULT CERT
*  start date: Apr 13 11:00:24 2025 GMT
*  expire date: Apr 13 11:00:24 2026 GMT
*  issuer: CN=TRAEFIK DEFAULT CERT
*  SSL certificate verify result: unable to get local issuer certificate (20), continuing
anyway.
* using HTTP/2
* [HTTP/2] [1] OPENED stream for https://webpage.localhost/
* [HTTP/2] [1] [:method: GET]
* [HTTP/2] [1] [:scheme: https]
* [HTTP/2] [1] [:authority: webpage.localhost]
* [HTTP/2] [1] [:path: /]
* [HTTP/2] [1] [user-agent: curl/8.7.1]
* [HTTP/2] [1] [accept: */*]
> GET / HTTP/2
> Host: webpage.localhost
> User-Agent: curl/8.7.1
> Accept: */*
>
* Request completely sent off
< HTTP/2 404
< content-type: text/plain; charset=utf-8
< x-content-type-options: nosniff
< content-length: 19
< date: Mon, 30 Dec 2024 16:45:40 GMT
<
* Connection #0 to host webpage.localhost left intact
```

Question 7

Create an egress network policy that blocks all traffic to IP address 169.254.169.254 from frontend and backend namespaces.

Step 1: Create the policy definition and create the policies.

```
---
apiVersion: networking.k8s.io/v1
kind: NetworkPolicy
metadata:
  name: deny-single-ip
  namespace: backend
spec:
  podSelector: {}
  policyTypes:
    - Egress
  egress:
  - to:
    - ipBlock:
        cidr: 169.254.169.254/32
---
apiVersion: networking.k8s.io/v1
kind: NetworkPolicy
metadata:
  name: deny-single-ip
  namespace: frontend
spec:
  podSelector: {}
  policyTypes:
    - Egress
  egress:
  - to:
    - ipBlock:
        cidr: 169.254.169.254/32

$ kubectl apply -f singleIP-policy.yaml
networkpolicy.networking.k8s.io/deny-single-ip created
networkpolicy.networking.k8s.io/deny-single-ip created
/ # wget --timeout=5 http://169.254.169.254
Connecting to 169.254.169.254 (169.254.169.254:80)
wget: download timed out
/ # wget --timeout=5 https://169.254.169.254
Connecting to 169.254.169.254 (169.254.169.254:443)
wget: download timed out
```

Question 8

A new developer in your team named mob-dev needs view, create, update, and delete permissions on the namespace mobile-app. Start by creating the CSR, certificate, roles, and role bindings for the user and test that the user can only perform operations in the mobile-app namespace.

Step 1: Generate user key and CSR.

```
$ openssl genrsa -out mob-dev.key 2048
$ openssl req -new -key mob-dev.key -out mob-dev.csr
You are about to be asked to enter information that will be incorporated
into your certificate request.
What you are about to enter is what is called a Distinguished Name or a DN.
There are quite a few fields but you can leave some blank
For some fields there will be a default value,
If you enter '.', the field will be left blank.
-----
Country Name (2 letter code) [AU]:
State or Province Name (full name) [Some-State]:
Locality Name (eg, city) []:
Organization Name (eg, company) [Internet Widgits Pty Ltd]:Lab
Organizational Unit Name (eg, section) []:TestPrep
Common Name (e.g. server FQDN or YOUR name) []:mob-dev
Email Address []:mob-dev@cksprep.local

Please enter the following 'extra' attributes
to be sent with your certificate request
A challenge password []:
An optional company name []:
```

Step 2: Generate CSR.

```
cat mob-dev.csr | base64 | tr -d "\n"
LS0tLS1CRUdJTiBDRVJUSUZJQ0FURSBSRVFVRVNULS0tLS0KTUlJQ3dEQ0NBYWdDQVFBd2V6RUxNQWtHQT-
FVRUJoTUNRVlV4RXpBUkJnTlZCQWdNQ2xOdmJXVXRVM1JoZEdVeAp…

$ cat <<EOF | kubectl aroot@terrapyauto-ubuntu:~# cat <<EOF | kubectl apply -f -
apiVersion: certificates.k8s.io/v1
kind: CertificateSigningRequest
metadata:
  name: mob-dev
spec:
  request: LS0tLS1CRUdJTiBDRVJUSUZJQ0FURSBSRVFVRVNULS0tLS0KTUlJQ3dEQ0NBYWdDQVFBd-
2V6RUxNQWtHQTFVRUJoTUNRVlV4RXpBUkJnTlZCQWdNQ2xOdmJXVXRVM1JoZEdVeAp…
  signerName: kubernetes.io/kube-apiserver-client
  expirationSeconds: 86400  # one day
  usages:
  - client auth
EOF
certificatesigningrequest.certificates.k8s.io/mob-dev created
```

Step 3: Sign CSR and create user context in **Kubeconfig** file

```
$ kubectl get csr
NAME        AGE    SIGNERNAME                                      REQUESTOR
REQUESTEDDURATION   CONDITION
mob-dev     102s   kubernetes.io/kube-apiserver-client             kubernetes-admin
24h                 Pending

$ kubectl certificate approve mob-dev
certificatesigningrequest.certificates.k8s.io/mob-dev approved

$  kubectl get csr fin-dev -o jsonpath={.status.certificate} | base64 -d > mob-dev.crt

$ kubectl config set-context mob-dev --user=mob-dev --cluster=kind-kind
Context "mob-dev" created.
```

Step 4: Create Role, RoleBinding, and test the permissions.

```
$ kubectl create role mob-dev-role --verb=get --verb=create --verb=update --verb=
delete --resource=pods --namespace=mobile-app
role.rbac.authorization.k8s.io/mob-dev-role created

$ kubectl create rolebinding mob-dev-binding --role=mob-dev-role --user=mob-dev -n=
mobile-app
rolebinding.rbac.authorization.k8s.io/mob-dev-binding created

$ kubectl config use-context mob-dev
Switched to context "mob-dev"

$ kubectl run nginx-test --image=nginx -n frontend
Error from server (Forbidden): pods is forbidden: User "mob-dev" cannot create
resource "pods" in API group "" in the namespace "frontend"

$ kubectl run nginx-test --image=nginx -n mobile-app
pod/nginx-test created

$ kubectl get pod nginx-test -n mobile-app
NAME         READY   STATUS    RESTARTS   AGE
nginx-test   1/1     Running   0          11s
```

Question 9

Create a new pod named **`sa-test-1`** in the sa-demo namespace. The pod should have permissions to view pods, services, configmaps, and secrets. Create a new **`serviceAccount`**, role, and role binding when solving the question.

Step 1: Create the namespace and service account.

```
$ kubectl create ns sa-demo
namespace/sa-demo created
$ kubectl create serviceaccount sa-test-demo -n sa-demo
serviceaccount/sa-test-demo created
```

Step 2: Create the role and role binding for the service account.

```
---
apiVersion: rbac.authorization.k8s.io/v1
kind: Role
metadata:
  name: sa-test-role
  namespace: sa-demo
rules:
- apiGroups: [""]
  resources: ["pods", "services", "configmaps", "secrets"]
  verbs: ["get", "list", "watch"]
---

apiVersion: rbac.authorization.k8s.io/v1
kind: RoleBinding
metadata:
  name: sa-test-rolebinding
  namespace: sa-demo
subjects:
- kind: ServiceAccount
  name: sa-test-demo
  namespace: sa-demo
roleRef:
  kind: Role
  name: sa-test-role
  apiGroup: rbac.authorization.k8s.io

$ kubectl apply -f sa-role.yaml
role.rbac.authorization.k8s.io/sa-test-role created
rolebinding.rbac.authorization.k8s.io/sa-test-rolebinding created
```

Step 3: Create the pod with service account and test the permissions.

```
apiVersion: v1
kind: Pod
metadata:
  name: sa-test-1
  namespace: sa-demo
spec:
  serviceAccountName: sa-test-demo
  containers:
```

```
  - name: sa-test-1
    image: nginx:latest

$ kubectl apply -f sa-demo-pod
pod/sa-test-1 created

$ kubectl exec -it sa-test-1 -n sa-demo -- /bin/bash

root@sa-test-1:/# curl -s -k -m 5 -H "Authorization: Bearer $(cat /var/run/secrets/
kubernetes.io/serviceaccount/token)" https://kubernetes.default.svc.cluster.local/api/
v1/namespaces/sa-demo/pods
{
  "kind": "PodList",
  "apiVersion": "v1",
  "metadata": {
    "resourceVersion": "13416"
  },
  "items": [
    {
      "metadata": {
        "name": "sa-test-1",
        "namespace": "sa-demo",
        "uid": "736e6222-5775-41ef-ac6f-cde998bbb7ad",
        "resourceVersion": "13325",
        "creationTimestamp": "2025-04-26T17:15:58Z",
        "annotations": {
          "kubectl.kubernetes.io/last-applied-configuration":
…
                    "f:terminationMessagePolicy": {}
"qosClass": "BestEffort"
      }
    }
  ]
}
```

Question 10

You need to create a new service account named **secret-view-sa**, which can list other service accounts and secrets in the cluster across all namespaces. You also need to create a secret name **view-sa-secret** for the service account, which will hold the service account token, and lastly, extract the token from the secret and validate that you can list the secrets in the cluster via curl.

Step 1: Create the **serviceaccount**, **clusterrole**, and **clusterrolebinding**. We will use the following YAML for the cluster role.

```
apiVersion: rbac.authorization.k8s.io/v1
kind: ClusterRole
metadata:
  name: secret-view-clusterrole
rules:
- apiGroups: [""]
  resources: ["serviceaccounts", "secrets"]
  verbs: ["list"]

$ kubectl apply -f clusterrole.yaml
clusterrole.rbac.authorization.k8s.io/secret-view-clusterrole created

$ kubectl create serviceaccount secret-view-sa
serviceaccount/secret-view-sa created

$ # kubectl create clusterrolebinding secret-view-binding --clusterrole=se-
cret-view-clusterrole --serviceaccount=default:secret-view-sa
clusterrolebinding.rbac.authorization.k8s.io/secret-view-binding created
```

Step 2: Create the secret token and validate access.

```
$ kubectl apply -f - <<EOF
apiVersion: v1
kind: Secret
metadata:
  name: sa-view-secret
  annotations:
    kubernetes.io/service-account.name: secret-view-sa
type: kubernetes.io/service-account-token
EOF
secret/sa-view-secret created


$ TOKEN=$(kubectl get secret sa-view-secret -o jsonpath='{.data.token}' | base64 -d)
$ APISERVER=$(kubectl config view --minify -o jsonpath='{.clusters[0].cluster.server}')
$ curl -s -k -H "Authorization: Bearer $TOKEN" $APISERVER/api/v1/secrets | jq .
{
  "kind": "SecretList",
  "apiVersion": "v1",
  "metadata": {
    "resourceVersion": "15088"
  },
  "items": [
    {
      "metadata": {
```

```
        "name": "sa-view-secret",
        "namespace": "default",
        "uid": "d939fbc6-c4d4-42ec-83f1-0e6b918760a2",
        "resourceVersion": "15088",
        "creationTimestamp": "2025-04-26T17:34:33Z",
        "labels": {
          "kubernetes.io/legacy-token-last-used": "2025-04-26"
        },
        "annotations": {
          "kubectl.kubernetes.io/last-applied-configuration": "{\"apiVersion
\":\"v1\",\"kind\":\"Secret\",\"metadata\":{\"annotations\":{\"kubernetes.io/
service-account.name\":\"secret-view-sa\"},\"name\":\"sa-view-secret\",\"name-
space\":\"default\"},\"type\":\"kubernetes.io/service-account-token\"}\n",
          "kubernetes.io/service-account.name": "secret-view-sa",
          "kubernetes.io/service-account.uid": "e787b273-c58e-4457-aeeb-8498dd4c2eb9"
…
```

Question 11

Create a new namespace called **secure-app**, within the namespace, all pods must adhere to the **restricted** PSS. Once you have the namespace, try deploying a new pod with **`allowPrivilegeEscalation: true`.** Verify the behavior and fix the deployment error.

Step 1: Create a namespace with restricted PSS in enforce mode.

```
apiVersion: v1
kind: Namespace
metadata:
  name: secure-app
  labels:
    pod-security.kubernetes.io/enforce: restricted

$ kubectl apply -f secure-app-ns
namespace/secure-app created
```

Step 2: Deploy pod with privilege escalation.

```
apiVersion: v1
kind: Pod
metadata:
  name: secure-app
  namespace: secure-app
spec:
  containers:
  - image: busybox:latest
    name: busybox-enforce-restrict
    command: ["sh", "-c", "sleep 3600"]
    securityContext:
```

```
      allowPrivilegeEscalation: true

$ kubectl apply -f secure-app
Error from server (Forbidden): error when creating "secure-app": pods "secure-app" is
forbidden: violates PodSecurity "restricted:latest": allowPrivilegeEscalation != false
(container "busybox-enforce-restrict" must set securityContext.allowPrivilegeEscala-
tion=false), unrestricted capabilities (container "busybox-enforce-restrict" must set
securityContext.capabilities.drop=["ALL"]), runAsNonRoot != true (pod or container
"busybox-enforce-restrict" must set securityContext.runAsNonRoot=true), seccompProfile
(pod or container "busybox-enforce-restrict" must set securityContext.seccompProfile.
type to "RuntimeDefault" or "Localhost")
```

Step 3: Update the manifest and redeploy.

```
apiVersion: v1
kind: Pod
metadata:
  name: busybox-enforce-restrict
  namespace: psa-enforce-restrict
spec:
  containers:
  - image: busybox:latest
    name: busybox-enforce-restrict
    command: ["sh", "-c", "sleep 3600"]
    securityContext:
      allowPrivilegeEscalation: false
      capabilities:
        drop: ["ALL"]
      runAsNonRoot: true
      seccompProfile:
        type: RuntimeDefault

$ kubectl apply -f secure-app
pod/busybox-enforce-restrict created
```

Question 12

Create a new secret **cks-test** with the following variables:

```
Username=myuser
Password=mypassword
```

Create a new pod with **`busybox:latest`** image, mount the **`cks-test`** secret inside the pod using two **environment variables** named **`USERNAME`** and **`PASSWORD`**, respectively. Open a shell to the pod and print the environment variable on the screen.

Step 1: Create the secret.

```
$ echo -n 'myuser' | base64
bXl1c2Vy
$ echo -n 'password' | base64
cGFzc3dvcmQ=

apiVersion: v1
kind: Secret
metadata:
  name: cks-test
type: Opaque
data:
  username: bXl1c2Vy
  password: cGFzc3dvcmQ=

$ kubectl apply -f secret
secret/cks-test created
```

Step 2: Create the pod with secret mounted as environment variables.

```
apiVersion: v1
kind: Pod
metadata:
  name: secret-pod
  namespace: default
spec:
  containers:
  - name: secret-container
    image: busybox:latest
    command: [«/bin/sh", "-c", "sleep 3600"]
    env:
    - name: USERNAME
      valueFrom:
        secretKeyRef:
          name: cks-test
          key: username
    - name: PASSWORD
      valueFrom:
        secretKeyRef:
          name: cks-test
          key: password

$ kubectl apply -f secret-pod
pod/secret-pod created

$ kubectl exec -it secret-pod -- /bin/sh
/ # echo $USERNAME
```

```
myuser
/ # echo $PASSWORD
password
```

Question 13

Use the following YAML definition file and scan it with **kubesec**. The scan should result in an overall negative score. Fix the observation from the scan to achieve an overall positive score.

```
apiVersion: apps/v1
kind: Deployment
metadata:
  name: insecure-app
spec:
  replicas: 1
  selector:
    matchLabels:
      app: insecure-app
  template:
    metadata:
      labels:
        app: insecure-app
    spec:
      containers:
        - name: insecure-container
          image: nginx:latest
          securityContext:
            privileged: true
            allowPrivilegeEscalation: true
          ports:
            - containerPort: 80
              hostPort: 8080
          resources:
            limits:
              cpu: "1"
              memory: "1Gi"
            requests:
              cpu: "500m"
              memory: "512Mi"
```

Step 1: Scan the file with **kubesec**.

```
# kubesec scan insecure-app
[
  {
    "object": "Deployment/insecure-app.default",
    "valid": true,
```

```
      "fileName": "insecure-app",
      "message": "Failed with a score of -33 points",
      "score": -33,
      "scoring": {
        "critical": [
          {
            "id": "Privileged",
            "selector": "containers[] .securityContext .privileged == true",
            "reason": "Privileged containers can allow almost completely unrestricted
host access",
            "points": -30
          },
          {
            "id": "AllowPrivilegeEscalation",
            "selector": "containers[] .securityContext .allowPrivilegeEscalation ==
true",
            "reason": "Ensure a non-root process can not gain more privileges",
            "points": -7
          }
        ],
```

Step 2: Update the YAML file.

```
apiVersion: apps/v1
kind: Deployment
metadata:
  name: insecure-app
spec:
  replicas: 1
  selector:
    matchLabels:
      app: insecure-app
  template:
    metadata:
      labels:
        app: insecure-app
    spec:
      containers:
        - name: insecure-container
          image: nginx:latest
          securityContext:
            privileged: false
            allowPrivilegeEscalation: false
          ports:
            - containerPort: 80
              hostPort: 8080
          resources:
            limits:
```

```
            cpu: "1"
            memory: "1Gi"
          requests:
            cpu: "500m"
            memory: "512Mi"

$ kubesec scan insecure-app
[
  {
    "object": "Deployment/insecure-app.default",
    "valid": true,
    "fileName": "insecure-app",
    "message": "Passed with a score of 4 points",
    "score": 4,
    "scoring": {
      "passed": [
        {
          "id": "LimitsCPU",
          "selector": "containers[] .resources .limits .cpu",
          "reason": "Enforcing CPU limits prevents DOS via resource exhaustion",
          "points": 1
        },
        {
          "id": "LimitsMemory",
          "selector": "containers[] .resources .limits .memory",
          "reason": "Enforcing memory limits prevents DOS via resource exhaustion",
          "points": 1
        },
        {
          "id": "RequestsCPU",
          "selector": "containers[] .resources .requests .cpu",
          "reason": "Enforcing CPU requests aids a fair balancing of resources across
the cluster",
          "points": 1
        },
        {
          "id": "RequestsMemory",
          "selector": "containers[] .resources .requests .memory",
          "reason": "Enforcing memory requests aids a fair balancing of resources
across the cluster",
          "points": 1
        }
      ],
…
```

Question 14

Use the following deployment manifest file and scan it with **`kube-linter`**. Apply the scan recommendations to fix all the observations.

```
apiVersion: apps/v1
kind: Deployment
metadata:
  name: insecure-app
spec:
  replicas: 1
  selector:
    matchLabels:
      app: insecure-app
  template:
    metadata:
      labels:
        app: insecure-app
    spec:
      containers:
        - name: insecure-container
          image: nginx:latest
          securityContext:
            privileged: true
            allowPrivilegeEscalation: true
          ports:
            - containerPort: 80
              hostPort: 8080
          resources:
            limits:
              cpu: "1"
              memory: "1Gi"
            requests:
              cpu: "500m"
              memory: "512Mi"
```

Step 1: Scan the deployment file.

```
$ kube-linter lint insecure-deployment.yaml
KubeLinter 0.7.2

/root/insecure-deployment.yaml: (object: <no namespace>/insecure-app apps/v1, Kind=De-
ployment) The container "insecure-container" is using an invalid container image,
"nginx:latest". Please use images that are not blocked by the `BlockList` criteria :
[".*:(latest)$" "^[^:]*$" "(.*/[^:]+)$"] (check: latest-tag, remediation: Use a con-
tainer image with a specific tag other than latest.)

/root/insecure-deployment.yaml: (object: <no namespace>/insecure-app apps/v1, Kind=De-
```

```
ployment) container "insecure-container" does not have a read-only root file system
(check: no-read-only-root-fs, remediation: Set readOnlyRootFilesystem to true in the
container securityContext.)

/root/insecure-deployment.yaml: (object: <no namespace>/insecure-app apps/v1, Kind=De-
ployment) container "insecure-container" has AllowPrivilegeEscalation set to true.
(check: privilege-escalation-container, remediation: Ensure containers do not al-
low privilege escalation by setting allowPrivilegeEscalation=false, privileged=false
and removing CAP_SYS_ADMIN capability. See https://kubernetes.io/docs/tasks/config-
ure-pod-container/security-context/ for more details.)

/root/insecure-deployment.yaml: (object: <no namespace>/insecure-app apps/v1, Kind=De-
ployment) container "insecure-container" is privileged (check: privileged-container,
remediation: Do not run your container as privileged unless it is required.)

/root/insecure-deployment.yaml: (object: <no namespace>/insecure-app apps/v1, Kind=De-
ployment) container "insecure-container" is not set to runAsNonRoot (check: run-as-
non-root, remediation: Set runAsUser to a non-zero number and runAsNonRoot to true in
your pod or container securityContext. Refer to https://kubernetes.io/docs/tasks/con-
figure-pod-container/security-context/ for details.)

Error: found 5 lint errors
```

Step 2: Update the deployment manifest and re-run the linter scan.

```
apiVersion: apps/v1
kind: Deployment
metadata:
  name: insecure-app
spec:
  replicas: 1
  selector:
    matchLabels:
      app: insecure-app
  template:
    metadata:
      labels:
        app: insecure-app
    spec:
      containers:
        - name: insecure-container
          image: nginx:1.23.0
          securityContext:
            privileged: false
            allowPrivilegeEscalation: false
            privileged: false
            runAsUser: 1000
            runAsNonRoot: true
```

```
          readOnlyRootFilesystem: true
        ports:
          - containerPort: 80
            hostPort: 8080
        resources:
          limits:
            cpu: "1"
            memory: "1Gi"
          requests:
            cpu: "500m"
            memory: "512Mi"

$ kube-linter lint insecure-deployment.yaml
KubeLinter 0.7.2

No lint errors found!
```

Practice Questions

1. Create 3 namespaces called frontend, backend, and database. Deploy a pod named **`backend-test`** in the backend namespace using **`alpine:latest`** image. Open an interactive shell to this pod. Check whether you can connect to the database pod from the backend-test pod.

2. Namespaces, with the right policies in place, can be used to isolate the workloads and share the cluster resources with multiple users. You need to implement the following scenario and use test pods to validate the policies.
   - All the pods in the frontend namespace should be able to communicate with and only with all pods in the backend namespace.
   - All the pods in the backend namespace should be able to communicate with and only with all the pods in the database namespace.
   - All other ingress and egress to/from the backend and database namespaces should be blocked.

3. Assume you are installing **`kubelet`** on a new node. Download the latest version of **`kubelet`** and validate its checksum to ensure that the file has not been tampered with.

4. Create a new namespace called practice. Create a default-deny **`NetworkPolicy`** name default-deny. The policy should deny all egress traffic from the namespace practice.

5. You need to ensure that anonymous access to the API server is not enabled. Update the API Server Configuration file to use the following flag.

   ```
   --anonymous-auth=false
   ```

6. Create a new namespace called development, create a new Deployment with **`busybox:latest`** image, set the replica count to 3. Create a new **serviceAccount**, **Role**, and **Rolebinding** for Kubernetes Dashboard. Ensure that the **serviceAccount** only has read-only access to resources deployed in the development namespace.

7. Download the binary for **`kubeadm`**, download the checksum for **`kubeadm`**, and validate the checksum for the file. Write the result in a text file called **`checksum_result.txt`**.

8. You are onboarding a new member, Sneha, to your team. Sneha is joining as a Kubernetes administrator and will be responsible for managing the production Kubernetes cluster. As part of the onboarding process, you need to create a new private key, certificate, and a new **`kubeconfig`** file with a default context for her. Use the following details when creating the mentioned objects.

    - Private key length should be 2048
    - Private key file should be named **`sneha_admin.key`**
    - You must also generate a new Certificate Signing Request (CSR) and set the subject name to sneha_k8admin.
    - Use the CSR to generate a new certificate and **`kubeconfig`** file, which can be shared with Sneha.
    - Make sure that there is only 1 context in the new **`kubeconfig`** file.

9. You are responsible for managing and monitoring the production Kubernetes cluster for your organization, and as part of operational streamlining efforts, you are implementing a new monitoring solution. The solution runs as an external service for fault tolerance and needs a service account to read all the cluster resources. You need to create a new service account named **`k8s-monitoring-sa`**. As the account will be used by an external application, you need to disable the token automounting at the service account level. You also need to generate a new secret for the service account to hold the service account token; the secret will be named **`monitoring-sa-token`**. Once you have the secret, extract the token from the secret and save it in a file named **`service-account-token.txt`**.

10. Let us build on our last question, you should now have a service account **`k8s-monitoring-sa`**, you need to build a new role with get, list, and view permissions for all pods, deployments, replicasets, services, configmaps, and volumes in the cluster. Assign this role to the service account and use the token from the last question to validate whether all operations are working. Also make sure that the service account cannot get the secrets.

11. You are given admin access to a new **Kuberentes** cluster, you need to share the access with a new user who has joined your team. Your task is to first create a new SSH key, CSR, and certificate. The user is named mark.

12. New user mark from the last question needs to be able to list all the pods, services, configmaps, secrets, volumes, and volumeclaims. He should also be able to get the details of individual objects if needed. Create a new cluster-wide role and rolebinding with name **admin-view-role** and **admin-view-rolebinding** for mark. Validate the rolebinding by getting the details of any configmap in the default namespace.

13. Create a new service account named audit-view, which has view-only permissions on all objects in the cluster. Validate the permissions of the service account by mapping it to a new nginx pod and running a curl command from inside the container to list all the services in the cluster.

14. Create a new nginx pod and map the audit-view service account to the pod. Make sure that **automounttoken** is disabled for the pod. Once the pod is up, run the same curl command to list all services from inside the container.

15. Create a new Kubernetes cluster with v1.30. Practice upgrading this cluster to the latest available release. You might have to perform the upgrade more than once depending on the latest Kubernetes release.

16. Use Seccomp audit profile to identify **syscalls** needed to run the following pod.

```
apiVersion: v1
kind: Pod
metadata:
  name: audit-syscall
spec:
  securityContext:
    seccompProfile:
      type: Localhost
      localhostProfile: audit.json
  containers:
  - name: audit-syscall
    image: busybox:1.28
    command: [ "sh", "-c", "echo 'Using audit Seccomp Profile!' && sleep 1h" ]
   securityContext:
     allowPrivilegeEscalation: false
```

17. Create a custom Seccomp profile to only allow **syscalls** identified in the last question. Apply default deny and the custom Seccomp profile, and make sure that the pod can run.

18. Create a new namespace called dev-test, and apply the baseline standard in audit mode. After the namespace has been created, try to deploy a new pod with security context **runAsUser: 0** in the same namespace. Validate the behavior of the deployment. Also, confirm that the pod has been created with the audit annotation matching the PSS profile and mode.
19. Create a new namespace called **migration-test**. Apply the PSS policy and PSA mode on the namespace which will warn the users when they deploy a mode which is violating the baseline Pod Security Standard.
20. Create a new image pull secret to pull images from the docker registry using your own credentials, use the **imagepullsecret** and create a new pod with the **nginx:latest** image.
21. Create a new secret name **db_creds**, the secret should have two values, **DB_USER=mydbuser** and **DB_PASSWORD=mydbpassword**. After creating the secret, mount the secret in a new busybox pod, and use the sleep command to keep the pod from exiting. After the pod is ready, read the secret directly from the **etcd** store.
22. Create a new container named **kata-pod** with **busybox:latest** image and **kata runtimeclass**. Use the sleep command in the pod to prevent the pod from exiting.
23. You need to verify that the pod is running in a lightweight VM. One way to do this is to look at the kernel version of the container by running the **uname** command. Your task is to confirm that the worker node kernel version and the kernel version seen by the container are different.

Conclusion

This chapter has equipped you with the knowledge and skills to tackle practical questions you might encounter in the exam. By focusing on hands-on application and problem-solving, it has bridged the gap between theoretical concepts and real-world scenarios. Remember to review the key concepts and practice similar questions to solidify your understanding and increase your confidence.

Index

A

B

C

D

L

M

N

S

U

V

W